PHILEAS DOGG'S
GUIDE TO
DOG-
FRIENDLY
HOLIDAYS
IN BRITAIN

Acknowledgements:
Jane would like to thank: Mum, Dad, Steph and Jerome, for support beyond the call of duty; Dodger, for getting me up in the mornings; Apricot, for cups of char; Elisa Llewellyn, for holidays to destinations where Attlee's passport isn't valid; Lindsay Calder and Vicky Powell, for red wine and ranting; Dave Ware, for Scandi box set therapy; Fran and Samm, for keeping me in beans on toast; La Lissaman (our travel inspiration) and Ella Buchan, for help organising trips; Tim Kent, for snaps; Amy Bratley, Frankie Mullin, Hannah Mattison and Joanne Mallon, for cheerleading and such; John Griffiths, for designing the website; Andi Godfrey, Karen Lloyd, and Sara Walker for encouragement on our first forays into the Fido fraternity and, biggest and best of thanks to Matt Tiller, a true believer.

Attlee would like to thank his pack – Alfie Schnauzer, Brix, Clover, Diva, Dora, Evie, Fenn, Gizmo, Hattie, Mitzy, Monty, Ozy, Plum, Skye, Stompy, Tess and Wilfred; Paddy, in whose paw steps he follows, and Paul the dog walker. (Attlee would NOT like to thank Annie for his couture collection. Jane would.)

Jane and Attlee would both like to thank Hugh at Constable and Robinson, for commissioning our BOOK!

PHILEAS DOGG'S
GUIDE TO
DOG-
FRIENDLY
HOLIDAYS
IN BRITAIN

JANE
COMMON

CONSTABLE • LONDON

Constable & Robinson Ltd
55-56 Russell Square
London WC1B 4HP

www.constablerobinson.com

First published in the UK in 2014 by Constable,
an imprint of Constable & Robinson Ltd

A copy of the British Library Cataloguing in Publication Data is available from the
British Library

ISBN 978-1-4721-1260-6 (paperback)
ISBN 978-1-4721-1341-2 (ebook)

Printed in China

10 9 8 7 6 5 4 3 2 1

CONTENTS

INTRODUCTION 7

CHAPTER 1
SCOTLAND 15

CHAPTER 2
THE NORTH EAST 53

CHAPTER 3
THE NORTH WEST 87

CHAPTER 4
WALES 113

CHAPTER 5
THE HEART OF ENGLAND 147

CHAPTER 6
THE EAST OF ENGLAND 183

CHAPTER 7
SOUTH EAST ENGLAND 217

CHAPTER 8
SOUTH WEST ENGLAND 253

INDEX 286

INTRODUCTION

I adopted Attlee – or Pickle, as he was then – from Battersea Dogs and Cats Home in November 2009, after two years of deliberating over whether to take on a dog or not. The responsibility; the money; the curtailing of spontaneous after-work drinking activity; rising early every morn to march the mutt around . . .

But, against that, was the simple fact that I wanted a dog – for companionship, as much as anything else. It was the best decision I've ever made.

Attlee, a charismatic little character, is an excellent companion. When we go for Sunday roast or a glass of wine in the local – just the two of us, as we sometimes do – strangers come over and chat. They are drawn to his expressive eyes and his waggedy stump of a tail – to his spontaneous 'chase my back leg because I don't have a tail to chase' performances.

My first holiday alone with Attlee was in the summer of 2011. I was about to turn 40 and had just been unceremoniously dumped by a boyfriend. The evening before departure I wept down the phone to my sister. I'd backpacked around the world as a single woman, but going on holiday in Britain on my own – to a holiday cottage in Shropshire for a week – seemed, somehow, a bit tragic? Spinsterhood writ large . . .

In fact, that week was one of the most joyful of my life. The sun shone; we walked for miles every day; we ate lunch in country pubs and then repaired to our local for the week in the evenings, to watch Andy Murray on a winning streak at Wimbledon.

Attlee hails a fellow traveller, Sir John Betjeman, at St Pancras Station

The Law on Dogs in Public Places

A lot of restaurateurs, hoteliers and publicans say that they would like to welcome dogs into their establishments – but that the law won't allow them. The truth is, the law does allow dogs into places where food is being served – just not into the actual kitchen itself.

If the owner of an establishment has made a decision not to allow dogs inside, that's fine. Some proprietors plain don't like dogs – others might be concerned about alienating customers who don't like dogs. But it irritates me, as a dog owner, to have a law that doesn't exist quoted at me.

For the record, the Food Standards Agency confirms that: 'the food hygiene rules do not prohibit the presence of dogs or other pets in catering establishments (e.g. pubs, restaurants, takeaways) which remains a decision at the discretion of the proprietor.'

Attlee, with his boundless energy and enthusiasm, found every turn in the woods and every chip discovered on the pub floor exhilarating and life-affirming – and that sort of enthusiasm is infectious. As for feeling self-conscious as a single woman on holiday in the UK, it's hard to feel self-conscious when a dog is beside you, licking his bits or introducing himself to the man at the bar eating a burger and chips or barking because he's happy and he wants his big, happy bark to be heard.

Phileas Dogg was born one Sunday in September 2011, a few months after that trip to Shropshire. I was making a cup of tea in the kitchen when I heard the tap, tap, tap of the keyboard in my study and lo – there was Attlee, typing away so fast it seemed impossible that his brain could be keeping pace with paws. A miracle!

So, with the assistance of a kind and incredibly able graphic designer called John Griffiths who created a site for us – gratis – Phileas Dogg was born, taking to the web waves in January 2012. It seemed to strike a chord. While there was a lot of information available on the Internet about holidaying with dogs, there was very little that was authored (or paw-thored, as in our case).

And the site was timely. More and more people – families, couples, singles – are taking their dogs on holiday. According to one survey, nine out of ten dog owners take their pets on trips with them; another says that the dog travel market is increasing by 6 per cent year-on-year.[1] Many major hotel chains now accept dogs – Travelodge, Best Western, Malmaison and Hotel du Vin.

Left, the dog-friendly Boat Inn, Cromford and right, Tony enjoys a dog's dinner at the Brandling Villa, Newcastle

Naturally I hope that the trend for dog travel continues to grow – not just for Phileas Dogg's sake, but for the sake of dog owners everywhere, who want to take their dogs on holiday rather than book them for a stint in the kennels. And for the sake of our dogs – in family photographs of happy times, the dog is always there, in the centre of the frame. Dogs win awards for valour and help disabled people lead independent lives. They work for us, in the army and the police and the fire service. They are there for the small child who can't sleep at night and for the old man whose stroll around the park with his dog is his one opportunity to chat to people all day. Dogs are at the very heart of their owners' lives. Isn't it right they should be at the heart of their holidays too?

Attlee says: I am a five-year-old mongrel – alumni Battersea School for Dogs, November 2009. I am good at chasing squirrels, pulling hangdog expressions and begging for treats. I am the current holder of the Best Rescue Dog title in the Brunswick Park (SE5) Dog Show. When I am not chasing squirrels, begging for treats or winning awards, I enjoy going on holiday with Jane. These are my traveller's tails . . .

---

[1] Surveys by Morethan insurance and Medic Animal.

JANE'S TOP TRAVEL TIPS FOR HOLIDAYING WITH A HOUND

- I always phone wherever I'm hoping to stay rather than booking over the Internet. Having a chat reassures me that a place is dog-friendly rather than just dog-tolerant and that Attlee will be welcome.

- Visit England's Welcome Pets! accreditation scheme is a good indicator of establishments where dogs will be given a warm welcome – criteria include a bowl being available upon request and rooms being located close to external access. Look for the red and blue paw prints Visit England logo.

- The PDSA produces a leaflet on the dos and don'ts of taking your dog on holiday, containing advice such as making sure your dog is wearing a tag listing your mobile phone number and grooming him before you set off so he doesn't overheat in the sun – good, common-sense stuff. Log on to www.pdsa.org.uk.

- Check that your dog's insurance covers him on holiday.

- Dogs travel free on trains! Attlee and I have largely conducted our travels by public transport – I don't drive – and, although my evidence is empirical, I have only ever met two ticket inspectors on trains who weren't dog lovers.

- Up until I discovered that collapsible dog bowls existed, a large part of my luggage on our travels was taken up by Attlee's plastic food bowl. Now I have discovered collapsible dog bowls, I can pack an extra pair of shoes.

- W H Smith and other newsagents at train stations don't allow dogs inside – worth knowing if you're travelling solo by public transport.

Dogs Trust

Dogs Trust works with Welcome Cottages whereby Welcome donates 10 per cent of the price of a holiday to the charity if the holiday maker books through www.dogstrust-cottages.co.uk – a deal Dogs Trust office dog Daniel the Spaniel is happy to take advantage of.

Dastardly is ready for a Wacky Race to his holiday destination.

- Whatever mischief Attlee suddenly embarks upon can usually be diverted by a TREAT. This is most definitely not recommended in dog training manuals but, when Attlee is barking at a guide dog at a train station concourse, I believe that distracting him with a Bakers Sizzler is a reasonable and responsible course of action.

- Whenever Attlee and I arrive somewhere new, we walk around so we both know the lay of the land. And I don't leave him alone somewhere until we've spent a while there and he knows he is secure.

- Local websites for waggers or books of dog walks dedicated to your holiday destination are invaluable. On my first holiday with Attlee, a book of local walks written by a dog called Boomer got us out and about – especially as it included details of dog-friendly pubs and cafes in the area. Check out www.bestdogwalksuk.com, which sells books of walks specifically for dogs in different parts of the country.

- If the worst does happen on holiday, and your dog goes missing, contact Dog Lost at www. doglost.co.uk. A voluntary organisation set up a decade ago by Jayne Hayes, who didn't know where to turn when she lost her own dog, it has a small army of volunteer dog owners across the country who will use their local knowledge to help you look for your missing mutt, as well as a national database and social media alerts where details of your pet will be posted.

The Little Dog Who Saved a Pub

In the run up to Christmas 2011, Mops Draper, 60, landlady at The Compass in Winsor, Hampshire, just on the edge of the New Forest, was facing a bleak festive season. After a decade and a half of running The Compass, she was, she believed, going to have to close down – a victim of the recession. Whereas once she'd ordered in nine and a half ton barrels of beer for the festive season, now she only needed to order one.

Mops believed that the Christmas cards she sent to her customers that December, and the annual Christmas message she placed in the local newspaper, were going to be her last. She used a photograph of her cute little Jack Russell puppy, Boris – 17 weeks old, then – as the image on the Yuletide greetings simply because, in difficult times, he cheered her up.

'There was no major strategy behind using Boris,' Mops says. 'He was just cute. But the floodgates opened. Customers I hadn't seen for years popped in to meet Boris and people in the area with puppies brought their dogs in to say hello. In the space of a couple of weeks, the pub changed from being empty most evenings to being packed – packed with people with dogs and people with dog-shaped holes in their lives that Boris could fill.'

Mops was inspired. She started organising Sunday dog walks from the pub, with Boris at the helm, followed by a roast for Rovers and their owners afterwards. She contacted a local dog trainer and held puppy training sessions in The Compass too. Now, three years on, Mops markets The Compass as the New Forest's dog-friendliest pub.

'Being dog-friendly turned my fortunes around,' Mop says. 'Now it's the major part of our business and we've transformed from a dying pub into a thriving pub. All thanks to Boris.'

The Compass, Winsor Road, Winsor, Hampshire, SO40 2HE: 02380 812237; www.compassinn.co.uk

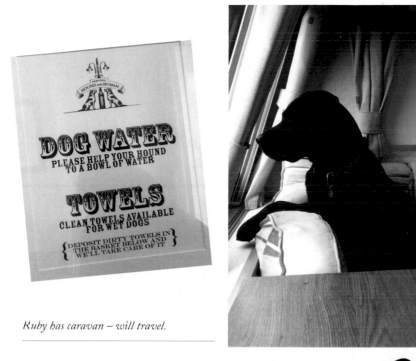

Ruby has caravan – will travel.

The Phileas Dogg Paw Print of Approval

We have included places that are, in our opinion, the most dog friendly in the country and that's dog-friendly, rather than merely dogs allowed. Establishments that really go above and beyond in making our dogs at home receive a Phileas Dogg Paw Print of Approval. All prices quoted are correct at time of going to print and are per double for one night B&B, unless otherwise stated. Prices for dogs are also per night, unless otherwise stated. We have endeavoured to get all our facts straight as of January 2014 but, of course, things can change so do double-check with establishments when ringing and booking. If there's anything you think we should know (for example, that a hotel has changed its policy on dogs since this book was printed) email Jane on jane@phileasdogg.com and tell us.

THE KINTYRE PENINSULA

I wonder how many times the pleasant lady in Campbeltown Tourist Information has had to smile patiently while asked where, exactly, Paul McCartney's farm is on the Mull of Kintyre and where, exactly, the video for the song was filmed. Quite a few times probably – probably even more than the number of SQUIRRELS there are in all of Britain. And that, as I can attest, is a very high number.

Jane is currently asking the pleasant lady that very question. And the pleasant lady is smiling patiently and marking the spots with crosses on the map.

We have travelled to the Kintyre Peninsula, as it's officially known, for a couple of days away with Jane's mum, Branwen. It's been a long journey but then it would be from anywhere – unless you're Paul McCartney who probably comes in a helicopter, with WINGS.

But if you're a dog, like ME, the Mull of Kintyre is worth the travel.

The scenery is amaze bones and there are wild minks – or minxes – to chase. Although I don't actually get to chase any of them, as I only glimpse them, from the car.

Jane says this is just as well because wild minxes are vicious. Even more vicious than the fox I recently had a scrap with who gifted me a scarlet gash across my snout. (You should have seen him, though – walking round on crutches for weeks afterwards!)

Kintyre Peninsula

Tarbert, Kintyre Peninsula

We start our trip in Tarbert, a pretty little fishing village at the top of the peninsula, on the banks of Loch Fyne. The houses are cheerfully painted and there's a castle up a hill – a good, bracing walk but leads on for the first part as there are SHEEPS.

Unfortunately, though, many of Tarbert's coffee shops and even pubs don't welcome dogs. 'We are dog-friendly but dogs aren't allowed in,' one man tells us. He must be speaking Gaelic because that sentence makes no logical sense to me.

Thank Dog, then, for the West Loch Hotel, two-or-so miles out of Tarbert, where we make our kip for the night. It is run by Andrew and his sister Rosalind and, most importantly, Andrew and Rosalind's two dogs, Mac and Molly, who are just 13 weeks old when we visit.

Normally, whenever I arrive somewhere, I am treated like a deity (like Dog, in fact) but not on this occasion as all the fuss surrounds the puppies, who are Spoodles, a cross between a Poodle and a Spaniel. (That's nothing compared to me, a cross between about 21 different types of dog and no one even knows what types they are.)

Fancy a wee nip? Shortie is King at the Ardbeg distillery on Islay.

Despite the attention lavished on the Spoodles, the West Loch is welcoming. It is very FOODIE and, at dinner, in the bar – dogs aren't allowed in the restaurant – there is a little bone on a fine, white china plate for me.

There's a games room next to the bar, with a big wooden table for large parties – and a piano, should Paul McCartney ever pop in and fancy performing a quick rendition of *Mull of Kintyre*.

Next morning, we head off down the 35-miles-or-so road to Campbeltown, which is near the bottom of the Mull of Kintyre. The drive is by rugged shoreline nearly all the way. We could have done this on paw – the route of the Kintyre Way is supposed to be very fine – but time is dog biscuits so we don't.

Now, being here is a bit like being on an island because it's a peninsula and feels so cut off from the rest of the world. And, as we drive along, we see other islands in the distance – Gigha, and Islay, and Jura.

The Mull of Kintyre is the start and end point for ferry journeys back and forth to these islands so a lot of the hail fellow-well-met travellers we encounter are island hopping. This is a bit like the island hopping that Greek dogs enjoy – except in Greece it is always sunny and in Scotland it often rains.

And in Greece there are no red deer, which we see plenty of on the Mull of Kintyre, although again, as

The beach at Bellochantuy

with the wild minxes, I can't chase them, because I'm in the car. Very frustrate-bones!

It is also possible to see seals on the Mull of Kintyre. But we don't see any, even though we go to the beaches right at the bottom tip of the peninsula, at Southend.

We do see some cows on the beach, however, and of this I do not approve at all. Cows are supposed to live in fields and they are supposed to stay in fields. They do not have the right to wander wherever they please, like us dogs.

After Southend, we go to Bellochantuy beach, to the Argyll Hotel, which several people have recommended to us. It has recently been taken over by Nick and Ian. Well, they may think they've taken over but it is obvious within five minutes of arriving that actually their Dalmatians Struan and Talaidh are in charge. They patrol from the bar to the beach terrace to the restaurant and back again and SPOT everything that's going on.

The Argyll Hotel is one of the best situated hostelries I've ever visited on my travels as it is right on six miles of beach. And, as this is Scotland and not – say, Faliraki – the beach is empty. When we stroll along we have it and the VIEWS to Gigha, Islay and Jura, and the mists rolling in from the sea all to ourselves.

PHILEAS PHACTS: Mull of Kintyre

WEST LOCH HOTEL

Campbeltown Road (A83), Tarbert, Loch Fyne, Argyll and Bute, PA29 6YF: 01880 820283; www.westlochhotel.com 🐾
Price: from £79 per double
Charge for dogs: £3.50 a night
Extras for dogs: bone served at dinner
Access all areas: not in the restaurant but in the bar and public lounges
Number of dogs: check when booking
Late night pee: ten-minute stroll to West Loch jetty
Owner's dogs: Mac and Molly

THE ARGYLL HOTEL

Bellochantuy, Campbeltown, Argyll and Bute, PA28 6QE: 01583 421212 www.argyllhotelkintyre.co.uk 🐾
Price: £80 per double per night
Charge for dogs: no
Extras for dogs: fitness weekends; dog beds in public areas; books of walks; toys, bowls and blankets
Access all areas: yes – in the restaurant, terrace, bar, public areas and the eight bedrooms
Number of dogs: just let Nick and Ian know the size of your pack!
Late night pee: miles of beach
Owner's dogs: Struan and Talaidh, the Dalmatians

I am aware, however, that Struan has SPOTTED us and is wondering what we're doing on HIS beach. Well, he'll need to get used to it because the Argyll Hotel is about to become even more dog-friendly. Soon welcome packs will be presented to all dogs on arrival, along with books of walks along the beach and in the hills and heather behind the hotel. Plans are also a-paw for fitness weekends for dogs and their humans who may need to lose a few pounds. Obviously I have no requirement of this, but, if Jane keeps eating PIE AND CHIPS on our travels, she may need to sign up pronto.

Resident Rover: Selkie's Day Out in the Highlands

'Awright dugs! Ahm wee Selkie Wilson, Sprocker fae the Clan Gunn, CEO of Highland Dogblog and the original Rufty Tufty, writing in tae ye fae the Heilans! Attlee asked me to write a wee piece fir ye oan some of oor brawest walks hereaboots and ahm the very dug fir the job!'

Hmph, Lauren says a little less accent and a little more focus. Honestly, some humans – no sense of the dramatic. But I do see that understanding us is a bonus in this project, so I'll be good and try again.

Hello there! My name is little Selkie – I'm a Sprocker Spaniel (that's a Springer/Cocker cross) from the Clan Gunn and I live with Lauren in Dingwall, Ross-shire in the Highlands. Lauren works for me at Highland Dogblog and we spend a lot of time out and about in this beautiful part of Scotland. Attlee asked us to share some of our favourite local walks with you because here in the Highlands we are spoilt rotten for choice.

There has been much woofing at meetings on the beach with other Highland dugs, seminars in the forests, deep conversations alongside salmon-filled rivers and so on. But, we have, at last, chosen to recommend a 'Dug's Day Oot on the Black Isle'. Lauren and I think it's the perfect combination for dugs and humans and all of you can have a cracking time – kids too!

Assuming that you're travelling north, drive past Inverness and cross the

Selkie's a mover and shaker at Highland Dog Blog

Beaches

Dogs are allowed on nearly all Scottish beaches, as long as owners are responsible. (Even on the four that are exceptions, there are still dog-friendly parts of the beach.) Here's Pugalier Mavis having the time of her wee life – she's only a year old – running along the coastline of the Dornoch Firth with her friends and struggling to keep up with Doris the Dane!

Kessock Bridge with its fabulous views across the Moray Firth, all the while looking out for my pals the Moray Dolphins. Keep heading north and turn off the A9 onto either the B9161 or A832 towards Munlochy, Avoch and on to Fortrose and Rosemarkie. We always drive 'country pace' and I ask Lauren to open the window so I can stick my nose out and smell the forest, farm and sea news as we roll along.

Wave a paw at the Highland Coo's and sheep on your way past, and don't get a fright when you go past Clootie Well – it's a little weird with lots of cloths (cloots) hanging off the trees but they say it's a blessed place and helps lots of sick people.

Then after Avoch, where my pal Spud (a beautiful Collie) is first boat dog at Dolphin Boat Trips, it's all the way alongside the sea, past the Chanonry Sailing Club and the old Fortrose Cathedral through Fortrose itself and out to Rosemarkie. Head for the North Beach car park – it's handy and there are no time limits.

There are three different ways to walk from here or you can just hang out on the beach, dig holes, swim, play ball and meet the locals. If you want a good walk, then hit the beach running and head north (Walk One) with the Beach Cafe on your left.

This stretch of beach goes for at least five miles all the way to Cromarty (check tides if you're planning on walking the whole distance) so you can really feel your freedom. I chase seagulls and oystercatchers and poke my nose in rock pools – there's always something going on there.

We usually do a couple of miles and then turn back – there's a natural turning

It's a hard life for hounds in the Highlands

point just after a small fresh water burn (stream) where you have to climb through some high rocks to get to the next section.

Keep your eyes open for seals, otters and of course, dolphins – as well as all kinds of birds. There are even a couple of caves to schnuffle in! This walk takes as long as it takes, especially if you see otters. And, depending on when you walk, you can be completely alone – just you and your humans with the whole place to yourselves – or there can be lots of other pals to play with. We're all used to being off lead here in the Highlands so call out and tell people if you need a little space so they have time to rein in their dugs.

Walk Two is for you if you prefer a wooded walk to sand – it's at Fairy Glen, following the Markie Burn. Stroll there from Rosemarkie beach, across the playing field and then down the path past the houses and under the bridge. Locals say that Fairy Glen is one of the last places where the 'little people' were seen on the Black Isle. I haven't seen any but I'm always looking – especially near the waterfalls.

This is a 1.75 mile round trip and we always turn around at the second waterfall and retrace our route, rather than going across the bridge and onto the main road, which is quite narrow and busy with cars. It's far more fun to skip

Highland hounds, clockwise from the left: Ollie, Wiggie, Indie (with panniers), Ozzy and Harvey.

back through the fairy forest.

For Walk Three, head down the beach to Chanonry Point where you can see the lighthouse and lots of people gathering on the end of the shoreline to watch dolphins. (Careful of jumping in on that side because the current can be very strong and there's a steep drop off into the bay which is why the dolphins love it so much.)

You can also watch seals, salmon, gannets and sometimes even pilot whales. Look out for my pals Hudson and Harvey, the Newfoundlands. They're the resident bears and they do daily patrols at the lighthouse. You'll often see them with their best friend Sam, a rescue German Shepherd. They all love to swim but beware – Sam will try to steal your water toys!

The best plan after any of these walks is to head back towards the main car park and for tea and cupcakes at the Rosemarkie Beach Cafe – we aren't allowed inside but we are allowed outside and there's always a biscuit to greet us.

If you want something more substantial, head to the Plough Inn, built in the 17th century for drovers and travellers. It has a little garden outside or, if it's cold, a great fire inside where dogs can warm their paws.

Another thing we like to do is drive to Fortrose to buy a 'chippy tea' and then on to Chanonry Point to eat it at the picnic tables. On the drive, you'll go straight down the middle of the Royal Dornoch Golf Course – you know how we Scots like our golf! You'll find the Fortrose Caravan Park here as well as the Rosemarkie Club campsite. Both are good – just jump out of the tent and you're on the beach!

Sadly, some of us can't stay and have to drive home at the end of the day, though.

Her name might be continental but when it comes to holidays, Paris' heart is in the Highlands.

22

PHILEAS PHACTS: Selkie's Day Out in the Highlands

ROSEMARKIE BEACH CAFE
off Marine Terrace, Mill Road, Rosemarkie, Highland,
IV10 8UW: 07957 412567;
www.rosemarkiebeachcafe.info

PLOUGH INN 48 High Street, Rosemarkie, Highland, IV10 8UF: 01381 620164

FORTROSE CARAVAN PARK
Wester Greengates, Fortrose, Highland, IV10 8RX: 01381 621927;
www.fortrosecaravanpark.co.uk
Price: from £10 per pitch (tent) and from £20 per pitch (caravan)
Charge for dogs: no
Extras for dogs: no
Access all areas: yes – on leads
Number of dogs: no restrictions
Late night pee: the beach

ROSEMARKIE CAMPING AND CARAVANNING CLUB SITE
Ness Road East, Rosemarkie, Fortrose, Highland, IV10 8SE: 01381 621117;
www.campingandcaravanningclub.co.uk/campsites/uk/highlands/fortrose/rosemarkie
Price: from £7.90 per member per unit; non-members add £7.20 per night
Charge for dogs: no
Access all areas: yes – on leads
Number of dogs: three maximum
Late night pee: wander down to the sea

Highland Dog Blog is a rapidly growing social network for dog lovers who live in and/or just love the Highlands and Islands of Scotland:
www.highlanddogblog.co.uk

It's a beautiful drive for the humans – especially if they do a loop of the Black Isle peninsula – but you dugs are sure to miss it because you'll be fast asleep in the back of the car with your noses tucked between your sandy paws and your tails wagging as you dream happy salty dreams.

ATTLEE IN EDINBURGH

My first visit to Edinburgh, back in 2011, when I was just a young pup of two years old, was a disaster, repast-wise. When we met up with Jane's friend Lorena and her baby Rosie, Edinburgh city centre recorded a big, fat FAIL in providing a dog-and-baby friendly eatery for us. (Rosie is not a baby any more – she is four. I am still a dog.)

Having a snout about in Auld Reekie

Pubs welcomed me but not Rosie. Cafes welcomed Rosie but not me.

I was unimpressed with Scotland's capital. It had promised so much, dubbed, as it is, Auld Reekie – a reference, I understood, to the smells that emanated from it. My nose had been twitching in anticipation. But, with this apparent lack of dog-friendly digs, the only thing I could smell was trouble.

Is Edinburgh not the home of Greyfriars Bobby – the faithful and loyal hound who visited his master's grave in Greyfriars Kirkyard every day for 14 years after he'd died?

And how has Edinburgh repaid the faith and loyalty of canine-kind? By turning us away at the door to every eatery? Still, I decided to visit Edinburgh again. I am all for second chances, having had one myself, when Jane chose ME at Battersea Dogs (and Cats – grrrrr) Home.

We stayed at the Travelodge on Queen's Street, which is two streets parallel to Princes Street, making it very, very central. Opposite the Travelodge there were some fine gardens containing smells and shrubs and very likely SQUIRRELS but these beautiful and beckoning gardens were closed to Travelodge guests. Only residents of the surrounding flats and houses were granted the keys to the kingdom and our Travelodge swipe card did not cut the mustard. However, the nice lady on reception said that the hotel was trying to organise for its guests to be granted temporary keys as well, which would only be fair because Jane and I were residents on that street, if only for one night, and I really wanted a snout around those gardens.

Anyway, Queen Street Gardens denied to us, Jane and I commenced our research on Hanover Street, just around the corner. It was a bright and sunny Saturday morning – Edinburgh was having a heat wave – and we were in high spirits.

Clover's a Beagle from the Bronx who took some time out to visit the Edinburgh Festival – a true holidaying hound from across the pond.

Edinburgh: home of Greyfriars Bobby!

Jane, being in one of her chatty moods, asked a lady on the street to recommend a cafe and she pointed us in the direction of Henderson's.

Well, there were two things wrong

PHILEAS PHACTS: Edinburgh

TRAVELODGE EDINBURGH QUEEN STREET
30-31 Queen Street, Edinburgh, EH1 1JX:
0871 984 6143;
www.travelodge.co.uk
Price: from £21 per double
Charge for dogs: £20 per dog per stay
Extras for dogs: no
Access all areas: the hotel is just reception and room
Number of dogs: ask at time of booking
Late night pee: hopefully guests will be granted keys to Queen Street Gardens!

GREYFRIARS BOBBY STATUE is at the corner of Candlemaker Row and George IV Bridge, Edinburgh, EH1 2QQ; **www.greyfriarsbobby.co.uk**

HENDERSON'S is at 92–94 Hanover Street, Edinburgh, EH2 1DR: 0131 225 6694; **www.hendersonsofedinburgh.co.uk**

RONDE CAFE AND CYCLE SHOP
66-68 Hamilton Place, Stockbridge, Edinburgh, EH3 5AZ: 0131 260 9888;
www.rondebike.com

HAMILTON'S BAR
16–18 Hamilton Place, Stockbridge, Edinburgh, EH3 5AU: 0131 226 4199;
www.hamiltonsedinburgh.co.uk

BLUE BEAR
9 Brandon Terrace, Edinburgh, EH3 5EA: 0131 629 0229;
www.cafebluebear.co.uk

AFFOGATO
36 Queensferry Street, Edinburgh, EH2 4QS: 0131 225 1444;
www.affogatogelato.co.uk

Dugs in Pubs

*Dugs n Pubs (**www.dugsnpubs.com**) is a listings site for dog-friendly pubs and places in Edinburgh and beyond, started in 2009 by Lhasa Apso Bailie and his owners. Many dog-friendly venues in Scotland now display their Dugs Welcome sticker. Here's Bailie enjoying the ambience in his Edinburgh local, The Stockbridge Tap.*

with Henderson's. One – dogs are only allowed outside in a tiny courtyard with two tables. That was liveable with, as it was a sunny day. But the second problem with Henderson's is that it's blimin' vegetarian.

So while its rolls and breads and cakes, all freshly made, might be the finest in Edinburgh, as everyone insisted on telling us, frankly, if there's no meat in your sausage, what's the point? (Actually, there was vegetarian haggis and it was pretty tasty – although how people can tell whether a haggis is vegetarian or carnivorous when they catch it on the Scottish moors, I do not know.)

Jane and I were not to be cowed by the lack of meat and the lack of indoor seating for dogs, however. Cows are stupid animals and Jane and I are not stupid. In fact, we are the Woofward and Barkstein of canine journalism. So we carried on.

'Are there any dog-friendly cafes in Edinburgh?' Jane asked a lady who was passing with a dog. The woman replied, yes – in Stockbridge. Stockbridge, 15 minutes' walk away, is the dog-friendliest part of town, she said. A 15-minute walk – that's a mere skip for an athlete like me. So off we went.

Stockbridge was a very proper little area with a river running through it and lots of old buildings. We decided we'd try the first cafe we ventured across and a strange place it was, too – half cafe, with big wooden tables and one of those spluttering, fizzing machines that coffee comes from, and half bicycle shop. Grrr-huzzah – dogs were allowed in Ronde.

A bird's eye view of Edinburgh

'Half our customers are dogs,' the manager smiled. Rover result!

The next place we came across in Stockbridge was Hamilton's, a pub/restaurant that had won lots of awards. Dogs welcome – tick. Cheered, it was time for the walk Jane had promised me up Arthur's Seat, which, she said, is an extinct volcano. We don't have any of them in South-East London!

It was a steep uphill climb but I could smell haggises in the undergrowth and so was undeterred. I didn't catch one of the blighters though – they'd obviously heard I was coming. Or perhaps they'd all been snaffled already by Evie, one of the many doggie denizens of Edinburgh who contacted me after she read about my visit. Evie wrote to tell me that her favourite cafe in the city is the Blue Bear at the bottom of Dundas Street – 'baby and dug friendly,' she reported. Or maybe Epix, who recommended Affogato, an ice cream and coffee shop on Queensferry Street, where: 'I'm allowed to go inside – just in the front area but that's okay because that's where the fun is. There are so many flavours of Gelato in a Frisbee that spins round – no gravy Gelato yet but I'm waiting!'

No, I believe the real snaffler of the haggis must be Jack the Lad, who sounds rather full of himself. 'The greatest things about Edinburgh are all the parks and wild places,' he reported in his missive. 'My own personal stomping ground is Blackford Hill – loads of rabbits, squirrels and dog crazy people to scratch my ears and admire my rippling physique. Then there are The Meadows, where all the hottest bitches hang out . . . . . . grrrr!'

Grrrr indeed, Jack the Lad!

FOUR SEASONS HOTEL, PERTHSHIRE

The waitress is hovering with pencil and pad poised and I'm weighing up the big decision. Should I have the Rooster and Rice or the Hearty Ham Hough and Jelly? The Mean Bean Fritter or the Hog and Heinz? It's the first time in my life I've been presented with a menu just for dogs at dinner and I want to make the right choice.

'Hairy Hamish's Highland Haggis sounds good,' Jane says. I know that she's trying to push me towards that because she fancies a taste herself. It's what I normally do when we're in restaurants – put my paw next to the order I want Jane to make. SAUSAGES!

We're at the Four Seasons Hotel in the village of St Fillans, Perthshire. The views over Loch Earn are serene and the woods on the hillsides full of adventure. There are boats to hire and walking boots to pull on. But forget all that – this is a top spot because of the extras for dogs: a pet butler, should I require breakfast in bed; a list of walks presented upon arrival; a big bowl of dog treats behind the bar; a welcome pack from Sham and Pagne, Resident Canine Reservation Managers; and, now, my own menu.

The Beatles spent two nights here, back in 1964. That's obviously when the hotel realised that celebrity guests – John, Paul, Ringo, George and now Phileas Dogg – require a higher level of service than the hoi polloi. As well as 12 bedrooms in the main house, there are six cabins in the woods and that's where the Beatles slept, in Cabins One and Six. I'm in cabin Four and the decor appears as if it hasn't changed much in the meantime. Amaze-bonios!

After the Beatles' stay, the local paper ran a feature about it: 'Police had to be called to disperse several car loads of teenagers and students who followed the group back to the hotel,' it reported. Apparently, a local hound snubbed John and Paul, who tried to 'entice a dog into the loch by throwing sticks for it to retrieve. The dog was not playing, however, and refused to do more than paddle.'

Good dog – refusing to bow and scrape . . .

Oh, my bowl of Hairy Hamish's Highland Haggis has arrived. Scrape – bow; paw in the air; bow again and scrape the bowl clean . . .

PHILEAS PHACTS: Four Seasons Hotel

Lochside, St Fillans, Perthshire, PH6 2NF:
01764 685333;
www.thefourseasonshotel.co.uk 🐾
Price: £144 per double; £108 per chalet
Charge for dogs: no
Extras for dogs: pet butler; dog menu; welcome letter and biscuits
Access all areas: everywhere bar the fine dining restaurant
Number of dogs: check at time of booking
Late night pee: the woods behind the hotel
Owner's dogs: Munsterlanders Sham and Payne

Clockwise: Musing the menu; dinner is served; Hairy Hamish's Highland Haggis and Loch Earn. Above, Phileas Dogg stayed here!

Resident Rover: The Travelling Bear in the Hebrides and Skye

Day One: I'm the Travelling Bear and I'm on holiday – hurrah. We have driven a very long way in my owner Vee's Mini – from the South of England to the town of Oban, Gateway to the Isles. After checking in to our hotel, The Oban Caledonian, I'm eager to explore. There are lovely views of Mull from the harbour and we find the ruins of Dunollie Castle and the fields behind – Scotland has an open countryside, right to roam policy, so we can go anywhere as long as we abide by the rules. I have a good run and a fox hunt!

Day Two: We set sail to Barra on a beautiful, calm day. It's a five-hour crossing on a Caledonian MacBrayne ferry from Oban to Barra – past Mull and the small isles and then out to open sea. I could go inside the ferry, to the designated pet area, but people are eating sarnies on deck so that's where I am. I take the journey in my stride – watching for dolphins; sunbathing; and accepting the admiring glances, pats and biscuits that pass my way. On arrival on Barra, we can see our hotel – the Castlebay – from the ferry so we're dropped at our door!

Days Three and Four: Highlights of Barra are the beautiful white sands and crystal blue waters of Cockle Strand, where the planes land at low tide, along with the apple core beaches of Vatersay – we could be in the South Pacific, especially as the weather is so fabulous. I love zooming around the *machair*, Gaelic for the heathery land next to the beach; tearing through the dunes – stopping to chase the odd bunny; and then chasing off across the beach after an Arctic tern or three which ends up with me racing through the shallow waters. Happy, happy, happy!

Days Five and Six: From Barra, we set sail on a much smaller Caledonian MacBrayne ferry to the Uists and Benbecula. We drive straight through South Uist and head for the RSPB Balranald nature reserve on North Uist. From the visitor centre there's an excellent walk across the *machair* to sandy-white beaches teeming with migrating birds, otters and seals out off the headland.

Later we find our hotel, The Langass Lodge, set on the edge of Loch Eport and overlooking Ben Eaval. The former shooting lodge is set in its own (sheep-free) estate and has a marked circular walk that takes in the Ben Langass stone circle and the Barpa Langass burial chamber, with incredible views across the landscape. There are voles to track and otters to spot. I'm a fabulous tracker – but,

Greer, the Skye on Skye
Here's Skye Terrier Greer, a London girl, researching her family tree on a trip to the Isle of Skye.

Time flies for a hound on hols

Vee says, a complete fidget when it comes to sitting still and waiting for otters to appear. Well, you can't have everything! In the evening, I'm allowed in the bar to sit by the fire but prefer to look out of the patio windows in our room, policing for pheasants!

Days Seven and Eight: We set sail again, this time to Harris where we check in at the Rodel Hotel and stroll around the little harbour and grounds. This is my favourite place on the trip as it's teeming with bunnies to chase through the gorse bushes. Heaven on Earth!

Harris boasts magnificent scenery and spectacular beaches like the famous Luskentyre and Huisinis – deserted apart from the odd cow hiding in the dunes. Buzzards, seals, dolphins and basking sharks are regularly sighted and we trek through the Harris hills to an observatory to spot some Golden Eagles – I had to keep a look out for quite some time. Luckily, Vee had a flask of tea and biscuits.

Eagled-eyed Bear on Harris

From Harris, we spent a day driving to Lewis and exploring the standing stones at Callanish and, best of all, Uig Sands. I was so happy racing around the huge, empty beach, through the sand dunes, climbing rocks and splashing through the crystal sea.

Days Nine, Ten and Eleven: Our final island on the trip is Skye. Staying in Flora MacDonald's cottage at the Flodigarry Country House Hotel, we had walks from the doorstep down to Staffin Bay to work up our appetites before breakfast!

I was determined to see as much as possible in our three days on Skye. We walked up to the Old Man of Storr on the windiest day ever – I thought I might fly off. We ventured across the Quiraing; tackled the Cuillins by walking Glen Brittle with its stunning views of Rum; and explored the three peninsulas – Trotternish, Waternish and Duirinish – taking in Coral Beach, Neist Point and a delicious lunch in Stein. (Most pubs and restaurants on Skye were dog-friendly.)

Then it was time to drive home via Loch Fyne and the Lake District. We'd travelled 2,300 miles on The Travelling Bear's Great Road Trip and had an amazing holiday, full of Fido fun!

Stone circle, North Uist

PHILEAS PHACTS: Hebrides and Skye

CALEDONIAN MACBRAYNE FERRIES are at www.calmac.co.uk

THE OBAN CALEDONIAN
Station Square, Oban, Argyll and Bute, PA34 5RT: 0844 855 9135;
www.akkeronhotels.com
Price: from £85 per double
Charge for dogs: £10 per night per dog
Extras for dogs: beds and bowls on request
Access all areas: dogs are allowed in the bedrooms and the back bar
Number of dogs: confirm when booking
Late night pee: the hotel is right opposite the harbour

CASTLEBAY HOTEL
Castlebay, Isle of Barra, HS9 5XD: 01871 810223;
www.castlebay-hotel.co.uk
Price: from £110 per double
Charge for dogs: no
Extras for dogs: no
Access all areas: not in the hotel's public areas but there's a dog-friendly bar next door
Number of dogs: maximum two
Late night pee: hotel gardens

LANGASS LODGE
Loch Eport, Isle of North Uist, HS6 5HA: 01876 580285;
www.langasslodge.co.uk

Price: from £95 per double
Charge for dogs: no
Extras for dogs: no
Access all areas: in the old part of the Lodge and in the bar
Number of dogs: check at time of booking
Late night pee: lots of open space

RODEL HOTEL
Rodel, Isle of Harris, HS5 3TW: 01859 520210;
www.rodelhotel.co.uk
Price: starts at £130 per double
Charge for dogs: no
Extras for dogs: biscuits behind the bar
Access all areas: in the lounge but not the restaurant
Number of dogs: maximum two
Late night pee: five acres of grounds
Owner's dogs: Black Labrador, Mullan

FLODIGARRY COUNTRY HOUSE HOTEL
Flodigarry, Isle of Skye, IV51 9HZ: 01470 552203;
www.flodigarry.co.uk
Price: from £130 per double
Charge for dogs: officially there is (but unofficially there isn't)
Extras for dogs: biscuits behind the bar
Access all areas: dogs allowed in the bar
Number of dogs: two maximum
Late night pee: in the sprawling grounds
Owner's dogs: two Friese Stabij

THE ISLE OF BUTE

Bute is the name of an island in the Firth of Clyde in Scotland and also the name of a horse tranquiliser. I have never taken horse tranquiliser so it's my experiences of the island I'll be sharing with you.

In some ways, Bute is my second home as Jane's parents Mick and Branwen live there. It is an island about 15-miles long and four miles wide and it's very far from South-East London. It is a bus and a train and a pee at Glasgow Central and another train from Glasgow Central to Wemyss Bay and then a half-hour ferry ride away. I am always exhausted by the time the ferry from Wemyss Bay arrives at Rothesay, Bute's main town. Still, I always do my 'Bisto-kid nose in the air' because I can smell the mussels and the sea instead of the fried chicken of South-East London. When I'm there, I eat the mussels that are swept up on to land. I have an eclectic palate like that.

In its day, Rothesay was very popular with holiday makers coming doon the watter from Glasgow but its allure diminished with the advent of package holidays. Not to worry Rothesay, with your castle and your museum and your fountains and putting green – you will become alluring again now that you're on Phileas Dogg's map!

Mick and Branwen live in a village called Port Bannatyne, about two miles from Rothesay. Here, there's a marina and a Post Office with a cafe and a hitching post for dogs to wait while their humans are inside the shop, and a pub called the Anchor, where I accompany Mick on occasion. The Anchor is not one of those pubs where there's gastro-this and gastro-that (the only gastro I've ever had is enteritis). The Anchor is a pub where the person goes in and orders a pint of beer and then sits down and drinks their pint of beer. Simple.

The main point of interest in Port Bannatyne for dogs is a Petanque Club – the only one on any Scottish island. Petanque is like the French game boules and it is interesting for dogs because it involves lots of BALLS to catch. One afternoon, I dashed onto the petanque piste and grabbed a little red BALL and ran away with it. I was in trouble because the ball I ran away with was called JACK.

Despite all this, when Jane is staying with her parents in Port Bannatyne, she sometimes complains that she is bored. There are no literary salons or private members' clubs on Bute but, whatever Jane might claim on Twitter, she doesn't go to those in London anyway.

I am never bored on Bute. No dog could be bored on an island with BEACHES! Ettrick Bay is a mile and a half of sandy beach near Port Bannatyne and we always have the whole beach to ourselves. I run and race and scoop up bits of seaweed in my mouth and throw them towards Arran, the island across the sea.

At the top of Ettrick Bay there's a cafe but nobody calls it a cafe – everybody calls it a tea room, and it's been there since the 1950s or some-such. After we've been for a walk the humans go there for a cup of tea and a big slice of coffee-and-walnut cake, which the Ettrick Bay Tea Rooms is famous for. Normally I wait, patiently, outside but, recently, I decided I should have a treat as well. So, I had a snout around on the beach and found a reddish wobbly thing that looked like jelly. I've eaten a scoop of jelly before, at a party, so I thought: 'grr-huzzah, a treat, foraged by me, the Hugh Fearnley-Whittingstall of the dog world!'

I ate it – and I was sick. Then I was sick again. I staggered over to the path beside the beach and chewed big clumps of grass, to make myself even sicker. Whatever I'd eaten was not good. When Branwen saw me being sick and saw the half eaten bit of jelly she screamed. It was a jellyfish, she cried – and jellyfish are poisonous.

But, thank Dog, after five minutes or so, I

Top to bottom: view of Port Bannatyne; getting hitched at the Post Office; The Winter Garden, Rothesay; seal spotting on Bute

 36

stopped being sick. The evil in my tummy was vanquished. Still, that is a lesson for my fellow dogs on beaches: do not eat jellyfish. And lucky I'd learnt my lesson because another of Bute's beaches – Scalpsie Bay – was covered in the wobbly warriors on my most recent visit. I wonder if a CAT who had sent me a death threat for visiting Scalpsie had put them there? 'WHAT! A dog on MY island. I had better not catch you on Scalpsie beach. Be warned. Varjak the Devon Rex – 100 per cent CAT,' he'd written. I will not be intimidated by a cat or by jellyfish, however. And, as Scalpsie is possibly Bute's finest beach, I shall visit there whenever I please.

On the way back from Scalpsie, we stopped at the Kingarth Hotel, near the village of Kilchattan Bay, for a drink. The Kingarth is famous because, when Stella McCartney married on the Isle of Bute, all of the wedding guests, including MADONNA, popped in for a drink. The wedding was at Mount Stuart, which is a grand Gothic mansion with lots of crazy architecture. (Jane has heard it was the first house in Scotland to have an electric lift but she's not 100 per cent sure so don't quote us.)

Mount Stuart has 300 acres of garden leading down to the sea and, since 2012, all of this has been open to us, fellow hounds of Britain. Some of the walks are through landscaped gardens and some are through conifer trees and there is even a spot called the Wee Garden – for dogs that need to wee. High Paw!

Lift your leg on Bute

Tell your humans to spend a penny in Bute's famous Victorian gents' toilets on Rothesay Pier. They're not dog-friendly but I am told they are very impressive. I lifted my leg against a lamp post outside the Victorian toilets on Rothesay Pier and can report that it, too, was very impressive.

Mount Stuart: grounds for hounds!

PHILEAS PHACTS: Isle of Bute

For information about travelling to Bute, log on to **www.calmac.co.uk**

MUNRO'S BED AND BREAKFAST

17 Ardmory Road, Rothesay, Isle of Bute, Argyll and Bute, PA20 0PG:
01700 502346;
www.visitmunros.co.uk
Munro's has beautiful sea views – it's at the top of a hill – and walks in the woods on the doorstep.
Price: from £85 per double
Charge for dogs: £10 per night
Extras for dogs: the odd cuddle
Access all areas: bedrooms only
Number of dogs: one large or two middle-sized per room
Late night pee: a large garden
Owner's dogs: two Black Labs and Winston, the cat, who thinks he's a Black Lab

ARDENCRAIG HOUSE APARTMENTS

High Craig, Isle of Bute, Argyll and Bute, PA20 9EP: 01700 505077;
www.ardencraig.org.uk
Self-catering apartments run by Mick's friend Elaine from the bridge club – tell her you read about Ardencraig in Phileas Dogg's book and you can be assured of a warm welcome.
Price: £445 per week and up
Charge for dogs: no

Extras for dogs: no
Access all areas: yes
Number of dogs: one regular guest stays with five dogs!
Late night pee: you're on a quiet road
Owner's dogs: Meg the Collie/Labrador cross and Millie the Collie

ETTRICK BAY TEA ROOM

Ettrick Bay, Isle of Bute, Argyll and Bute

KINGARTH HOTEL

Isle of Bute, Argyll and Bute, PA20 9LU:
www.kingarthhotel.co.uk

MOUNT STUART

Isle of Bute, Argyll and Bute, PA20 9LR:
01700 503877;
www.mountstuart.com

PORT BANNATYNE POST OFFICE

46 Marine Road, Port Bannatyne, Isle of Bute, Argyll and Bute, PA20 0LW:
01700 503914;

THE ANCHOR TAVERN

32 Marine Road, Port Bannatyne, Isle of Bute, Argyll and Bute, PA20 0LL

PORT BANNATYNE PETANQUE CLUB

www.portbannatynepetanque.org.uk

38

Resident Rover: Beanie in Shetland

Hello, my name is BeAnne Duvet; I'm a Patterdale Terrier and I live in Shetland, Britain's most northerly outpost. Shetland is 100 miles north of the British mainland, making me Phileas Dogg's Rover Reporter from furthest afield. Mostly I spend my days at our croft – that's what farms are called on Shetland – sitting at Frances' feet so I am ready in case she attempts to go somewhere without me. Frances breeds Shetland and Icelandic ponies. I like horsing around with the ponies and sometimes I ride them. Frances is also a photographer, which is lucky as I love having my picture taken.

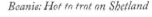

In the summer, Shetland is beautiful. The sun can shine for almost 24 hours non stop and there are lots of wild flowers and amazing wildlife – otters, puffins and whales. But in the winter Shetland is not for the faint-hearted – it is a rough, tough place almost continuously battered by wind and rain. Having said that, there is an infinite amount of rabbits, as they have no predators on Shetland, so chasing them is worth braving the weather for. Shetland has very few houses and lots of open space – and because of Scotland's right to roam, dogs, and people, are allowed everywhere. The beaches in Shetland are beautiful and ALWAYS dog-friendly. I like the beaches because there are no woolly maggots on them – and by woolly maggots I mean SHEEP. Apart from the beaches, woolly maggots are everywhere. And I'm not allowed to chase them.

Lerwick is the only town in Shetland. Mum shows me off there as I am very pretty and I roll

Beanie: Hot to trot on Shetland

on my back to impress people. I am allowed in most shops, as long as permission is asked. One lady said it was okay as long as I didn't pee. As if (I'm very well-bred).

One place on Shetland that is totally dog-friendly is Foords Chocolates on Unst, the most northerly of the over 100 islands. Unst is accessible from Lerwick by car or bus route 24, hopping on two ferries along the way. It's worth the journey as every dog who visits is given a treat and has their photograph taken for the wall of dogs. There are over 200 pictures of dogs on that wall! There's not one of me though – I'm a local.

PHILEAS PHACTS: Shetland

For information about travelling to Shetland, log on to **www.northlinkferries.co.uk**

FOORDS CHOCOLATE FACTORY AND CAFE
Saxa Vord Resort, Haroldswick, Unst, Shetland, ZE2 9TJ: 01957 711393;
www.foordschocolates.co.uk

HERRISLEA HOUSE HOTEL
Veensgarth, Tingwall, Shetland, ZE2 9SB: 01595 840208
www.herrisleahouse.co.uk
Prices from £130 per double per night
Extras for dogs: no
Charge for dogs: none
Access all areas: everywhere except the restaurant
Late night pee: miles of open space outside the front door
Owner's dogs: Teal, a Springer Spaniel

THE ISLE OF ARRAN

Where am I? The temperature is 25 °C; there is not a rain cloud in the sky; I am racing up and down a beach of golden sand on an exotic island and sitting at a beach bar, eating haggis and drinking whisky.

The answer is: this paradise island is Arran, in the Firth of Clyde, the ninth largest island off the British coast. It is about 50 miles to drive right round. There are no midges – not today, anyway. And it is the most interesting place I have ever visited because of the SMELLS. There are so many smelly things on Arran – mountains, trees, beaches, the sea and SHEEP. There are sheep ON the beach at Lochranza, at the northern end of Arran – the aroma of the sea salt and the sheep poo mix together in a way that almost makes my nose explode. And that's saying something as I understand SMELLS better than anyone. *Even a Parisienne perfumer would lose out to me in a battle of le nez . . .*

We are staying in Arran's capital Brodick at the Shorehouse – dog-friendly self-catering apartments just 500 yards' walk from where the ferry dropped us. Easy! They are right next door to the McLaren Hotel, which is a pub and a hotel and an Indian restaurant and another restaurant too. It is wearing lots of HATS! The barman had time to be friendly, though, despite his many HATS. He was

Arran Castle (top); Lochranza (left); The beach at Brodick (right)

Seaweed snaffling, Kildonan

from Glasgow and Jane asked him if people on Arran have a certain accent – so that she can talk it and I can bark it. But he explained, the locals are from all over the world – they have come on holiday and fallen in love with the island and never left – so an Arran accent might be Glaswegian or English or even Australian.

Arran is all about the beaches – that must be why Australians appreciate it. (I will visit Australia one day – I just have to keep digging the tunnel through the centre of the EARTH I am constructing in the park.)

The beach at Brodick, a few minutes' walk from the Shorehouse, leads into a forest through which you can walk (run in my case, obviously) up a hill to Brodick Castle. Behind the castle is a mountain called Goat Fell – Bark Out Loud. Why didn't the goat stay on its feet? Silly billy! *You'd never find a mountain called Attlee Fell as I am very sure-footed.*

(Brodick Castle is owned by the National Trust for Scotland and dogs are not allowed inside. But we are allowed in the grounds, which have views over the Firth of Clyde.)

The next settlement along from Brodick is Lamlash, a pretty village stretched along the coastline. But Jane wouldn't let me off the lead on the BEACH as it's next to the road. Still, the best beach bar in the world is in Lamlash – the Drift Inn. Inside it's like a regular pub in Glasgow but its beer garden is a green meadow leading to the beach, with views across to Holy Isle – a Buddhist retreat where people go to meditate.

Kildonan BEACH is on the southern tip of Arran and everyone there told us it is the sunniest place on Arran and that even in February it is sweltering in tropical heat. (I haven't been in February so I'm unable to confirm this.) From Kildonan you can see an island called Pladda and behind that Ailsa Craig, which sounds like a person but is in fact a turret-shaped grey rock rising from the sea. There is a sport called curling and nearly all of the curling stones in the world are made of granite from Ailsa Craig – PHACT!

PHILEAS PHACTS: Arran

For ferry sailings to Arran, log on to www.calmac.co.uk.

SHOREHOUSE SELF-CATERING APARTMENTS

Shore Road, Brodick, Isle of Arran, KA27 8AJ : 01770 302377; www.theshorehouse.co.uk
Sleeps: two to four
Price: from £68 per apartment
Charge for dogs: £10 per dog per stay
Extras for dogs: no
Access all areas: yes
Number of dogs: two
Late night pee: 500 yards to the harbour
Owner's dogs: Archie the Spaniel

KILDONAN HOTEL

Kildonan, Isle of Arran, KA27 8SE: 01770 820207;

www.kildonanhotel.com
Price: from £99 per double
Charge for dogs: £5 per dog per night
Extras for dogs: biscuits behind the bar
Access all areas: yes, except the dining room
Number of dogs: two maximum
Late night pee: the beach
Owner's dogs: Kasha, a Pointer Lurcher Cross

THE MCLAREN HOTEL

Brodick, Isle of Arran, KA27 8AJ: 01770 302226; www.arran-hotels.co.uk

THE DRIFT INN

Shore Road, Lamlash, Isle of Arran, KA27 8JN

Resident Rover: Scuba

Scuba is a regular at the dog-friendly Ormidale Hotel in Brodick and star of the hotel's 'Dogs of the Ormidale' calendar.

ORMIDALE HOTEL

Brodick, Isle of Arran, KA27 8BQ: 01770 302293; www.ormidale-hotel.co.uk
Price: from £90 per double
Charge for dogs: no
Extras for dogs: regulars have the opportunity to feature in the 'Dogs of the Dale' calendar
Access all areas: everywhere
Number of dogs: no limit
Late night pee: grounds and country lanes

SCOTLAND DIRECTORY

THE ANDERSON

Union Street, Fortrose, Highland, IV10 8TD:
01381 620236;
www.theanderson.co.uk

It's whisky galore at this favourite with Phileas Dogg readers, praised for its food and friendliness. Rooms are quirky and unpretentious in a hotel which dates back to the 1870s. Owner Jim is a former travel guide writer.

Price: from £95 per double

Charge for dogs: no

Extras for dogs: doggie menu, biscuits and water bowls

Access all areas: in the rooms and the pub (where a cow was once a patron) but not in the whisky bar

Number of dogs: check at time of booking

Late night pee: 200 metres to the beach

Owner's dogs: Sheba, a Collie Cross rescue

APPLECROSS INN

Shore Street, Applecross, Strathcarron, Highland, IV54 8LR: 01520 744262;
www.applecross.uk.com/inn

Tucked away in the remote Applecross peninsula, all the rooms have sea views in this cosy, informal pub which has garnered many awards over the years for food and beer.

Price: £120 per double for the first night and £100 after that

Charge for dogs: £10 per stay

Extras for dogs: treats at bar

Access all areas: there are two dog-friendly bedrooms and dogs are allowed everywhere except the dining room

Number of dogs: maximum two

Late night pee: a skip to the beach

ARDANAISEIG HOTEL

Kilchrenan, Taynuilt, Argyll and Bute, PA35 1HE
01866 988155;
www.ardanaiseig.com

The collection of wellington boots in the hall of this listed 19th century baronial mansion will have your dog in a constant state of excitement about the next walk – and, with 240 acres of grounds to explore, Rover's got the right idea.

Price: from £173 per double

Charge for dogs: £20 per stay

Extras for dogs: no

Access all areas: allowed in all bedrooms but not in public areas, including the bar

Number of dogs: as many as the hotel can fit

Late night pee: ask for the bedroom called Orchy, with direct access to the garden

Owner's dogs: no.

ARDVERIKIE ESTATE

Kinlochlaggan, Newtonmore, Highland, PH20 1BX:
01528 544300;
www.ardverikie.com

Your dog can be Monarch of the Glen in one of the six self-catering properties on the estate where the BBC1 programme was filmed

Sleeps: from two in the lodges up to 13 (and four dogs) in the farmhouse

Price: from £400 to £1650 for a week depending on the property

Charge for dogs: £20 per dog per stay

Extras for dogs: no

Access all areas: yes

Number of dogs: it depends on which property you're renting

Late night pee: the estate is 40,000 acres!

SYHA

Dogs aren't allowed at youth hostels in England and Wales but, in 2013, the Scottish Youth Hostel Association piloted a dog-friendly scheme in two of its hostels – Cairngorm Lodge and Torridon. Hopefully, by the time you're reading this, the trial period will have been extended and dogs will be a permanent fixture. Flynn was one of the first dogs through the door at Cairngorm Lodge – with owners Mark and Natalie. Log on to www.syha.org.uk for more information.

B+B EDINBURGH

3 Rothesay Terrace, Edinburgh, EH3 7RY: 0131 225 5084;

www.bb-edinburgh.com

A boutique bed and breakfast with a restaurant, bar, library and views over Edinburgh Castle – sturdy Scottish breakfasts are provided in the mornings as energy for the hike up Arthur's Seat.

Price: starts at £90 for a small double

Charge for dogs: £50 refundable deposit in case of 'unforeseen cleaning'

Extras for dogs: no

Access all areas: except the restaurant

Number of dogs: two maximum

Late night pee: access to a communal, secure garden.

BEN LOMOND YURT

Trossachs Yurts, West Mossside Organic Farm, Thornhill, Stirlingshire, FK8 3QJ: 01786 850428;

www.westmossside.com or **www.trossachsyurts.com**

Set in a valley close to pretty Callander with its wool and tea shops, dog-friendly Ben Lomond yurt is one of three on a working organic farm. It's cosy with a wood-burning stove, thick rugs and a big dog blanket, should the Scottish evening turn chilly.

Sleeps: four max

Price: £240 for a three day weekend

Charge for dogs: no

Extras for dogs: blankets, bowls and towels

Access all areas: yes

Number of dogs: two, if you speak nicely to Kate on the phone

Late night pee: the yurt leads on to woodland – take a torch.

THE BOTHY

Isle of Canna, Inner Hebrides, Highland, PH44 4RS: Call the National Trust for Scotland on 0844 493 2018

www.nts.org.uk/Holidays/Accommodation/The-Bothy-Canna If splendid isolation is what you're after, look no further than the Bothy (a Scots word meaning estate worker's cottage or shelter) on the tiny island of Canna. With a population of less than 20, Canna is the furthest west of the Small Isles of the Inner Hebrides. It doesn't have any pubs but does offer beaches and birdlife in abundance.

The Bothy, Canna

Sleeps: four
Price: £300 to £500 a week
Charge for dogs: £15 per week
Extras for dogs: no
Access all areas: yes, but not on beds
Number of dogs: maximum two
Late night pee: the whole island!

COLINTRAIVE HOTEL

Colintraive, Argyll and Bute, PA22 3AS: 01700 841207;
www.colintraivehotel.com
This award-winning hotel in a small coastal village in Argyll boasts beautiful views across the Kyles of Bute and plentiful peaceful walks in the hills. As well as being dog-friendly, it is boat-friendly, with moorings at the beach 100 yards opposite.
Price: from £90 per double
Charge for dogs: no
Extras for dogs: dog treats
Access all areas: everywhere but the restaurant
Number of dogs: ask at time of booking
Late night pee: enclosed garden at the side of the hotel
Owner's dogs: Caesar, a black Labrador

CRAIGARD HOUSE HOTEL

Low Askomil, Campbeltown, Argyll and Bute, PA28 6EP: 01586 554242;
www.craigard-house.co.uk
Craigard is a grand old house perched on a hill with amazing sea views. It used to house Campbeltown's maternity hospital and many of the babies born here check in as adults and sign the Babies of Craigard visitors' book.
Price: from £85 per double
Charge for dogs: no
Extras for dogs: no
Access all areas: dogs aren't allowed in the restaurant but are welcome in the lounge
Number of dogs: maximum two
Late night pee: massive gardens at the front of the hotel
Owner's dogs: Beanie (pictured below), a hotel dog to her bones, will accompany you on walks

THE CROSS KEYS

Main Street, Kippen, Stirlingshire, FK8 3DN:
01786 870293;

www.kippencrosskeys.co.uk

This traditional village inn has changed a lot since
Jane used to work here 25 years ago and her inept
waitressing skills would not pass muster in what's now
a pretty slick operation, winning plaudits for food from
Kippen locals and national newspaper journalists alike.

Price: £70 per room upwards

Charge for dogs: no

Extras for dogs: biscuits behind the bar

Access all areas: yes

Number of dogs: enquire at time of booking

Late night pee: The Cross Keys is on Kippen's main
street

Owner's dogs: Jessie, a Labradoodle

FARR BAY INN

Berryhill, Sutherland, KW14 7SZ: 01641 521230;

www.farrbayinn.co.uk

Known locally as the FBI, it doesn't take much
investigation to work out quite how dog-friendly
the Farr Bay Inn is – very! It's cheerful, clean and
comfortable, offering a haven for locals (of whom

Zippy at Cross Keys

there aren't many in this remote part of the world) to
relax over a whisky, and tourists to de-stress amidst
stunning scenery.

Price: £74 per double

Charge for dogs: no

Extras for dogs: treats in rooms; beds and blankets
available

Access all areas: yes!

Number of dogs: maximum two

Late night pee: 350 metres to the beach

Owner's dogs: German Shepherd Bruin (pictured
below) earns his biscuits behind the bar

THE FINTRY INN

23 Main Street, Fintry, Stirlingshire, G63 0XA:
01360 860224;
Traditional Scottish pub with rooms in the village of
Fintry, nestled in the Campsie Hills — there's no public
transport but the local walks and views make it worth
the half-hour drive from Glasgow. The inn dates from
1750 but, under risk of closing forever, was recently
taken over by a collective from the village and is
being extensively refurbished. A top chef now runs the
kitchen and everything is homemade — down to the
tomato ketchup.

Price: The Fintry Inn has a self-catering flat for
overnighters, sleeping up to six and costing £30
per person per night. Eight new bedrooms are being
refurbished for guests, due for completion in spring 2014.

Charge for dogs: no

Extras for dogs: no

Access all areas: yes

Number of dogs: enquire at time of booking

Late night pee: a little park by a stream 200 yards
away

GEORGE HOTEL

Main Street East, Inverary, Argyll and Bute, PA32 8TT:
01499 302111;

www.thegeorgehotel.co.uk

Plaudits all round for the dog-friendliness of the
George, now run by the seventh generation of the same
family of hoteliers, in the small town of Inverary at the
top of Loch Fyne. If your dog misbehaves send him to
Inverary Jail — a dog-friendly attraction in town.

Price: from £75 per double

Charge for dogs: no

Extras for dogs: no

Access all areas: everywhere except the conservatory

Number of dogs: no maximum as long as they're
well-behaved

Late night pee: Inverary's main street

Owner's dogs: Labradors Belle and Fudge

GLENCAIRN HOUSE

Morar, Mallaig, Highland, PH40 4PD:
01687 450600;

www.glencairn-house.com 🐾

Dogs are made more than welcome at Glencairn, in both
the B&B and the static caravan. There's even a dog
agility course in the grounds for more energetic canine
guests. No televisions in the rooms so relax instead
gazing out at the wonderful views towards Skye.

Price: £60 per double and up

Charge for dogs: no

Extras for dogs: biscuits and beds in rooms. Gary is a
leatherworker and his handmade dog collars and leads
are available for sale.

Access all areas: yes

Number of dogs: one man arrived with six German
Shepherds!

Late night pee: the garden

Owner's dogs: Bernese Mountain Dogs Gillen and
Keller

GLENVIEW B&B

Luss, Loch Lomond, Argyll and Bute, G83 8PA:
01436 860606;

www.bonniebank.com

Luss is a pretty little village on the shores of Loch
Lomond, where Scottish soap opera *Take the High Road*
was filmed. Dogs will love leaping off the bonny banks
into the loch and can dry off at the two self-catering
cottages adjoining the Glenview B&B.

Sleeps: both cottages sleep four

Price: £120 per night

Charge for dogs: no

Extras for dogs: no

Access all areas: in the cottages, yes

Attlee at Luss, Loch Lomond

Number of dogs: one per cottage
Late night pee: a gated garden
Owner's dogs: a Bichon called Benzie

INNSEAGAN HOUSE HOTEL

Achintore Road, Fort William, Highland, PH33 6RW:
01397 700841;
www.innseaganhousehotel.com
There are excellent views of the loch from the
Innseagan – the hotel dogs will rush to point them out
to you upon arrival.
Price: from £65 per double
Charge for dogs: £6.50 per dog per night
Extras for dogs: no
Access all areas: everywhere except the restaurant but
meals can be taken in the bar and lounge
Number of dogs: maximum two
Late night pee: gardens at the front of the hotel
Owner's dogs: Bear, the Golden Retriever, and Sheila,
the Collie.

MUASDALE CAMPSITE

Muasdale, Tarbert, Kintyre Peninsula, Argyll and Bute,
PA29 6XD: 01583 421207;
www.muasdaleholidays.com

This 10-pitch campsite, on the Kintyre Peninsula, is
right on the beach and as laid-back as they come. The
village of Muasdale meanders along the shore road,
with a village shop for essentials but, other than that,
on a sunny day, there's no reason to go anywhere but
the beach with views across to Gigha and Jura.
Price: £10 for a no-electric pitch plus £2 per adult and
£1.25 per child.
Charge for dogs: £1.25 per night per dog
Extras for dogs: no
Access all areas: dogs aren't allowed in the toilet and
kitchen block
Number of dogs: maximum three
Late night pee: pull back the canvas and step onto
the beach.

OTTER AND ISLAND LIGHTHOUSE COTTAGES

Kildalloig Estate, Campbeltown, Argyll and Bute,
PA28 6RE: 07979 855930;
www.kintyrecottages.com
The beam from the now automatic lighthouse will
illuminate your stay at Otter Cottage or Island Cottage
on the Mull of Kintyre – both are the original lighthouse
keepers' homes. Situated on Davaar Island, only

accessible on foot at low tide, the cottages provide cosy hideaways with just goats and sheep for company.

Sleeps: two
Price: Start at £35
Charge for dogs: no
Extras for dogs: no
Access all areas: not in the bedrooms
Number of dogs: discuss at time of booking
Late night pee: enclosed gardens

ROXBURGHE COUNTRY HOUSE HOTEL

Heiton by Kelso, Borders, TD5 8JZ: 01573 450331;
www.roxburghe-hotel.com
This sumptuous 4-star pad in the Borders employs its own ghillie (attendant on shoots) – charming Alistair Ferguson who roams the grounds with his lovely Lab Lady, giving a warm, waggy welcome to all the guests.

Price: £135 per double
Charge for dogs: no
Extras for dogs: no
Access all areas: there are six dog-friendly rooms – including a two-storey suite – overlooking the courtyard. Dogs aren't allowed in the hotel itself, though.
Number of dogs: depending on size, two
Late night pee: wander on the golf course looking for stray balls

RUFFLETS COUNTRY HOUSE

Strathkinness Low Road, St Andrews, Fife, KY16 9TX: 01334 472594;
www.rufflets.co.uk
There are treats on arrival for dogs at Rufflets and a dog-sitter on hand should guests fancy a day out sans Fido but dogs aren't actually allowed into the main hotel itself, instead being offered accommodation in one of the three Gatehouse rooms or self-catering lodges. Still, the ten acres of grounds more than

Ben at the Sonachan

compensate for being relegated to gatekeeper status, especially as dogs are allowed off-lead to explore. The beaches of St Andrews, should your dog wish to re-enact the famous running scene from *Chariots of Fire*, are just a five minute drive away.

Price: from £150 per double
Charge for dogs: £10 per night
Extras for dogs: welcome pack on arrival with list of walks in the grounds, poo bags and a 'dog in room' sign for the door
Access all areas: not the main house
Number of dogs: maximum two
Late night pee: ten acres of grounds

SONACHAN

Kilchoan, Highland, PH36 4LN: 01972 510211;
www.sonachan.com
The most westerly hotel on the British mainland offers B&B and bunkhouse accommodation with talk of opening a campsite with yurts.

Price: £80 per double

Charge for dogs: £5 per stay

Extras for dogs: no

Access all areas: all the action's in the bar – breakfast and evening meals – and dogs are allowed on the upper level

Number of dogs: ask at time of booking

Late night pee: country roads – take your torch!

Owner's dogs: Finlay, a friendly Border Collie

STONEFIELD FARM WIGWAMS

Tarbert, Argyll and Bute, PA29 6SX:
01880 821554;

www:stonefieldfarmholidays.co.uk

Just a short walk from the village of Tarbert on the Mull of Kintyre, Stonefield Farm's six wigwams nestled in the mountains are cosy when the Scotch mist descends. The wigwams are horse-friendly too, with livery available.

Sleeps: two

Price: £64 per wigwam per night

Charge for dogs: £10 per stay

Extras for dogs: no

Access all areas: dogs aren't allowed in the on-site cafe and farm shop

Number of dogs: two dogs

Late night pee: you're in the mountains

TRIGONY HOUSE HOTEL

Closeburn, Thornhill, Dumfries and Galloway, DG3 5EZ:
01848 331211;

www.countryhousehotelscotland.com

A former shooting lodge in Dumfriesshire, the family run 4-star Trigony House doesn't need to rely on trendy gimmicks to entice – its commitment to old-fashioned service and standards are enough. Dog owners should request the Garden Suite, which has its own conservatory and enclosed section of garden.

Price. a classic double is £110

Charge for dogs: £7.50 per night per dog

Extras for dogs: a welcome pack on arrival with biscuits, chews and a map of local walks; a chest of drawers in the hall full of towels for muddy waggers and dog shampoo available upon request at reception

Access all areas: everywhere except the restaurant

Number of dogs: maximum three

Late night pee: four acres of grounds

Owner's dogs: Golden Retriever Roxy and Mini Dachshund Kit

WHITBY, NORTH YORKSHIRE

Aaaaaaaaaar-oooooooooooooooooooooh!

I am recreating the howl of the hound of Dracula and greeting every dog we encounter with blood-curdling baying at the moon. My canine cohorts, from Poodle to Patterdale, respond in kind.

We are in Whitby and if I choose to howl at the moon on occasion, this is the town to do it in. Not only are Jane and I staying in Whitby, Britain's most Gothic of towns, we are staying in Bats and Broomsticks, Whitby's most Gothic of guest houses. *Hound of Dracula sound effects at double volume, Phileas Dogg soundman please!*

Upon arrival at Bats and Broomsticks, we're greeted by a six-foot Dracula outside the Victorian villa. I am not frightened. He is plastic. We are also greeted by Kev, the proprietor – a chatty chap who leads us to our room past another life-size Dracula, holding a tray laden with lollipops, and a six foot coffin with RIP written on it. In the room, a bat hangs above the four-poster and my water is Gothic too – heavy metal and decorated with pentacles. A lesser dog might be chilled to the bone but not me. I bark at the plastic bat. My bones are warm.

'Sleep well – if you dare . . .' Kev pantomimes.

Attlee at Bowes Castle, County Durham

Whitby Harbour

And, after a few stiffeners in The Fleece and The Dolphin in Whitby town, I do – although Jane wakes me by screaming when a raucous Whitby seagull screeches in the night. The daft bat thought it was the plastic bat. Luckily Kev had placed a couple of Kit Kats in our hospitality tray and munching on them calms her fraying nerves.

Breakfast is in the basement, past a library of horror films, and all the tables are decorated with elaborate candlesticks borrowed from Meat Loaf's 'Anything for Love' video and Dracula teapots. Incense burns and the sound track is the Sex Pistols. A bit left-field but I'm a left-field, left-pawed kind of dog.

'Every other B&B is the same, but we're different – we give people an experience,' Kev says as he serves me SAUSAGES. He introduces us to 14-year-old Chihuahua Kizzy – one of four resident Bats and Broomsticks barkers. She is unscathed by spending her days in a Gothic guesthouse and informs me of the whereabouts of Whitby's most hospitable-to-hounds hostelries.

Out to explore. Whitby's a strange town because, while it prides itself on its horror connections, it's also cheery in the finest English seaside tradition, with sticks of rock and candy floss and brightly painted fairground rides. I notice this incongruity and mark it down in my reporter's notepad but Jane's too busy buying a Dracula ice cream (blackcurrant and liquorice with raspberry blood) to notice.

In Bram Stoker's *Dracula*, when a ship runs aground in Whitby, a big black dog dashes up the 199 steps to Whitby Abbey. This dog is Dracula himself, who can take on any form he chooses. But I am not a hell hound – I am a (relatively) well-behaved mongrel from Battersea School for Dogs and I take the steps at a sedate pace.

After all that exertion, though, I am sure I will be prevented from entering the abbey, as I am from many famous British buildings, on

Whitby Abbey – dogs welcome!

the simple grounds that I am a dog. But I am proved wrong. A lovely lady at the entrance hall tells me that not only am I allowed into this English Heritage site, I am allowed into over 300 English Heritage sites. Paws up English Heritage for recognising that we dogs are a vital part of England's heritage . . .

Pickles, who found the 1966 Jules Rimet World Cup trophy; Petra, the first Blue Peter dog; Mary Queen of Scots' dogs, who stayed by her side, even as she was executed – I salute you as I march into Whitby Abbey

Built in 600 and something and ransacked by the Vikings and again by Henry VIII, the abbey is now a glamorous Gothic ruin. Jane won't let me lift my leg against it, despite my best efforts to leave my mark to deter any more Vikings from attempting another ransack. I am allowed to wander all around, though, having a good old sniff and soaking up the mood of the ancient monument.

Then Jane needs a coffee, as she often does within a quarter of an hour of arriving at a cultural event or a historical monument, so we head back down the 199 steps and find The Grapevine caff. It has a wall decorated with photographs of dogs from around the country, all of whom have holidayed in Whitby and become pen pals with The Grapevine's houndfrau, Molly.

Bella the fairground dog (left); The Elsinore (right)

History and caffeine fix achieved, we wander. We meet Bella, who runs the fairground at the corner of Pier Road, and Jane buys some bunting made out of old copies of the *Beano*. Then we meander through the old town to The Elsinore, a proper pub in the old-fashioned beer and bar mats tradition where scampi and chips (the starter portion alone is massive) and a lime and soda costs less than a fiver.

But, by the time we reach the part of the beach where dogs are allowed during summer, just past Whitby theatre and beyond the beach huts, there is no beach to be seen – just sea. We have made an error of Gothic proportions. The tide's in.

As our train home is at 4pm, I am denied a scarper along the sand. I howwwwwwl in frustration and attempt to summon Dracula's Hell Hound to turn the tide for me . . .

Whitby Goth Weekend takes place every April and November – **www.whitbygothweekend.co.uk**

PHILEAS PHACTS: Whitby

BATS AND BROOMSTICKS
11 Prospect Hill, Whitby, Yorkshire, YO21 1QE: 01947 605659; **freespace.virgin.net/batsandbroomsticks** 🐾

Price: from £65 with a bathroom down the corridor with ducks with devil horns perched on the bath!

Charge for dogs: no

Extras for dogs: a pentacle engraved dog bowl; biscuits on arrival and sausages at breakfast

Access all areas: yes

Number of dogs: check on time of booking

Late night pee: there's woodland a few hundred yards up the hill

Owners' dogs: four, including Gothic Chihuahua Kizzy

WHITBY ABBEY
Abbey Lane, Whitby, North Yorkshire, YO22 4JT; **www.english-heritage.org.uk**

THE FLEECE
Church Street, Whitby, North Yorkshire, YO22 4AS: 01947 603649

THE DOLPHIN HOTEL
Bridge Street, Whitby, YO22 4BG: 01947 821455; **www.dolphinhotelwhitby.co.uk**

Kizzy vamps it up

THE GRAPEVINE CAFE
2 Grape Lane, Whitby, North Yorkshire, YO22 4BA: 🐾

Dogs are allowed on all Whitby beaches from September 30 to April 30. During the summer, they are allowed from the Pavilion along the beach to Sandsend, a good walk on a fine day, and Tate Hill.

All the boat trips from Whitby harbour, including the old lifeboat that takes visitors out, are dog-friendly.

THE ELSINORE
Flowergate, Whitby, North Yorkshire, YO21 3BB Tel: 01947 603975

ASKRIGG, YORKSHIRE DALES

It is Jane's friend Vicky's birthday and we are in Kirklea Cottage in Askrigg, a village in the Yorkshire Dales, to celebrate. Askrigg is famous because a television programme from the 1970s, *All Creatures Great and Small*, was filmed here. It was about a vet – I hope he's not around this weekend.

We have just arrived in the cottage and I am enjoying a lot of fuss. But then Vicky arrives with her chocolate Labrador Jess and I am not the sole recipient of the fuss. I bark at Jess to let her know that I'm top dog, but she ignores my barking and swishes her big Labrador tail from side to side. It bashes my nose.

Next morning, when we go for a walk, I decide that if I'm a naughty dog everybody will pay me – and not Jess – attention. We walk up a hill through Askrigg and through a gate into a field. Simon checks there are no livestock and – grrrr-huzzah! – I'm off the lead. It is terrific – one field leads to another and I

Askrigg (left); The Little Cheese Shop (above)

sprint through them, my fine terrier legs working fast as blood pumps around my body and the cold wind buffets me. I smell rabbits and sheep in the clods of reedy grass and I know there are adventures to be had. Then I see it – a dead rabbit, lying in the field. Its scent is wonderful – rich and pungent – and I gobble it up and crunch its bones and feel its juice running down my throat.

Jane shouts at me, rustling the bag of doggie treats she always carries in her handbag. As if doggie treats are going to distract me! Then Simon and Jane try to herd me as if I am a sheep and Jess looks at me, a pious and proper Goody-Two-Paws. When I've finished crunching, I walk up to Jane and allow her to clip my lead on as if nothing in the world has happened.

Back at the cottage, Jane tells everyone how naughty I've been but instead of ignoring me, because I'm bad, everybody talks to me kindly and tells me I'll have an upset tummy for my troubles. 'He might need the vet,' someone says and I panic – so he is around this weekend!

But I don't have a sore tummy! I have had gastroenteritis three times from street food in South-East London but fresh country meat doesn't give me gut ache in the slightest. I'm full of beans.

The people decide to go to a little town called Hawes for another walk but, as soon as we step out of the car, it begins raining. It's diagonal, slicing into your body and even though I'm a hardy little fellow it's making my insides cold. Hawes is a town made of grey stone and the rain makes it even greyer. So we go to a pub, The Crown Hotel, which has a silver plaque on the wall saying: 'We are a dog-friendly pub.' The Crown has a real fire and there are two other dogs in front it – a graceful girl greyhound and a Bulldog. The Bulldog stares at me and I stare straight back. This may be his local but I won't be intimidated.

In the pub everybody says they hope the rain will stop so we can go for another walk. But it doesn't. Jane dashes out into the rain to buy some cheese from the cheese shop – apparently Hawes is famous for Wensleydale cheese. (A dog called Gromit, on television, and his master, Wallace, eat a lot of this.) Then Tracey dashes out to buy a bottle of wine. Then we all dash back to the car and home to Askrigg.

Back at the house, the humans sit and talk and Jess and me sit and stare at each other with the rain lashing outside.

Then we walk around Askrigg, even though it's still raining. We peer in a gift shop that takes dogs, and a coffee shop – Sykes Tea Rooms – that takes dogs, and then decide on the pub opposite the cottage – The Crown. This is a great gig as, rather than having to sit on the floor, as I usually do in pubs, I'm allowed to sit on a seat, in between Vicky and Jane. They even place a pint of beer in front of me.

Pup with a Pint

It isn't long before I'm in trouble again, though and this time it's BIG trouble. Next morning, Jane and Hazel take me for a walk, up the hill again, and into the same fold of fields, with the public footpath sign, as the day before. Jane can't see any sheep so I'm off the lead, hurtling and hurdling.

I gallop from one field to the next to the next, all the smells triggering every nerve in my body with newness. And then I see them, behind a grey stone bothy – two SHEEP with curly horns on their heads. Before I even have time to process this, instinct has kicked in and I am chasing them. Then Jane is screaming and chasing me and Hazel is screaming and chasing her and it is like a Benny Hill sketch, us all chasing each other. Except it's not funny . . . The sheep run through two fields and into a small stone barn while I bark and bark to tell them to stop and listen to me.

Dogs and Sheep

The DEFRA website says the following on the matter of dogs worrying sheep: Under the Dogs (Protection of Livestock) Act 1953 the owner, and anyone else under whose control the dog is at the time, will be guilty of an offence if it worries livestock on agricultural land. For more information, log on to **www.gov.uk/defra**

Then Jane appears, teary and red in the face, and grabs me. I struggle because I want to keep barking but Jane doesn't let go. She puts my lead on in silence – I am in trouble – and then we are hurrying through the fields and through the gate back to the cottage.

'You could have been shot,' Jane says, shaking. 'If the farmer had seen you chasing sheep, he could have shot you.' I don't like that one bit – I have seen people being shot on television and know that it's not good.

PHILEAS PHACTS: Yorkshire Dales

KIRKLEA COTTAGE (right)
Askrigg, North Yorkshire:
Book through Yorkshire Cottages:
01228 406701;
www.yorkshire-cottages.info
Sleeps: up to six
Price: from £310 for a three night stay
Charge for dogs: no
Extras for dogs: no
Access all areas: not the bedrooms
Number of dogs: two
Late night pee: a two-minute walk and you're in the countryside

THE CROWN HOTEL
Market Place, Hawes, North Yorkshire, DL8 3 RD : 01969 667212;
www.crownhawes.co.uk
Price: £70
Charge for dogs: no
Extras for dogs: biscuits on arrival and sausages for breakfast
Access all areas: everywhere
Number of dogs: no limit
Late night pee: car park with grass and poo bins 100 yards away
Owner's dogs: two lively Jack Russells Pickle and Buddy

SYKES HOUSE TEA ROOM AND B&B
Askrigg, North Yorkshire, DL8 3HI:
01969 650535; **www.sykeshouse.co.uk**
Price: £75
Charge for dogs: £10 per dog per stay
Extras for dogs: no
Access all areas: yes – dogs are allowed in the breakfast room
Number of dogs: two per room
Late night pee: fields across the road

THE CROWN INN
Main Street, Askrigg, North Yorkshire, DL8 3HQ: 01969 650387

THE LITTLE CHEESE SHOP
Ivy Cottage, Hawes, North Yorkshire, DL8 3R7;
www.ribblesdalecheese.wordpress. com or **www.thelittlecheeseshop.co.uk**, where cheese can be ordered online

If I was shot, I'd definitely need the vet.

Back at the cottage, everyone is very stern with me. It is a relief to be on the train to London, to escape the sternness. I have done a very bad thing.

I will never ever chase sheep again. I will repeat it a hundred times until I remember.

Resident Rover: Jack the Pug in Harrogate, North Yorkshire

I am Jack the Pug and, whatever that silly blue rosette round my neck says, I am second to none. I'm a pugnacious pug and, in between my gruelling fitness regime to keep trim, I have put paw to paper to celebrate Dog's Own County – Yorkshire – and Harrogate, my home.

Harrogate is famous as a spa town with lots of lovely old buildings but the best part of town for us dogs is the 200-acre parkland called The Stray in the town centre. There's lots of straying to be done and fun to be had chasing children on bicycles. The park is lined with cafes and pubs – I'm partial to a pork pie – and The Coach and Horses, dog-friendly after 3pm, is my favourite boozer. Good food and it stocks lots of Harrogate beers – essential for a party animal like me!

The Harrogate Ringway is a glorious 20-mile path circling the town – a bit much for my little legs all in one day so I take it in stages. Almscliffe Crag is a nice spot for a scramble and within easy walking distance of Braythorne Bees, a farm which serves good Yorkshire lunches in its gardens. Or pop into The Square and Compass in the village of North Rigton – biscuits for pugs on demand!

I am a lucky enough pug to live in Dog's Own County but if you're a holidaying hound, I heartily recommend Harrogate Holidays for self-catering accommodation. I work (five days a week; no slacking) in the office there, with 13 other animals, including some hens and half a pony. (As in, one pony who is only with us half the time.) At weekends I am dog-tester for Harrogate Holidays' dog-friendly cottages.

My favourite is Newby Farm Cottage, as the lane it stands on is a 'no-through' road meaning no nasty vehicles interrupt my morning constitutional. In Harrogate itself, my favourite is Daisy House. It's only five minutes from Valley Gardens Park, which has more mineral springs erupting than anywhere else on the planet.

When Harrogate lass Lola the Cockerpoo isn't working at the car wash, her favourite place to be is Valley Gardens.

PHILEAS PHACTS: Harrogate

THE COACH AND HORSES
16 West Park, Town Centre, Harrogate, North Yorkshire, HG1 1BJ: 01423 561 802;
www.thecoachandhorses.net

BRAYTHORNE BEES
The Honey House, Braythorne Lane, Stainburn, Otley, West Yorkshire, LS21 2LW:
0113 284 2982

THE SQUARE AND COMPASS
North Rigton, Harrogate, North Yorkshire, LS17 0DJ: 01423 733031;
www.thesquareandcompass.com

Jack's favourite Harrogate Holidays properties are:
NEWBY FARM COTTAGE
The Sleights, Gravelly Hill Lane, Huby, Leeds, West Yorkshire, LS17 0EX
Book through Harrogate Holidays on 01423 523333; **www.harrogateholidays.co.uk**
Sleeps: up to five
Price: starting at £465
Charge for dogs: £20 a stay
Extras for dogs: dog biscuits alongside all the produce from the garden awaiting guests in the kitchen
Access all areas: not in bedrooms
Number of dogs: check at time of booking
Late night pee: enclosed garden although dogs on leads as there are chickens

DAISY HOUSE
39 Strawberry Dale, Harrogate, North Yorkshire, HG1 5EA
Sleeps: up to six
Price: starting at £560 per week
Charge for dogs: £20 per stay
Extras for dogs: no
Access all areas: not upstairs
Number of dogs: one
Late night pee: enclosed courtyard garden

The beach at Low Newton, top, and, inset, The Ship Inn, Low Newton

ALNMOUTH AND LOW NEWTON, NORTHUMBERLAND

We always pass through Alnmouth on our train journeys from London to Scotland and back – the views out of the window are very dramatic around that part of the Northumbrian coastline. But, one day, to my great consternation, we didn't pass through – we alighted. There was a bit of confusion at Alnmouth taxi rank about how far it was to the village itself. Quarter of an hour's walk, someone said – a mile and a half reckoned someone else.

'It's only £3 in a taxi,' a cabbie told us but, when he dropped us off two minutes later outside the Hope and Anchor, our bed and board for the weekend, the price had mysteriously risen to six quid. *A bit rum . . .*

Still, the Hope and Anchor, where a chatty lady and a chatty Jack Russell checked us in, appeared hopeful – a traditional pub with whitewashed walls and a cosy bar. Never mind that our bathroom light didn't work (I perform my ablutions al fresco) or that, according to Jane's sister Steph, there was a bit of dust.

No dust in Alnmouth itself – it was as sparkling as a just-out-of-the-dishwasher dog bowl. The good people of the village – as pleasant a seaside village as I've ever visited – obviously take a great deal of pride in maintaining it. Alnmouth is one long street with friendly pubs, tea rooms and shops lining it and then, at the end, the beach and the crashing great North Sea. In terms of amount of beach per canine capita, I would estimate that we dogs have two miles of sand each. Grrrr-huzzah!

At the entrance to the beach, there's a sign saying that a Methodist called John

Wesley described Alnmouth as a 'small seaport town famous for all kinds of wickedness.' But, when I barked at the kites that beachgoers were flying – an act of all kinds of wickedness on my part – I was given disapproving glances. Obviously, these days, wickedness is frowned upon in Alnmouth.

I had hoped we might patronise the Hope and Anchor for evening repast, as part of the pub houses an Italian restaurant and spaghetti is my favourite food, with just one strand transforming me into Placido Dom-dingo – world renowned opera howler. But Steph has a CAR – something Jane does not possess – and the sisters were determined to take advantage of this fact by exploring the Northumbrian coastline further.

'Come on,' Steph ordered. 'There is a good pub called The Ship Inn at Low Newton-by-the-Sea and we must research that for the book.'

I gave her a hard stare – I am in charge of what we will research for the book, being as I am a travel writer and Steph is a psychologist. (I did once attempt to psychoanalyse Dodger on the couch but he spat at me. Clearly he is a cat with issues.)

Oh one minute. We have just pulled up at a little square with white stone fisherman's cottages and a pub on miles of empty beach . . .

'That is the Ship Inn,' Steph announces. Rarely, for me, I am humbled – not just by the vastness and remoteness of the beach and the charm of the cottages but also by my cruel dismissal of Steph's attempts at travel journalism.

'This place is in all the posh travel books,' Steph says and I am grateful to her. If it's in all the posh travel books, it's sure as all hell going to be in mine. So here goes: The Ship Inn, Low Newton, is a lively pub with hearty food and its own micro-brewery. Take that Alistair Pawday!

On the sands at Alnmouth

PHILEAS PHACTS: Alnmouth and Low Newton

HOPE AND ANCHOR

44 Northumberland Street, Alnmouth,
Northumberland, NE66 2RA:
01665 830363;
www.hopeandanchorholidays.co.uk
Price: from £100 based on two
people sharing
Charge for dogs: no
Extras for dogs: no
Access all areas: the Italian
restaurant isn't dog-friendly but
pasta can be eaten in the pub
Number of dogs: check at time of
booking
Late night pee: step out of the door
and you're on Alnmouth's main street
Owner's dogs: Jack Russell Bow
(pictured)

with tables and chairs just off it for dogs
and their owners
Number of dogs: two maximum
Late night pee: car park out the back
with a bin
Owner's dogs: no – they're too busy
running the B&B, so they make an extra
fuss of any visiting mutts

THE SADDLE B&B

24 Northumberland Street, Alnmouth,
Northumberland, NE66 2RA:
01665 830476;
**www.thesaddlebedandbreakfast.
co.uk**
This is a well-run and old-fashioned
but charming-for-it B&B on
Alnmouth's main street
Price: £70
Charge for dogs: no
Extras for dogs: SAUSAGES at
breakfast
Access all areas: not in the breakfast
room but there's a little ante-room

THE SHIP INN

Low Newton by-the-Sea,
Northumberland: 01665 576262;
www.shipinnnewton.co.uk

Every beach in Northumberland is dog-
friendly all year round except for Newbiggin.

YORK

I am a guest at a wedding: Jane's sister Steph is marrying Jerome at York Register Office and an exception to the rules about dogs not being allowed in register offices has been made on the grounds that I am small and well-behaved. (I am neither but Steph had to fudge the facts a little when pleading with the registrar!)

To celebrate the fact I am a wedding guest, Annie in the park made me a top hat and tails. I felt a right prat in it and refused to wear it on the streets, as when other dogs saw me they laughed. But it seemed to give the humans, especially the little ones, a kick and sometimes we have to do things for others at the expense of our dignity – or so Jane kept reminding me.

The correct way to dress for a wedding

The service, in the register office, was a bit boring for dogs but the reception was amaze-bones. I ate Parma Ham, pumpkin pasta, chorizo, bread and butter pudding and cheese and biscuits. A feast! After the reception the bride and groom caught the train from York to London to stay the night at the St Pancras Hotel. Everyone threw confetti, which I had to spend hours shaking from my fur afterwards. Then the wedding party – now bride- and groom-less – commenced a pub crawl!

We kicked off in The Lamb and Lion Inn – a very fine establishment built into the city walls, with corridors from olden days to sniff my way along, a beer garden for summer and fireplaces for winter. There was also a private dining room, into which, had I not already eaten enough for ten dogs (and three of them Great Danes), I would have been welcomed.

Then we staggered down the street to the Three Legged Mare, also known as

No dogs allowed in Betty's famous Tea Rooms

the Wonky Donkey. It is quite grungy and reminded Jane of her student days, so we stayed until closing, which was rather a long time for me, as I had missed my afternoon nap.

After throwing out time, Jane and Steph's friend Jo returned to their room at the Holme Lea Manor Guest House. The previous night there had been three single women sleeping in single beds but now there were just two as Steph had slipped off the dusty spinster shelf. This worked in my favour as it meant one single bed was free for me!

(I don't think the Holme Lea would approve so keep it under your toppers, chaps. The Holme Lea, while perfectly homely, didn't exactly roll out the red carpet for us Rovers – it was dogs *allowed* rather than dogs welcome. But Steph struggled to find a hotel in York which would even allow me through the door so we cannot knock it.)

The following day, we had a stroll around the city streets. There was a lot happening, including some strange men with feathers on their backs playing pan pipes. I barked at them because people aren't supposed to have feathers and I felt like ruffling a few.

Then we strolled along the city walls for half an hour – until we noticed a sign banning dogs from strolling along the city walls. Sorry York. I am not a Viking mutt, about to maraud through your fine city but still you do not wish me to set paw on your ancient buttresses and bulwarks. I don't understand your reasoning but I have to respect it.

At least Dickinson's Coffee Shop welcomed me – and then we walked past the strangest-smelling place ever. There was a peaty smell and the smell of some

PHILEAS PHACTS: York

HOLME LEA MANOR
18 St Peter's Grove, York, YO30 6AQ:
01904 623529;
www.holmelea.co.uk
Price: from £80
Charge for dogs: no
Extras for dogs: no
Access all areas: bedrooms only
Number of dogs: one small dog only
Late night pee: stroll on the street

THE LAMB AND LION INN
2–4 High Petergate, York, YO1 7EH:
01904 654112;
www.lambandlionyork.com

THREE LEGGED MARE
15 High Petergate, York, YO1 7EN:
01904 638246;
www.york-brewery.co.uk

DICKINSON'S COFFEE SHOP
14 Tower Street, York, YO1 9SA

rubbish and a pig-sty smell, all mixed together. A peculiar woman with long plaits and a ring through her nose greeted me. Apparently she was a Viking and we were standing outside the Jorvik Centre, which recreates York's Viking past, complete with authentic SMELLS.

Of course I wanted to investigate – I may be well-travelled but I've never travelled back in time. But I wasn't allowed inside Jorvik – humans only. Didn't they have dogs in Viking times? I rarely fart, being very well behaved, as the registrar at York register office can attest, but I could have let slip a doggy fart to ensure the visitors to Jorvik had a proper cultural experience.

Three-year-old Cairn Terrier Indy Powell enjoyed sitting outside Jamie's Italian on a sunny day in York because of the possibility of SCRAPS!

Middlethorpe Hall, near York

Middlethorpe Hall, a ten-minute drive from York city centre, is William and Mary's house. William and Mary were so keenly aware of the privilege I was bestowing on them by visiting, that I was afforded the best room in the house – not so much a room, as a whole cottage, down a little country lane from the hall itself. It had its own garden and antique furniture and a plump sofa (not that I tested it; I'm just guessing, William and Mary).

But then, WOE, when I fancied a nose around the big posh hall itself, William and Mary would not allow me in. I was stuck on the doorstep! Now, this is clearly wrong. Anyone who has watched *Downton Abbey* knows that dogs are definitely not below stairs – we are above stairs, like Lord Grantham's dog. THE CORGI'S AT BUCKINGHAM PALACE LIVE IN A POSH HOUSE. I rest my case.

Oh sorry – interruption from Jane. She is informing me that we were not staying at William and Mary's house at all – but in a William and Mary house, which is a different thing altogether. A William and Mary house is a house that was built during the reign of William and Mary – three hundred years ago. So there's no William and Mary at this William and Mary house now. Major confuse-bones!

MIDDLETHORPE HALL

York, YO23 2GB: 01904 641241;
www.middlethorpe.com
Sleeps: the cottage suites sleep up to three
Price: £197 and up
Charge for dogs: no
Extras for dogs: map of walks on arrival
Access all areas: dogs aren't allowed in the main house
Number of dogs: check at time of booking
Late night pee: 20 acres of grounds

BOWES, COUNTY DURHAM

Bowes – take a bow! Phileas Dogg's dog-friendliest village accolade is up for grabs and Bowes, in County Durham, sweeps the honours. It has three amenities – a pub, a working men's club and a castle ruins, overseen by English Heritage – and they're all dog-friendly. Bowes is 100 per cent dog-friendly!

Furthermore, within half an hour of my arrival, two locals had dug their hands in their pockets and presented me with dog treats. They weren't even dog owners, they said, but carried them on the off chance of meeting a canny canine.

The reason we'd come to Bowes is to have a look at its 16th century coaching inn, The Ancient Unicorn, which we've heard is haunted – Attlee Common, Ghost Hunter. But the bar maid said she'd never sensed a ghost in the pub so my sniffing out spirit skills weren't put to the test.

(There was evidence, however – Canine Scene Investigation fans – in the grounds of Bowes Castle of something a little more earthly but just as exciting. RABBITS! I tracked their poo and was just about to nip one on its fluffy little tail when Jane caught me and nipped my fun in the bud.)

The Ancient Unicorn is imposing and from the outside appears all strict and rigid. Inside, though, it's cosy and welcoming. It's a favourite with walkers tramping the Pennine Way and has dog-friendly bedrooms – clean but no frills, apart from the potential frill of seeing a ghost.

I bumped into Rufus – a proper hound on the ground in Bowes, as he was staying for a week in a holiday cottage (called Unicorn Cottage) right next to the Ancient Unicorn.

Rufus's hound bites are: 'I enjoy my visits to the Ancient Unicorn, as the walkers in the bar make a fuss of me. My favourite stroll is to High Force waterfall. However, I am not keen on the midges and the horse flies.'

Left to Right: Bowes Castle; Rufus Hound; The Pennine Way

PHILEAS PHACTS: Bowes

THE ANCIENT UNICORN,

Bowes, Barnard Castle, County Durham, DL12 9HL: 01833 628321;
Price: £60
Charge for dogs: £10 per stay
Extras for dogs: dog biscuits behind the bar
Access all areas: yes
Number of dogs: five Golden Retrievers stayed in autumn 2013
Late night pee: through the archway at the back of courtyard into fields

UNICORN COTTAGE

Bowes, County Durham, DL12 9HL
Book through Sykes Cottages at 01244 356666 or **www.sykescottages.co.uk**
Sleeps: three
Price: from £222
Charge for dogs: no
Extras for dogs: no
Access all areas: except bedrooms
Number of dogs: two maximum
Late night pee: through the archway shared with the pub into the fields

DURHAM

I visit Durham often, as I have family there and it is, in my estimation, one of Britain's dog-friendliest cities. Other cities should take the LEAD from Durham and plonk a lot of countryside right in the middle of their city centres, like it has. I don't mean parks, like in London – parks aren't countryside. I mean proper countryside – in Durham's case, walks along the River Wear, which is banked by trees and forest and where I am allowed to SQUIRREL freely. All this space and freedom, yet I am only two minutes stroll away from Barks and Spencers, which, as everyone knows, is the epicentre of any thriving burgh.

Durham has lots of things that humans like to tick off their 'I am a proper tourist and I have taken lots of photographs' lists. It has the Cathedral, where people

go to worship DOG. (Strangely, we canines aren't allowed inside.) It has a university and cobbled streets. There is a market in the main square on Saturdays, with a stall selling amaze-bones home-baked bones.

The best walk in Durham is along the river and through the woods to Shincliffe, a village in a conservation area, two miles from the city centre.

Above, walking in Teesdale, and, inset, a boat trip on the River Wear

We do it on a Sunday – and that means Sunday roast in the Seven Stars Inn. Once, when I was there with Steph and Jerome, a fellow diner, tucking into lamb and mint sauce, asked why I looked sad. Jerome replied that, while I have a sad face, my personality is happy. *Jerome should have said: Attlee is sad because he would like some kind stranger to share their lamb and mint sauce with him, thank you very much!*

As well as the Seven Stars, the other Durham pubs that are in receipt of the Phileas Dogg High Paw of Approval are The Dun Cow, for proper real ale drinkers, and The Victoria Inn, which has hardly changed since Victoria was on the throne and my great-great-great-great-great grandfather was the highest paid performer in circuses across the land.

There are also lots of grand days out for dogs around Durham. My favourite is to Eggleston Hall, which is in the middle of a heavenly heap of countryside. Sadly the cafe in the Hall doesn't allow dogs inside – a bit rotten, since so many of us go there. Broom House Farm is also very good for a WALK, followed by a Sunday roast, which comes with a free pudding.

Beamish, 12 miles from Durham, is also worth a NOSE. It is a village from years and years ago and is like a massive museum that people and dogs can walk around, buying sweets in the old-fashioned sweet shoppes and riding on the old-fashioned trams. The trams aren't as interesting as the no. 12 buses in South-East London – there weren't any Ye Olde Fryed Chicken Shoppes in the olden days so there are no scraps to be snaffled.

73

PHILEAS PHACTS: Durham

THE VICTORIA INN
86 Hallgarth Street, Durham, DH1 3AS:
0191 386 5269;
www.victoriainn-durhamcity.co.uk
Price: £75 and up
Charge for dogs: no
Extras for dogs: biscuits behind the bar
Access all areas: everywhere but the breakfast room
Number of dogs: maximum two
Late night pee: on the river bank

BEAMISH MUSEUM
Beamish, County Durham, DH9 0RG:
0191 370 4000;
www.beamish.org.uk

BROOM HOUSE is at Witton
Gilbert, County Durham, DH7 6TR:
0191 371 9697;
www.broomhousedurham.co.uk

EGGLESTON HALL
Barnard Castle, County Durham,
DL12 0AG:
01833 650553;
www.egglestonhall.co.uk

SEVEN STARS INN
High Street North, Shincliffe, Durham,
DH1 2NU:
0191 384 8454;
www.sevenstarsinn.co.uk

THE DUN COW
37 Old Elvet, Durham,
DH1 3HN:
0191 386 9219

No-Bones bones are sold at Durham Market every Saturday and at
www.no-bones.co.uk

The Northumberland Coast by Willow the Coton de Tulear

I am Willow and I'm positively bursting with excitement to tell you about my SUPER-DOGGY-DUPER holiday with Hannah and her mum in Northumberland. My tail hasn't stopped wagging since!

Beadnell: Our holiday cottage – three-bedroomed Gullsway – was in Beadnell, just south of the popular harbour town of Seahouses. It was perfect for me. The garden was enclosed, meaning lead-off freedom, and it was opposite the beach. Location, location, location! Cross the road, follow a path through the dunes and there was the sand and the sea – deserted and waiting for ME!

Just a stroll away lay another huge stretch of sand – Beadnell Bay. We walked all the way along it to a nature reserve – then rejoined the coastal path and walked back

*Life's a beach in Northumberland
for Willow*

to Beadnell through the sand dunes, which I discovered the joy of digging in. We finished with some well-earned refreshment at the dog-friendly Craster Arms

Seahouses: One day we walked along the beach from our cottage all the way to Seahouses, a bustling resort full of shops and places to eat and drink. The Bamburgh Castle Inn welcomes dogs and the pet shop in the town is brilliant. There's a busy harbour, which the Inn overlooks, where you can take one of the (dog-friendly) boat trips to the Farne Islands.

Bamburgh: One day we walked from Seahouses along the beach to Bamburgh – yet another AMAZING and empty beach, overlooked by the imposing Bamburgh Castle. In the village, there's a large green as well as a few shops and the Grace Darling Museum. We went to the Copper Kettle Tea Rooms – apparently it does the best cream teas in the WORLD but as I wasn't allowed one I can't comment. Still, it was very pleasant sitting outside in the courtyard – a real suntrap and always a dog or two to make friends with.

PHILEAS PHACTS: Northumberland Coast

GULLSWAY
14 Harbour Road, Beadnell,
Northumberland, NE67 5BB:
Book through **www.
gracedarlingholidays.com** or **www.
gullswaybeadnell.co.uk**
Price: short breaks from £350
Charge for dogs: £25 per stay
Extras for dogs: no
Access all areas: not in bedrooms
Number of dogs: one or two, if they're small
Late night pee: enclosed garden

THE CRASTER ARMS
The Wynding, Beadnell, Northumberland,
NE67 5AX: 01665 720272;
www.crasterarms.co.uk
Price: doubles from £85
Charge for dogs: no
Extras for dogs: no
Access all areas: dog area in the bar with a fireplace
Number of dogs: no maximum
Late night pee: the pub is next to a field

THE BAMBURGH CASTLE INN
Seahouses, Northumberland, NE68 7SQ:
01665 720283;
www.bamburghcastleinn.co.uk
Price: £85
Charge for dogs: £5, however many dogs
Extras for dogs: no

Access all areas: part of the bar is open to dogs
Number of dogs: within reason
Late night pee: dog-friendly rooms have patio doors on to garden
Owner's dogs: Murphy, a Chocolate Labrador

THE COPPER KETTLE TEAROOMS
21 Front Street, Bamburgh,
Northumberland, NE69 7BW:
01668 214315;
www.copperkettletearooms.com

THE JOLLY FISHERMAN
Haven Hill, Craster, Northumberland,
NE66 3TR: 01665 576461;
www.thejollyfishermancraster.co.uk

SHORELINE CAFE
1 Church Street, Craster, Northumberland,
NE66 3TH: 01665 571251

ROSS BACK SANDS BEACH
Turn right off the A1 past Belford on a minor road towards Ross;
OS Map Ref: NU 148377

THE WHITE SWAN
Warenford, Belford, NE70 7HY:
01668 213453

Craster: Also worth a visit is Craster, a short drive down the coast. This picturesque fishing village is starting point for several walks – most notably the bracing stride over the cliffs to Dunstanburgh Castle. It's one of the more popular routes – although this just meant more people to fuss me. Craster is home to a famous kipper smokehouse, which smelt VERY intriguing, as well as the Jolly Fisherman pub, which welcomes dogs, and the Shoreline Café. A café that lets dogs inside – jackpot!

Ross Back Sands: Now I'll tell you about the next place I visited only if you PROMISE – Pup's Honour – not to tell anyone else . . . Ross Back Sands is Northumberland's best-kept secret – partly because it's so well hidden. Park on the road leading to the tiny hamlet of Ross and then it's over a mile's walk through fields and sand dunes to the beach. But it's worth it! A golden beach stretches as far as the eye can see in either direction, framed between Lindisfarne Castle to the north and Bamburgh Castle to the south. We had a lovely picnic, as if we were on our own private beach.

Warenford: Finally I have to recommend an excellent, dog-friendly pub we went to for dinner on our last night in Northumberland – The White Swan in Warenford. It's cosy and traditional and the food is award winning – everything is locally sourced, with the menu telling you exactly which farm the produce comes from. It's best to book, because it's so popular!

Jess in Bamburgh

I am Jess the Dog – a ten-year-old rescue lab living in Durham. When we arrived to check in at the Victoria Hotel in Bamburgh and the receptionist saw what a grand and stately lady I am, we were upgraded to a room with a four pawster bed. Now that's something worth wagging – sorry, bragging – about!

THE VICTORIA HOTEL,
Front Street, Bamburgh, Northumberland, NE69 7BP:
01668 214431; **www.victoriahotel.net**
Price: from £95
Charge for dogs: £7.50 per stay
Extras for dogs: dog biscuits and beds
Access all areas: not in the restaurant – breakfast for dog owners is in the bar
Number of dogs: confirm when booking
Late night pee: grassy area opposite the hotel

It Shouldn't Happen to a Pet

Not every day in the life of a canine travel correspondent goes to plan – for example, my eight hours of research in Corbridge, a town half an hour on the train from Newcastle, which everyone had extolled to us as the prettiest town in Northumberland, with beautiful countryside walks, a Roman settlement on the outskirts, tea shops for cake, traditional pubs for real ale and a town square with an independent book shop. The sort of place, in other barks, which any dog worth his SAUSAGES would love to explore – except, when we explored, it was the least dog-friendly town we'd ever visited.

I was allowed in the Roman Town to stroll down the ruins of the oldest Roman high street in England. But I could not stroll through Corbridge itself, popping in here so Jane could have a coffee, and there so she could have a Sauvignon. We were turned away at nearly every door.

Every coffee shop – dogs not allowed.

Only one of the five pubs we enquired at welcomed dogs.

In fact, the lady at the tourist information said, glancing at me with an embarrassed expression, apart from the Golden Lion, there's only one other place in Corbridge that allows dogs – the Fellcroft B&B, close to the train station.

Well, Phileas Phans, it is just plain madness. I have a science bit here. Pet travel is increasing by 6 per cent, year-on-year. It is a growing THING. And what was really foxing me – to turn a noun I don't like into a verb I do – was how a town, set in the middle of such prime dog-walking country, could be so un-canine canny.

We sought out the proprietors of the Fellcroft B&B – our own angels of the north when it came to finding some canine kindness in Corbridge. Very glad to see us Arnold and Tove were too – and very sympathetic when we told them about our less than warm welcome.

'Dogs are less trouble than some humans we've had to stay here,' Tove said, placing a bowl of water in front of me.

High Paw Arnold and Tove!

For liquid refreshment of an evening, there's a pub – The Dyvels – next door to Fellcroft, with the finest beer garden I've ever seen. Just as well the beer garden's fine because – what a surprise – the Dyvels doesn't allow dogs inside. Devils!

PHILEAS PHACTS: Corbridge

FELLCROFT B&B
Station Road, Corbridge, Northumberland, NE45 5AY: 01434 632384;
www.fellcroft.co.uk 🐾
Price: £65
Charge for dogs: no
Extras for dogs: bowls
Access all areas: in the sitting room but not in the breakfast room
Number of dogs: check at time of booking
Late night pee: step onto the street

Resident Rover: Henry the mini Dachshund

My name is Henry and I'm a Black and Tan Mini Dachshund with Silver Dapple splodges. I've been living with Mum, Dad and my brother Dyson the Weimaraner on a farm called The Cud Life, between Harrogate and Ripley, since I was seven weeks and six days old, on 21 August 2013. (I was so cute Mum and Dad couldn't wait to collect me.)

Life on the farm is brilliant. As well as our home, we have two holiday cottages – Cowslip and Humble Bee – and a campsite with 15 pitches. Every Saturday evening we light a campfire and I make new friends.

There is also a cook shop on the farm, where I work very hard, sitting behind the counter and providing customer service with cuddles and cuteness. I keep unruly children entertained, meaning their parents can browse and (hopefully) buy in the shop without distraction. I'm good at this and definitely earn my wages (treats).

THE CUD LIFE

Spruisty Hall Farm, Ripon Road, Killinghall, Harrogate,
North Yorkshire, HG3 2AU: 01423 506385;
www.thecudlife.co.uk
Price: cottages start at £460 per week; pitches on the campsite £20
Charge for dogs: free on the campsite; £20 per stay in the cottages
Extras for dogs: designated dog walking areas; dog bowls; taps to wash paws after muddy walks and towels
Access all areas: not upstairs in the cottages
Number of dogs: check at time of booking
Late night pee: country lanes
Owner's dogs: Henry and Dyson

NORTH-EAST DIRECTORY

BATTLESTEADS HOTEL

Wark on Tyne, near Hexham, Northumberland, NE48 3LS: 01434 230209; **www.battlesteads.com**

Dogs love Battlesteads and Battlesteads loves dogs – well, how could a place that has invented its own sausage, The Great Battlesteads Banger, not? This attractive stone brick 18th Century farmstead is in the middle of prime walking country too, with Hadrian's Wall and Wark Forest close by.

Price: £115 up

Charge for dogs: £5

Extras for dogs: welcome pack including Bonios, blankets, poo bags and towels and a guide featuring walks starting at Battlesteads' door

Access all areas: the bar and a small section of the restaurant so dogs can eat with their owners

Number of dogs: general manager Katie says they have hosted dogs from Chihuahuas to Great Danes

Late night pee: two-acre garden

Owner's dogs: Winston the Black Lab (pictured) keeps an eye on things

BLACKSMITHS ARMS

Main Street, Naburn, York, YO19 4PN: 01904 623464; **www.blacksmithsarmsnaburn.co.uk** 🐾

Now this is something – the Blacksmiths has a bar just for dogs, where pints of water and packets of treats are served, with all monies raised going to Dogs Trust. The pub is in a village, four miles from York, and has a self-catering cottage attached. Book it for a break and there'll be no need to cook as pub grub can be delivered straight to your door!

Sleeps: the cottage sleeps two

Price: £350 a week

Charge for dogs: no

Extras for dogs: the bar in the boozer

Access all areas: everywhere except for the restaurant

Number of dogs: no maximum

Late night pee: two minutes' walk to the river

Owner's dogs: Shandy, a Heinz 57, and Bailey, a Sprocker Spaniel

BRANDLING VILLA

Haddricks Mill Road, South Gosforth, Newcastle upon Tyne, NE3 1QL: 0191 284 0490; **www.brandlingvilla.co.uk**

Newcastle's Brandling Villa is the pub of choice for any self-respecting dog on the Tyne. Frank, the boozer's Beagle, is in charge of the mutts' menu, which changes every couple of months to ensure pup patrons don't tire of the same old offering. Get your sausage on, Geordie Paws

THE BRIDGE INN

Whorlton, Teesdale, DL12 8XD: 01833 627341;
www.thebridgeinn-whorlton.co.uk
The Bridge Inn, a picturesque pub serving good food, is
on the green in the pretty village of Whorlton and has
a shop attached, selling treats for dogs returning from
long walks in the surrounding countryside.

17 BURGATE

Pickering, Yorkshire, YO18 7AU: 01751 473463
www.17burgate.co.uk
Pickering is a genteel old market town and 17 Burgate,
a B&B in a striking Georgian house in its centre,
epitomises that elegance, with period features aplenty
and tea served in the walled garden. Pickering Castle
is a short walk away (the grounds are dog-friendly)
with woods and fields behind.
Price: from £76
Charge for dogs: £5 per stay
Extras for dogs: biscuits and towels if required
Access all areas: the dog-friendly rooms are at the
back of the property, with doors opening onto the
garden. Dogs aren't allowed in the breakfast room
Number of dogs: two. Cats are also welcome!
Late night pee: enclosed garden
Owner's dogs: Dudley the Cocker Spaniel and ginger
tomcat Koshka meet and greet every guest – human,
canine or feline

CASTLE HOWARD

York, YO60 7DA: 01653 648333;
www.castlehoward.co.uk
Revisit Brideshead on four paws – dogs are welcomed
into the grounds of Castle Howard, where the 1980s
television series of Evelyn Waugh's novel was filmed,
and into the nearby Castle Howard holiday park, which
is managed by the estate. Campers are given discount
vouchers for entrance into the estate grounds.

Price: from £14 per non-electric pitch
Charge for dogs: £1 per pitch however many dogs
Extras for dogs: no
Access all areas: the holiday park has a designated
dog-walking area
Number of dogs: check at time of booking
Late night pee: there are 70 miles of public rights of
way within Castle Howard estate

THE DEVONSHIRE ARMS COUNTRY HOUSE HOTEL

Bolton Abbey, Skipton, North Yorkshire, BD23 6AJ:
01756 710441; **www.thedevonshirearms.co.uk** 🐾
The Yorkshire estate of the Devonshire's boasts 30,000
acres of countryside, with a dog-friendly kip at a
country house hotel bang in the centre of it. The hotel
even has a lounge especially for dogs, where they can
chew over the day's adventures with their mates.

Price: from £160

Charge for dogs: £10

Extras for dogs: a welcome pack on arrival; a bed, a bowl and biscuits

Access all areas: everywhere except the restaurant

Number of dogs: within reason

Late night pee: 30,000 acres

THE LAMPPOST CAFE

13-15 Bridgegate, Hebden Bridge, West Yorkshire, HX7 8EX: 01422 845475; **www.thelamppostcafe.co.uk** 🐾

Applause from the paws for this truly dog-friendly cafe where hounds and humans are treated as equally important customers – indeed, the Lamppost prides itself on being a place where 'wet dogs and muddy wellies are wholeheartedly welcome.' There are seats for dogs, towels for muddy paws and, of course, mutts have their very own menu, as tested by Hebden hounds Dilly and Sybil (pictured below).

LAVEROCK HALL HOLIDAY COTTAGES

Laverock Hall, Eggleston, Barnard Castle, County Durham, DL12 0AY: 07557 309952, **www.freewebs.com/comebyanaway** 🐾

These award-winning cottages take the form of two converted byres on a working farm in the beautiful Teesdale countryside. Mandy and Marcus train Border Collies as well – there are currently nine on the farm – and will willingly put your pup through his paces in the 120-foot indoor agility arena.

Sleeps: each cottage sleeps five

Price: starts at £325 for a week

Charge for dogs: no

Extras for dogs: indoor shower room for dogs; treats; throws and tags with Mandy's phone number on in case of missing mutts

Access all areas: yes

Number of dogs: four dogs go free – more than this are charged

Late night pee: each cottage has an enclosed garden and shared use of a six-acre field

Owner's dogs: nine Border Collies, ranging in age from 17 to four-months-old

THE LISTER ARMS

Malham, near Skipton, Yorkshire, BD23 4DB. 01729 830330; **www.listerarms.co.uk**

The Lister is an ivy-clad brick building on the village

green in the pretty Dales village of Malham and ten of its fifteen bedrooms are dog-friendly. Enjoy Pimms on the lawn in the summer and whisky by the coal fire in winter. Malham Cove is a mile's walk away – just be careful your dog doesn't fall off the edge chasing a rogue squirrel!

Price: £80 and up

Charge for dogs: £15 one-off charge

Extras for dogs: treats behind the bar and plenty of bowls of water around

Access all areas: everywhere except the restaurant

Number of dogs: check at time of booking

Late night pee: the village green

LOOK OUT COTTAGE

Alnwick, Northumberland:

Book through the National Trust on 0844 3351287 or at **www.nationaltrustcottages.co.uk**

The amazingly isolated, National Trust-owned, Look Out Cottage has a whole beach to itself and is where the coastguards lived – now holidaymakers can sleep in their original bunk beds. The coastguards have been replaced by mechanical equipment, housed in the north room of the cottage and the odd beep and buzz may disturb your slumber but it's all part of the fun!

Sleeps: four

Price: from £392 for three nights

Charge for dogs: no

Extras for dogs: bowl and blankets

Access all areas: yes

Number of dogs: two

Late night pee: enclosed walled garden

THE OLD WELL INN

21 The Bank, Barnard Castle, County Durham, DL12 OPH: 01833 690130; **www.theoldwellinn.co.uk**

Barnard Castle is a little market town with a strong community spirit – there are pots where people grow vegetables for anyone to pick. (Careful where your dog lifts his leg!) The Old Well is on the main street and has a dog-friendly room on the ground floor with its own little courtyard garden.

Price: £75 for the (double) dog-friendly room

Charge for dogs: no

Extras for dogs: a tap for dogs to cool down in the summer in the beer garden

Access all areas: in the bar but not the breakfast room

Number of dogs: check at time of booking

Late night pee: the enclosed garden

POSTGATE INN

Egton Bridge, Whitby, YO21 1UX: 01947 895241; **www.postgateinn.com**

Take your hairy heartbeat to the middle of Heartbeat country – to the pub that poses as the show's Black Dog, in fact – and, after a long walk through the Esk Valley, relax in the beer garden with amazing views over the surrounding countryside. Or settle in for a couple of nights and take a day trip out on the steam train to Pickering.

Price: £85 and up,

Charge for dogs: £5 per dog

Extras for dogs: no

Access all areas: yes, apart from the restaurant

Number of dogs: one (or two small)

Late night pee: a footpath leads into open countryside

Owner's dogs: two Jack Russells, Peanuts and Ruby; two Black Labradors, Trueman and Boycie; and mini Yorkie, Duchess

SKIPWITH STATION

North Duffield, North Yorkshire, YO8 5DE: 07753 961093/01757 282288; **www.skipwithstation.com**

You and your dog will have a first-class holiday in one of the converted train carriages in the grounds of an old railway station in the beautiful Derwent Valley. Two of the three carriages are dog-friendly and all have been re-furbed to a really high standard.

Price: starts at £180 for three nights

Charge for dogs: no

Extras for dogs: book of local walks in each carriage

Access all areas: not in the bedroom areas

Number of dogs: check at time of booking

Late night pee: step out into countryside

Owner's dogs: Chocolate Labradors Mimi and Mocha

TEMPEST ARMS

Elsack, Skipton, North Yorkshire, BD23 3AY: 01282 842450; **www.tempestarms.co.uk**

A proper pub with hearty meals, the Tempest is going down a storm among dog owners and is barking mad on Saturday afternoons when the local wags go for walks.

Price: from £70

Charge for dogs: no

Extras for dogs: blankets and dog bowls

Access all areas: in the two dog-friendly bedrooms and the bar

Number of dogs: check at time of booking

Late night pee: the two dog-friendly bedrooms open directly onto open space

Owner's dogs: Milly and Lottie; Dolly and Buddie — they're not all on duty at the same time though!

WESTFIELD LODGE

New Westfield Farm, Upper Marsh Lane, Oxenhope, Keighley, West Yorkshire, BD22 9RH: 01535 646900; **www.westfield-lodge.co.uk**

Bones — proper meaty ones straight from the butcher's — are kept in a big bucket at reception for dogs who visit these holiday lodges in the heart of Bronte country. There are 20 (17 dog-friendly) apartments, set around a pleasant courtyard and there's a dog-shower in the grounds for washing off mud after the 20-minute tramp over the moors to Haworth.

Price: starting at £180 for three nights

Charge for dogs: no

Extras for dogs: weekly bone delivery; dog wash facility; bowls and treats

Access all areas: dogs aren't allowed in bedrooms

Number of dogs: they have accommodated seven!

Late night pee: large enclosed field

Owner's dogs: an Alsatian, Tara, and a Spanish Water Dog, Tillie

WILD NORTHUMBRIAN TIPI'S AND YURTS SHEPHERD'S HUT

Thorneyburn, Tarset, Hexham, Northumberland: 01434 240902; **www.wildnorthumbrian.co.uk**

We've searched far and wide for a dog-friendly shepherd's hut so your dog can release his inner sheepdog, and, deep in a forest in the Northumberland National Park, we've found one. And what a shepherd's hut it is — made of reclaimed wood, it's a bespoke, totally one-off design, up a fell and nestled under a solitary pine tree, with its own wood-burning fire. Come-by, indeed!

Price: two night stay for two people and a dog is £180

Extras for dogs: no

Access all areas: yes

Number of dogs: two maximum

Late night pee: the shepherd's hut has its own garden, enclosed by a chestnut picket fence

THE NORTH WEST

AMBLESIDE AND KESWICK, LAKE DISTRICT

I wandered lonely as a cloud . . .

But I don't want to wander lonely as a cloud in the Lake District – I want to romp through the countryside with a great big pack of dogs with nothing lonely or cloudy about it. And, when we arrive at our holiday cottage for the weekend in Ambleside, I realise I'm not going to be as lonely as a cloud for a second as I have two canine companions for the weekend – bossy Jess, the ten-year-old Chocolate Labrador, and bouncy Angus, the ten-month-old Labradoodle. They're both considerably larger than me but I'm a terrier so I can handle it.

Jane's friend Vicky has booked 3 Swiss Villas, a traditional grey slate Lake District dwelling, for the weekend, as, unusually, it allows three dogs and has an enclosed yard, enabling us to get some peace and quiet away from our humans. Keswick in the Lakes has been named Britain's dog-friendliest town by the Kennel Club but, in my hound's opinion, Ambleside should be a contender. The paper shop – dogs welcome; the mountaineering shops – hello to dogs; the butchers – come on in, hounds, and smell the SAUSAGES.

And the walks – hello! We parked our car at Rydal Hall, a mile and a half from Ambleside, and tramped off on a five-mile hike around Rydal Water, where I pinched two cheese sandwiches from the packed lunch of a fisherman sleeping by

Rydal Water, the Lake District

Jess, Attlee and Angus (left to right) at Faery Land Cafe, Grasmere

the lake. *Sorry sleeping fisherman but you snooze; you lose!*

Then it was through White Moss Wood to Grasmere, where we sat on the banks of the lake beside a cheerful red gypsy caravan at Faery Land Cafe, eating their delicious fruit cake. Then off again, through Grasmere, past William Wordsworth's Dove Cottage and up the hill, back to Rydal Hall along the rather oddly named Coffin Trail. Jane had to put me on the lead every so often as the demon SHEEP were around.

After all that exercise, the humans needed refreshment. First stop, the traditional grey stone Ambleside Tavern, on the main street in town. Outside it looks charming and old-fashioned but inside it is modern and there was live music on. The singer fancied himself a comic as well as a tune-smith. When Jess, Angus and I walked in he scoffed: 'What's this? Crufts?'

Either he was commenting on my good looks or he was being extremely cheeky. I gave him a hard stare, in case it was the latter. But he was unabashed, commenting: 'Those dogs look old.' Now that is cheek considering I was but three at the time and Angus still just a young pup! Then Jane explained he may have been being rude not about the canines in our pack – but the humans. I snapped at his heels for this affrontery towards Jane, who is most definitely still in middle youth, and we moved swiftly on to The Golden Rule, where my canine companions and I were presented with dog biscuits as soon as we set paw inside. Now this is a *proper* pub – no insolent entertainers and just booze and biscuits.

The following day, we headed to Keswick – Britain's dog-friendliest town? I have to admit, I've never seen so many hounds in one place, browsing the stalls in the market square, Barking Out Loud and generally having a jolly good time. I asked my canine cohorts for Rover recommendations in Keswick. Of all the pubs, the Dog and Gun gathered the most paws up, so Jane and I repaired there. It was mobbed – walkers, dogs, shoppers – all crowded into a cosy traditional dark woods and red carpets sort of boozer, the specialities of which are Hungarian goulash and real ale. Massive portions of food too, meaning plenty of scraps fall below the table to a grateful snaffler like myself.

I did some Rover research on Keswick's best dog-friendly cafe too – dog-friendly cafes are the Holy Grail and I always sniff one out for my readers. (So many cafes won't let us in and this is a problem if our humans have pesky kids as well as canines.)

High paw, then, to The Lakeland Pedlar – Jess, Angus and I were welcomed while the humans glugged coffee, hot chocolate and, this caff being licensed, alcoholic ginger beer. The Pedlar is vegetarian but the ambience made up for the lack of tasty meat products. The owner told Jane that I was the most handsome dog she'd seen in a long time. *Take that Labrathingies. Mongrel Power!*

We had a wander round the shops too and I didn't have to do any of that boring sitting outside nonsense – I was allowed in every one, even the Peter Rabbit and Friends shop. RABBITS! Top marks to Mountain Warehouse, where the sales staff welcome every dog that sets paw inside as if we're the ones with the credit cards. Down at Derwentwater, a ten-minute walk from the town centre, there were ducks – horrid, squawking things that have to be barked at. Angus, undeterred, jumped in for a swim. I don't need to worry about making a splash – I achieve that every day through my career as Britain's top dog about town.

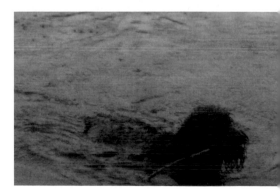

Doggy paddling in Derwentwater

Phileas Phacts: Ambleside and Keswick

3 SWISS VILLAS

Vicarage Road, Ambleside,
Cumbria, LA22 9AE: 01539 432691;
www.swissvillas.co.uk
Sleeps: six
Price: from £560 a week
Charge for dogs: no
Extras for dogs: no
Access all areas: not upstairs
Number of dogs: three maximum,
depending on size
Late night pee: there's a little park two
minutes away

THE AMBLESIDE TAVERN

Ambleside, Cumbria, LA22 9DR:
01539 433306

THE GOLDEN RULE

Smithy Brow, Ambleside, Cumbria,
LA22 9AS:
015394 32257;
www.goldenrule-ambleside.co.uk 🐾

FAERYLAND CAFE

Boat Landing, Grasmere, Cumbria

PETER RABBIT AND FRIENDS

17 Lake Road, Keswick,
Cumbria, CA12 5BS:
017687 75189;
www.peterrabbitshop.co.uk

MOUNTAIN WAREHOUSE

15-17 Market Square, Main Street,
Keswick, Cumbria, CA12 5BQ:
017687 75305;
www.mountainwarehouse.com

THE DOG AND GUN

2 Lake Road, Keswick, Cumbria,
CA12 5BT:
017687 73463

THE LAKELAND PEDLAR

Bell Close, Keswick, Cumbria, CA12 5JD:
017687 74492;
www.lakelandpedlar.co.uk

Pugsey, a cross between a Shih-tzu and a Pug, might only have little legs but he's a heroic hiker on holiday in the Lake District.

Resident Rover: Monty Spaniel's tour of Cheshire

Ah, Cheshire. Home of Cheshire Cheese, the Cheshire Cat (grrr!) and me, Monty Spaniel, acclaimed travel writer and Phileas Dogg re-paw-ter. I live in the south of the county, amid pretty Cheshire brick villages, fields, woodlands and distant plains. To the east I can see the hills of Derbyshire, while to the west are the mountains of Wales. Cheshire is a big farming county, and my local landscape is a place of lush green pastureland dotted with black-and-white cows. I can't see the point of cows but they are picturesque. I've picked out the crème de la crème (that's foreign for 'top dog!') of Cheshire's pubs and walks so here's my pick of where you'll find a woof-fully warm welcome.

THE SWETTENHAM ARMS

Swettenham Lane, Swettenham Village, near Congleton, Cheshire, CW12 2LF
01477 571284;
www.swettenhamarms.co.uk
Pretty and rural, this traditional country Inn dates back to the 16th century. Dogs are welcome in the stone-flagged bar and pub dining area, and there are real log fires, most suitable for sprawling in front of in winter.

THE BLACK SWAN

Trap Street, Lower Withington, Cheshire, SK11 9EQ:
01477 571770;
www.theblackswancheshire.com
The Black Swan gets my personal paws-up for most stylish Cheshire pub. They've thought of everything for canine comfort, from a jar of dog biscuits and water bowl to a log fire. There's also a lovely roofed, sheltered outdoor seating area, made from a former stable block.

QUINTA ARBORETUM

Swettenham Village, Congleton, Cheshire, CW12 2LD: 01477 537698
The Quinta Arboretum is right next to the Swettenham Arms, and only a couple of miles from
the Black Swan. The arboretum covers 28 acres and is planted with around 5,000 trees
covering 2,000 species so you're bound to find somewhere to lift your leg in peace (although
it's leads on sadly, chaps). From the arboretum, walk out along the Dane Valley or to nearby
Brereton Heath Country Park.

THE STAG'S HEAD

Mill Lane, Great Warford, near Alderley
Edge, Cheshire, SK9 7TY: 01565 872350;
www.stagsheadgreatwarford.co.uk
The Stag's Head receives my vote for
dog-friendliest Cheshire pub, and
visiting canines attract pats and
cuddles from staff and clientele alike.
Officially, dogs are allowed in the back
rooms only, but the landlady is fairly
flexible where well-behaved pups like
me are concerned. For walks, Lindow
Common and the National Trust site Alderley Edge are both nearby. The Edge is a ridge
of sandstone with stunning views across the plain while Lindow is an ancient peat moss
common famous for wildlife. Dogs can go off-lead in both areas although there are some
restrictions at Alderley.

THE GREYHOUND

Cow Lane, Ashley, Altrincham, Cheshire, WA15 0QR:
0161 871 7765;
www.thegreyhoundashley.co.uk
Originally part of the Egerton Estate, this pub was renamed The Greyhound in honour of
Lord Egerton's favourite dog. It's a traditional inn over 100 years old, with log fires and a
greyhound theme in the decoration. In honour of Lord E., as I like to call him, why not stroll
around his former family home, Tatton Park in Knutsford. There are 1,000 acres, including
two lakes, gardens and a stately home, all within five minutes drive of The Greyhound.
Dogs are allowed off the lead everywhere, as long as we stay under control, which naturally
I always do. The only drawback is that at certain times of year there are flocks of sheep
and herds of red and fallow deer grazing in MY park, and I have to tiptoe around them, like
they've got as much right to be here as I have! GRRRR!

Monty has a dunk in the Mere at Tatton Park

THE SWAN WITH TWO NICKS

Park Lane, Little Bollington, Altrincham, Cheshire, WA14 4TJ:
0161 928 2914;
www.swanwithtwonicks.co.uk

The origins of this quintessentially Cheshire pub go back over 250 years, and they definitely have the right attitude – dogs welcome, children tolerated. The pub name refers to the old system of counting the royally-owned swans by nicking their beaks, and the building itself is nestled against Dunham Massey Park, another of Cheshire's stately homes and former seat of the Stamford family. Dogs have to stay on leads in the deer park but are allowed off lead in the north park.

SUTTON HALL

Bullocks Lane, Sutton, Macclesfield, SK11 0HE:
01260 253211;
www.brunningandprice.co.uk/suttonhall

This 480-year-old former manor house was the family home of the Earls of Lucan. It's a great place for pooches, with a stone-flagged bar area and plenty of outdoor space. I recommend the fish and chips. For walks, Tegg's Nose Country Park, three miles away, has stunning views across the Cheshire plains and nearby Macclesfield Forest. Dogs are allowed off lead everywhere but watch out for sheep. ('Tegg' is an old local word for 'sheep'.)

THE FISHPOOL INN

Fishpool Road, Delamere, Cheshire, CW8 2HP:
01606 883277;
www.thefishpoolinn.co.uk
Newly refurbished, the Fishpool Inn is sumptuously decorated to a standard worthy of my discerning presence. Their dog biscuits are tasty, too. There's also a spacious outside eating area, if the weather's fine. The pub is right by Delamere Forest, a Forestry Commission site covering almost 2,500 acres. There are miles of wide, easy, sandy trails; two cafes; lakes and fantastic views if you climb a little.

THE DOG

Wellbank Lane, Over Peover, Knutsford, Cheshire, WA16 8UP:
01625 861421;
www.thedogpeover.co.uk
How could I leave out a pub called The Dog in a place called pee-over? (It's actually pronounced 'peever' but that's not so amusing.) The Dog is famous locally for its beers and dogs are welcome on all non-carpeted areas. A network of footpaths and bridlepaths run through the grounds of nearby Peover Hall – visit in May when the woods are thickly carpeted with bluebells.

Monty proves his pedigree at Tatton Park

Lowther and the Eastern Lakes, by Midge the Lowland Patterdale

What a dog-friendly time we had on a recent jaunt to Cumbria – me, my humans and MINNIE THE PEST, a very annoying Jack Russell who has taken to following me around.

Our first stop was Lowther Castle, just off the A6 about halfway between Shap and Penrith. The castle was home to the Earls of Lonsdale until 1937 but became too expensive to maintain and was abandoned after the Second World War. Later, the ornamental gardens were planted with commercial forestry, the lawns became a chicken farm and the castle ruins were closed to visitors. Now the ruins are being stabilised, the chicken farm has gone and the castle gardens are being restored for everyone – especially dogs – to enjoy. (Actually, the sign did say only well-behaved dogs were admitted so I was shocked to see the little PEST trotting through, happy as Lassie.)

I had a wonderful time exploring the ponds, summerhouses, ruined rock gardens and the avenues, lawns, woods and flowerbeds. Afterwards I sat in the autumn sunshine at the cafe in the old stable yard, chatting to the other dogs who were minding their humans and having a drink from the bowls of water thoughtfully provided. It was a jolly sociable spot. We then adjourned to the George and Dragon in the nearby village of Clifton – a civilised establishment which welcomes the canine visitor into its bar and bedrooms. The bar was busy with dogs returning from days out exploring the Lake District fells and Eden Valley.

Our bedroom was comfortable and we had our own secret staircase so we could pop out last thing at night and first thing in the morning without disturbing other guests. I was disturbed from my beauty sleep, however – woken at dawn by the Little PEST who was raring to explore some more.

So, after SAUSAGES, we drove to Ullswater, the nearest of the lakes, and along the western shore to Martindale, where there's a brilliant hour-and-a-half stomp around Hallin Fell, with great views of the lake. I spotted red squirrels – equally

Midge at Lowther Castle

annoying to me as the grey ones, but my humans appeared to appreciate them.

Then – big excitement for my humans – we drove to a village that shares the same name as me. PATTERDALE. I was made to have my photograph taken by the village sign, which pleased my humans greatly but made me feel a bit silly.

Life's a laugh for Minnie the PEST

CHESTERS BY THE RIVER

Skelwith Bridge, near Ambleside, Cumbria LA22 9NJ
015394 34711;
www.chestersbytheriver.co.uk 🐾

Chesters by the River has the rather confusing motto Bad Dog, No Biscuit – printed on tea towels, mugs and sweets – as well as a 'dog wall of fame' featuring every good dog who has set paw inside (and received a biscuit!).

The Bad Dog, No Biscuit motto relates to a naughty English Bull Terrier – the eponymous Chester – who was pub dog at the Drunken Duck in the 1980s and ruled the roost with an iron paw, stealing sandwiches and the mat which the draymen delivering the beer rolled the barrels on to. Legend has it that Chester even came out on top in a scrap with a Land Rover Defender!

PHILEAS PHACTS: Lowther and the Eastern Lakes

THE GEORGE AND DRAGON
Clifton, near Penrith, Cumbria, CA10 2ER: 01768 865381; www.georgeanddragonclifton.co.uk
Price: £95 and up,
Charge for dogs: £10 per stay, however many dogs
Extras for dogs: a dog pack in each room with poo bags, a map of local walks and a chew. There's a dog bed in reception too.
Access all areas: everywhere but the restaurant

Number of dogs: maximum two
Late night pee: courtyard garden
Owner's dogs: Bailey, a Golden Retriever, and Porter, a Patterdale Terrier

LOWTHER CASTLE,
Penrith, Cumbria, CA10 2HH: 01931 712192; www.lowthercastle.org

Apparently I come from Patterdale but this makes no sense to me as I know for a fact I was born on a farm in Lincolnshire. As for Minnie, I would very much like to know where she comes from. I am guessing it's PESTon-Super-Mare and am awaiting confirmation of this from the Rover Records Office.

Resident Rover: Liverpool by Murphy the Old English Sheepdog

Alright, la! I know what you're thinking. Liverpool is a city of music, football and fashion – so what could I, Murphy, the Old English Sheepdog, have to say of interest to mutts about Merseyside?

Well, Liverpool is a real doggie area – with loads of places for walks and for my mum and dad to have a pint afterwards. Even in the centre of town, dogs are welcome. I HATE waiting outside the shops for Mum or Dad but lots of the city pubs let us dogs in to take the weight off our paws after a long day staring into shop windows. My favourite is The Dispensary, where I'm allowed in the parts with tiled floors. Then I favour a walk past the Albert Dock with the breeze from the Mersey ruffling my fur.

What most people don't realise is that Merseyside has its own beaches – good ones, too. I'm lucky to live by Crosby Beach on the north side of the city. It has miles of open sand where I have a stroll every morning (not run – I'm getting on a

WATERMILL INN

Ings, near Windermere, Cumbria, LA8 9PY:

01539 821309;

www.watermillinn.co.uk 🐾

In the middle of prime dog-walking countryside, the Watermill Inn has its own micro-brewery with the beers – and pump clips – all celebrating our canine companions. Take your faithful Fido to this totally dog-friendly digs and you never know – he or she might be immortalised in beer!

Price: £81 and up

Charge for dogs: £4 per dog, a proportion of which goes to Dogs Trust

Extras for dogs: biscuits and bowl of water on arrival; map of walks

Access all areas: the smaller bar is dog-free but dogs are welcome everywhere else, including the big bar

Number of dogs: check when booking

Late night pee: gated traffic-free road

Owner's dogs: two German Shepherds Ruby and Scarlet

Ales with Tails at The Watermill in Ings

Who's that on Murphy's beach?

bit now) and dunes where me and Mum like to watch the young pups chase each other of a morning.

Now Crosby Beach has turned into a tourist attraction because artist Antony Gormley's 'Another Place' is here. It's a spooky installation of 100 cast-iron life-size replicas of Gormley's own body, stretching along the beach and into the sea. Humans stare at the statues against the changing sea and sky and make profound comments about the meaning of life. We dogs know they're only there for us to lift our legs against.

Mum likes to walk from Crosby to Formby where there are red squirrels at the National Trust place. I'm not so keen as Mum insists I go on the lead when we're close to them – apparently they're 'vulnerable'.

Everyone's a critic these days: Murphy lifts his leg against an Antony Gormley statue on Crosby Beach

PHILEAS PHACTS: Liverpool

THE DISPENSARY
87 Renshaw St, Liverpool,
L1 2SP:
0151 709 2160

NATIONAL TRUST FORMBY
Victoria Road, Freshfield, Formby,
Merseyside,
L37 1LJ:
01704 878591;
www.nationaltrust.org.uk/formby/

THE WHEATSHEAF INN
Raby Mere Road, Raby Village,
Wirral,
CH63 4JH:
0151 336 3416;
www.wheatsheaf-cowshed.co.uk

Though I'm a north Liverpool dog, sometimes we go south for a walk in Sefton Park. There are 235 acres of grass for me to stretch my legs while Mum visits the bandstand she reckons was the inspiration for Sergeant Pepper's Lonely Hearts Club Band.

If I'm really lucky, we go 'over the water'. Nope, it's not abroad – it's just across the Mersey. And I don't even go 'over' properly as I'm not allowed on deck on the ferry. Instead, I jump into the car boot and my chauffeur takes me across. (Okay – Mum.) Our favourite place 'over the water' is The Wheatsheaf Inn in Raby Village, in Cheshire. We walk up the picturesque Wirral Way and then go there for lunch. Mum loves the bar food. (I have the impression that she's been to the adjoining Cowshed Restaurant without me, because I heard her saying the slow-braised lamb shank there is yummy. But that's all right because I never share my tea with her either.)

Grasmere, with Monty Spaniel

I have discovered doggy paradise – in Grasmere, where almost every cafe, restaurant and hotel has a sign outside welcoming dogs.

Grasmere is a pretty little town in the Central Lake District, with its own lake (called, ahem, Grasmere), and lots of fells for walking. Apparently it's famous because some bloke called William Wordsworth lived here and called it, 'The loveliest spot that man hath ever found.' Well, now dogs have found it too so move over William! We're staying at The Swan Hotel, which is very nice, with deep, comfortable carpets. My only quibble is that the welcome sign says 'everybody

welcome – even dogs.' Surely it's supposed to say 'everybody welcome – ESPECIALLY dogs'?

We walk to Easedale Tarn, which involves strolling through the town and then up to the fell behind. The initial path along the valley floor is well-defined and easy, following a lively stream for splashing purposes. As we go through the gate up onto the fell, the going becomes a little harder, but we're gifted with some great views. One or two Lakeland sheep peer at me from the bracken – they probably want my paw-tograph – but otherwise we have the trail to ourselves until we reach the top of the rise, where a few people are picnicking. After a couple of hours walking, we settle down for our own lunch at the head of the tarn – but we take a different route back and Sara misses her footing and slips into a peat bog. A decisive victory for four legs over two!

Back in Grasmere, we require a teashop so that Sara can remove half the Lake District from her hands. And what's this I see? Almost everywhere has a dog bowl outside. We stop at a little shop/gallery called The Attic, admire their enamel dog bowl and 'Dogs Welcome' sign – then I go inside and select a lovely new treat tin from their 'dog' section. How cool is this?

Next up is Heidi's of Grasmere, a teashop and B&B. They've got a 'doggies welcome' sign, and greet us with gravy-bone biscuits.

Finally, we visit Baldry's teashop. Its 'dogs welcome' sign is a proper permanent one made from local slate, and I like the look of their bowl, which says 'Life is good' on the side. Sara orders the drinks and hoses herself down but, when the manager brings our tea tray, he's most indignant.

'Why didn't you say you had a dog? Just a moment,' he says, dashing off.

He returns with a handful of dog biscuits. Oh, yes. I like it here. In fact, there's a self-catering cottage attached, so I might just stay.

"The loveliest spot that dog hath ever found"

PHILEAS PHACTS: Grasmere

THE SWAN HOTEL
Keswick Road, Grasmere,
Cumbria, LA22 9RF
0844 879 9120;
www.macdonaldhotels.co.uk
Price: from £115
Charge for dogs: £15 per dog
Extras for dogs: no
Access all areas: in the bar, where
breakfast can be taken
Number of dogs: maximum two
Late night pee: car park and gardens

BALDRY'S TEA ROOMS
Red Lion Square, Grasmere,
Cumbria, LA22 9SP:
015394 35301;
www.baldryscottage.co.uk
Sleeps: five
Price: from £350 a week
Charge for dogs: no
Extras for dogs: a water bowl
Access all area: not on the furniture
Number of dogs: two
Late night pee: a little park
two minutes away

THE ATTIC
Grasmere, Cumbria, LA22 9SX:
015394 35827;
www.the-attic.co.uk

HEIDI'S GRASMERE LODGE
Red Lion Square, Grasmere,
Cumbria, LA22 9SP:
015394 35248;
www.heidisgrasmerelodge.co.uk

Molly from Carlisle loves the Lake District and will squeeze through any gap in the wall – however small – if it means she can carry on exploring.

PC Puppy!

Finding dog-friendly digs on the Isle of Man isn't as easy as it could be – a shame for an island that produces such fine police dog puppies! Nine new Rover recruits were born over the summer of 2013 and they're the prettiest police line-up you've ever seen. Ah well – if they need some time out from the tough training regime that will see them from police dog pups to police dogs proper the Hydro on the Promenade in Douglas offers a warm, waggy welcome.

THE HYDRO HOTEL

Queens Promenade, Douglas, Isle of Man, IM2 4NF:
01624 676870;
www.hydrohotel.co.im
Price: doubles start at £80
Charge for dogs: no
Extras for dogs: no
Access all areas: allowed in the lounge area and in the bar if it's quiet
Number of dogs: check when booking
Late night pee: promenade along The Promenade.

Wherever you lay your hat . . . that's my home

NORTH-WEST DIRECTORY

THE ALBION INN

Park Street, Chester, CH1 1RN:

01244 340345;

www.albioninnchester.co.uk

The Albion is a proper, traditional pub filled with First World War memorabilia and pub cat Charlie is raging a war of his own – against visiting dogs. So, while canine clientele will be served a cold sausage on arrival in The Albion, they shouldn't expect a place in front of the coal fire in winter – Charlie (below) has that covered. As for The Albion's two B&B rooms upstairs, Charlie has put his paw down and dogs are definitely not welcome as overnight guests. Miaow!

CHESTERFIELD HOTEL

5 Wellington Road, Blackpool, FY1 6AR:

01253 345979;

www.chesterfield-hotel.com

Owners Steve and Julie's attitudes to canine clientele could illuminate others – Blackpool's the Chesterfield, built in 1898 as a guesthouse and welcoming tourists ever since, is truly dog-friendly. Humans are greeted on arrival with tea and biscuits – dogs with water and biscuits. The bar is the place for a bow-wow of an evening.

Price: from £54

Charge for dogs: no

Extras for dogs: biscuits, towels and a dog mat in the bedrooms

Access all areas: yes

Number of dogs: no maximum

Late night pee: the beach is 50 metres from the door

Owner's dogs: Staffordshire Bull Terrier Barney

CRAKE TREES MANOR,

Crosby Ravensworth, Penrith, Cumbria, CA10 3JG:

01931 715205;

www.www.craketreesmanor.co.uk

When our correspondent arrived to take up residence in the Shepherd's Hut on the farm at Crake Trees Manor, the wood burner was lit and a pot of tea ready for pouring. As well as the Shepherd's Hut, Crake Trees Manor operates the self-catering Brew House, on the green in the village.

Price: the Brew House starts at £260 for three nights; the Shepherd's Hut is £70-90 a night B&B

Charge for dogs: £5 per dog

Extras for dogs: in the Brew House bowls are laid out on the slate floors for dogs and there's a small wet room which muddy mutts are welcome to use. A laminated leaflet of local walks is also provided.

Access all areas: on leads around the farm

Number of dogs: one small dog in the Shepherd's Hut; the Brew House can accommodate more

Late night pee: the Brew House has an enclosed

courtyard garden. On the farm, there are three public footpaths to follow

Owner's dogs: Jack Russells Maisie (above) and Casper

THE CUCKOO BROW INN

Far Sawrey, Ambleside, Cumbria, LA22 0LQ:
015394 43425;

www.cuckoobrow.co.uk

Clock onto the Cuckoo — it's one of the Lake District's most nurturing nests for dogs. There's a place in front of the coal fire for wet and weary walkers, waggy-tailed or otherwise, and a menu of hearty favourites like traditional Cumbrian Tatty Pot to revive flagging spirits.

Price: from £110
Charge for dogs: £10 per dog per stay
Extras for dogs: treats in the bar
Access all areas: yes
Number of dogs: depends on size of room
Late night pee: a country lane 20 yards away leading to open fields
Owner's dogs: Poppy, a German wire-haired Pointer

DRYBECK FARM

Armathwaite, near Carlisle, Cumbria, CA4 9ST:
0785 4523012;

www.drybeckfarm.co.uk

Take your pick between a gypsy caravan and three

Maisie in the Shepherd's Hut.

yurts at this quirky campsite on a working farm with pigs, rare breed cows, poultry and horses. The setting is pastoral — indeed, the site is in the valley of Eden — and there's a river to swim in and an outdoor wood-fired hot tub. One of the horses is a driving cob and provides a taxi service to the locals along the country lanes of an evening.

Sleeps: caravan sleeps two; yurts sleep up to eight.
Price: from £150 per weekend in the caravan; yurts from £240
Charge for dogs: £5 per dog
Extras for dogs: no
Access all areas: on leads in the campsite area — dogs aren't allowed on the working farm
Number of dogs: two
Late night pee: enclosed field
Owner's dogs: Rhodesian Ridgeback Eva; Siberian Husky Jack and Dogue de Bordeaux Boudica

HOPE STREET HOTEL

40 Hope Street, Liverpool, L1 9DA:
0151 709 3000;

www.hopestreethotel.co.uk

Hope springs eternal for hounds at this hip Liverpool hang-out. While the decor might be minimalist, the friendliness of staff is maximalist. Harper is often to be found snoozing the afternoon away on one of the leather sofas in the lounge — well, he blends in with the colour scheme.

Price: doubles from £89
Charge for dogs: £30 per dog per stay
Extras for dogs: blankets, bowls and toys
Access all areas: everywhere but the restaurant
Number of dogs: two
Late night pee: a park five minutes away
Owner's dogs: Harper the Dachshund

HORSE AND JOCKEY INN

9 The Green, Chorlton, Manchester, M21 9HS:
0161 860 7794;

www.horseandjockeychorlton.com

This is the hang-out if your hound likes a drop of the
hard stuff – there's a gravy-flavoured tipple on tap for
dogs. When your pup's had a pint, he might even feel
bold enough to enter the pub's annual Halloween dogs'
fancy dress fiesta!

THE INN AT WHITEWELL

Dunsop Road, Clitheroe, Lancashire, BB7 3AT:
01200 448222;

www.innatwhitewell.com

This is THE Clitheroe kid. With a terrace looking
out over green fields leading to fells and a river for
fishing in, the 14th Century Inn at Whitewell occupies
a nigh-on perfect spot. Inside it's glamour, but with
tongue firmly planted in cheek – the website states:
'this is a haven for those who like to walk, fish, paint
or just want to stroke their partner and talk to the dog.'
Indeed, Resident Rover Bedlam is always up for a bit
of a chat.

Harper at the Hope Street Hotel

Price: from £120 for a double
Charge for dogs: no
Extras for dogs: selection of dog beds in the hall
Access all areas: everywhere but the dining room
Number of dogs: confirm on booking
Late night pee: straight into fields
Owner's dogs: Bedlam

LOW NEST FARM B&B

Castlerigg, Keswick, Cumbria, CA12 4TF:
017687 72378;
www.dogfriendlylakedistrict.co.uk

Low Nest is in receipt of a clutch of Kennel Club awards
for its dog-friendly accommodation and rightly so –
the combination of the adventures to be had in the
surrounding countryside and the treats and surprises
at the cottages make this a real Disneyland for Dogs.
There's a choice of B&B, in the old farmhouse, or
self-catering, in one of three self-catering studios in
a converted barn. Proprietor Alison is the author of
a series of books on dog walks in the Lake District.
Sleeps: self-catering studios sleep up to three
Price: B&B prices start at £65 for the first night and
then £60; self-catering starts at £180 for three days
Charge for dogs: £3 per dog per day to a maximum of
£40 per party per holiday
Extras for dogs: dog pack in every room with throws,
treats, towels, tags with Low Nest contact details and
poo bags; a warm outdoors dog wash, an agility course
and a canine crèche.
Access all areas: everywhere
Number of dogs: from two in the B&B to six in the
self-catering
Late night pee: enclosed fields
Owner's dogs: four Weimaraner's – lasses Billie and
Lucy and lads Max and young pup Riley

Lucy from Low Nest Farm

OVERWATER HALL,
Ireby, Cumbria, CA7 1HH:
017687 76566;
www.overwaterhall.co.uk 🐾
Overwater Hall is a comfortable, quality establishment, with good old-fashioned service to make you comfortable indoors – and 18 acres of grounds to make your dog comfortable outdoors. Tread the boarded walkway through woodland – you can keep your wellies relatively mud-free while Rover can go overboard and slosh about in the undergrowth to his heart's delight.
Price: from £85

Overwater Hall's Bafta and Mitch

Nando's been a regular at Thurstaston beach on the Wirral since he was just a young pup but now he's two he's a bit of a Bow Brummel and has a regular scrub up at the local dog wash!

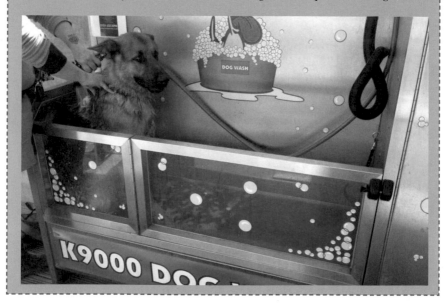

Charge for dogs: no

Extras for dogs: treats in rooms

Access all areas: dogs are allowed in one of the lounges and in the bar

Number of dogs: no limit

Late night pee: 18 acres of grounds

Owner's dogs: Black Labrador BAFTA and Chocolate Labrador Mitch

RUBY'S CAFE

Bridge Street, Appleby, Cumbria, CA16 6QH: 017683 51923

There might only be four tables in this cosy little cafe but proprietor Lynn always makes room for dogs. And, while owners have a cuppa and a slice of the caff's much-vaunted cheesecake, dogs are treated to a slice of toast. Pawfect!

THE SUN INN

6 Market Street, Kirkby Lonsdale, Cumbria, LA6 2AU: 015242 71965;

www.sun-inn.info

The sun certainly does shine on this 17th Century traditional inn, with every guest who stays full of praise for the warm atmosphere, tasteful decor and quality of the food. It's bang in the centre of Kirkby Lonsdale, a fine market town, and on the borders of three counties – Cumbria, Lancashire and Yorkshire – all ripe to explore. A boot wash tub for walkers outside the door doubles as a muddy paws wash.

Price: from £104

Charge for dogs: £10 per dog per stay

Extras for dogs: bowl, towel and biccies

Access all areas: in the bar but not in the restaurant

Number of dogs: maximum five

Late night pee: the river is two minutes away

Owner's dogs: Betsy, a Cockerpoo

WADDINGTON ARMS

Waddington, near Clitheroe, Lancs, BB7 3HP: 01200 423262;

www.waddingtonarms.co.uk 🐾

The Waddington is a cosy village pub in the heart of the Ribble Valley. The welcome is as warm as the Lancashire hot pot on a cold winter's eve and the bells from the church across the street only add to the pub's pastoral appeal.

Price: £85

Charge for dogs: no

Extras for dogs: water bowls and treats

Access all areas: except the restaurant

Number of dogs: confirm when booking

Late night pee: country lanes

WINDERMERE MANOR HOTEL,

Rayrigg Road, Windermere, Cumbria, LA23 1JF: 0845 6030051;

www.visionhotels.co.uk

The Windermere Manor is operated by Vision Hotels, specifically designed to cater for blind and partially sighted people but open to all. Given the Windermere Manor's experience in catering for assistance dogs, it's one of the most canine canny hotels in the country – even if your dog is of no assistance at all! It occupies a prime position, overlooking Lake Windermere, and Bowness is a 20-minute stroll away.

Price: doubles start at £59

Charge for dogs: £3 per dog

Extras for dogs: beds, fleeces and bowls in the rooms; warm dog towels in the entrance hall and a grooming room for dogs, with a shower

Access all areas: apart from the restaurant and the bar during meal times

Number of dogs: confirm when booking

Late night pee: several enclosed areas

WALES

LAUGHARNE, CARMARTHENSHIRE

Portrait of the Artist as a Young Dog

I'm at the bar of Browns Hotel in Laugharne, ordering another drink and regaling my fellow booze hounds with tall tails of my life as the angry young dog of British literature. Other curs pile into the pub to hear me talk, my waggish humour is at its most cutting, Alfie and Pepper are hanging on my every word . . .

Another of your strongest bowls of water please, bar tender.

Can we have your phone number? Pepper pleads, keen, obviously, to be able to access my muttologues on tap whenever she needs cheering. I give her Browns' number instead. Well, I am following in the footsteps of Dylan Thomas – and it was this pub's number he used to distribute when the hoi polloi requested his.

Browns has been scrubbed up since Dylan's day and is now a boutique hotel but the bar is old fashioned in mood and SMELLS – scrubbed wooden tables and polished leather – and has photographs of him on the wall. Opposite, is a reading room with shelves stacked with his tomes. I wonder if my local – the Hermit's Cave in Camberwell – will one day house such a homage to me?

Strolling around Laugharne I can understand why Thomas was so inspired when he lived here. It's a peaceful but cheerful little township with an estuary and a castle where he would wander to cure writer's block. Not something I ever

Dylan Thomas' Boathouse at Laugharne

suffer from and, on the odd occasion I do, I normally find chasing a squirrel gets the blood pumping again.

We visit the shed where Thomas wrote every day. It's a blue, wooden kennel – uninspiring in itself but the VIEWS across the water make it. I will concede, though, that Thomas' home, the Boathouse – now a museum and a cafe – is magnificent. I sit in the great man's garden in the sun and gaze out across the estuary. Inspiration strikes and, in my mind, I pen the first few lines of my auto-bi-dog-raphy.

Ah – the pups will be weeping salt tears when they read these words about how I grew to greatness from humble origins as a stray on the streets of London. It's moving stuff.

Jane – stop pulling my lead. I'm being creative. No – I am not ready to go. The muse has struck. Jane – arrrrrgh. Bloody philistines . . .

PHILEAS PHACTS: Laugharne

BROWNS HOTEL

King Street, Laugharne, Carmarthenshire, SA33 4RY: 01994 427688;
www.browns-hotel.co.uk
Price: from £95
Charge for dogs: £5 per dog
Extras for dogs: biscuits behind the bar
Access all areas: yes
Number of dogs: check when booking
Late night pee: Browns is on the main street

Alfie and Pepper, regulars at Browns

The Harbour at Solva

Pembrokeshire, West Wales, with Holly the Collie

I knew something was afoot – ahem, apaw rather – when I was rather unceremoniously chucked into the bath one morning. This means that I've either been rolling in something smelly or that I'm going on my jollies. Jollies it was, in this case!

The day after the bath, with my fur still smelling, much to my disgust, of Pet Head Chillaxin Spearmint and Lemongrass Calming Shampoo, I was in the back of the car with my travel bed, my toys and all the other essentials a Border Collie needs for a week's break in Wales. After three hours of rather rough sailing across the Irish Sea from my home on the Isle of Man to Liverpool on a sea c.a.t. (we don't mention the c word in our house) and a seven-hour drive in the car we arrived in Solva, Pembrokeshire.

First impressions were good. At our digs for the week – the Sail Loft – we were met by Simon, who is owned by a dog himself. He was very friendly to me and straightaway made sure Mum and Dad knew about the many dog walks in the area.

After a quick snoop round the apartment, which was very comfortably equipped, we headed down to the harbour to admire the bay. It was full of water that evening, but sometimes, over the following few days, it was miraculously transformed into a long narrow sandy beach where I could run and play.

Then Mum and Dad decided a gin and tonic was in order so we stopped at the Harbour Inn. There are four pubs in Solva – the Harbour Inn, the Ship Inn, the Royal George and the Cambrian Inn – and all except the Cambrian allow dogs. The Cambrian has tables outside though, so we were able to sample all four – rather too much time was spent sampling the pubs in my opinion but it was the humans' holiday as well as mine so I kept quiet. The Harbour Inn and the Ship Inn were my favourites, as I was made a fuss of and kept well supplied with water.

The next morning we drove – just a few minutes – to St Davids, the smallest city in Britain. Overlooked by a huge cathedral, several of its shops and pubs welcome dogs. When the humans ate at The Bishops, I was one of several dogs in the bar.

Our walk that afternoon started at the tiny harbour of Porthclais, just outside St Davids, and followed the coastal path around St Non's Bay to St Non's Chapel and Holy Well. Pilgrims have travelled there to drink the healing water for centuries so I had a good slurp to ensure I stayed healthy for the rest of the holiday.

Cliff top walks in West Wales

The following day we visited Broad Haven. There's a massive beach there – clean and sandy – and it was tempting to have a run but I was told dogs aren't allowed on the beach during the day in the summer. I got over my sulk when we set off on a lovely walk through Haroldston Woods, linking with the coastal path back to the village. Then we headed to Little Haven where there are no dog restrictions and I was able to cool my paws in the sea. (I don't do that swimming lark – just a paddle is enough for me.) There were three pubs, all of which were dog-friendly. We chose the St. Brides Inn

Holly gets her paws wet

and sat in the pretty beer garden because it was such a lovely afternoon.

The next day we headed north from Solva to Porthgain, which was once a commercial harbour exporting slate from the nearby mines. After the slate industry finished, Porthgain turned to brick-making and there are still relics of both industries in the land around the harbour. I wasn't interested in that, though – I wanted a walk. The headland is steep in places, and Mum put me on the lead on the more exposed areas. The humans were impressed by the views along the coast path but I was more interested in the smells.

Afterwards the humans watched a sheepdog demonstration at Pembrokeshire Sheepdogs, close to St Davids. Why? I'm a sheepdog and I demonstrate stuff to them all the time. Dogs were allowed into the arena to watch (I should think so too) but we were told that if any of the audience dogs became excited and barked, they'd be sent outside in case they put the performers off. What a load of prima donnas these theatrical types are!

Another outing was to Tenby with its brightly coloured houses clustered around the harbour. It was frustrating for me, though, as the beaches were out of bounds to dogs. Luckily I'd had a good walk earlier that day at the village of Llangwm (midway between Solva and Tenby) where I paddled in the Cleddau Estuary. We'd sat outside the Cottage Inn for lunch and, when it started to rain, the barman invited us inside, despite me being a little damp after paddling.

We also explored the Fishguard area with lunch at the Globe and a walk from Goodwick, Fishguard's twin town to the west, along the coastal path to Carreg

Tenby Harbour

Wastad Point, where the humans were excited about seeing seals sunbathing on the rocks. Seals don't run and are useless for chasing so I ignored them.

On our last day, we walked to St. Davids Head – a wild, rocky place where I was told off for picking up stones. (Don't humans understand how much fun stones are? Never mind if I damage my teeth!) Our route brought us back over the summit of

Carn Llidi, next to Whitesands Bay, before lunch in another dog-friendly pub – the Farmers Arms. Then we strolled around the rather impressive St. Davids Lifeboat Station, where the resident Border Collie took a fancy to me and followed me around the rocky beach, gazing at me adoringly. I couldn't blame him – I'm constantly told how pretty I am. Shame it was the last day or I could have had a holiday romance!

A holiday romance for Holly?

118

THE SAIL LOFT
19a Main Street, Solva, Haverfordwest,
Pembrokeshire, SA62 6UU:
01437 721114;
www.simonswinfield.com Sleeps: four
Price: from £295 a week
Charge for dogs: £30 per stay for two dogs
Extras for dogs: bowls in the cottage
Access all areas: everywhere but the
bedrooms
Number of dogs: maximum two
Late night pee: 50 yards to the beach

THE HARBOUR INN
Main Street, Solva, Haverfordwest,
Pembrokeshire, SA62 6UT:
01437 720013;
www.harbourinnsolva.com

THE SHIP INN
15 Main Street,
Solva, Haverfordwest,
Pembrokeshire, SA62 6UU:
01437 721528;
Price: from £55
Charge for dogs: no
Extras for dogs: no
Access all areas: not allowed in the
restaurant but breakfast can be taken
in the bar
Number of dogs: three, if they're small
Late night pee: 100 metres to the beach

THE ROYAL GEORGE
13 High Street, Solva, Haverfordwest,
Pembrokeshire, SA62 6TF:
01437 720002;
www.theroyalgeorgesolva.co.uk
Price: £65

Charge for dogs: no
Extras for dogs: biscuits behind the bar
Access all areas: yes
Number of dogs: ask at time of booking
Late night pee: car park with bins
Owner's dogs: Marni, a Chocolate Labrador

THE BISHOPS
22–23 Cross Street, St Davids,
Pembrokeshire, SA62 6SL:
01437 720422;
www.thebish.co.uk

THE FARMERS ARMS
14–16 Goat Street, St Davids,
Pembrokeshire, SA62 6RF:
01437 721666

ST BRIDES INN
St Brides Road, Little Haven,
Pembrokeshire, SA62 3UN:
01437 781266;
www.saintbridesinn.co.uk

THE COTTAGE INN
Llangwm, Haverfordwest,
Pembrokeshire, SA62 4HH:
01437 891494;
www.www.cottageinn-llangwm.co.uk

THE GLOBE
28 Main Street, Fishguard,
Pembrokeshire, SA65 9HJ:
01348 873999;
www.theglobefishguard.co.uk

For information on summer dog restrictions on
Pembrokeshire beaches, log on to
www.visitpembrokeshire.com

CRAIG-Y-NOS CASTLE, BRECON BEACONS

This is a wonderful place. It's a bit of a topsy-turvy place, to be sure, but Jane and I can be a bit topsy-turvy ourselves. So, while some Trip Advisor correspondents might cavil, your Pup Advisor correspondent is giving Craig-y-Nos Castle five stars – scores on the paws.

We visited Craig-y-Nos with Jane's Mum, Branwen, who was brought up in Neath – when she was a little girl, the drive to visit her grandmother in the West Midlands was past Craig-y-Nos and she used to wonder about it. It stands alone, on the side of the road in a dip among the mountains and looks like a puppy's drawing of a castle – with Gothic turrets, a spire and a gold fountain in the shape of a BIRD at the entrance.

When the sun shines, the castle appears hewn from gold – I am showing my poetic side here – but, when it rains it is grey and forbidding and eerie.

Now I am going to parrot-phrase the discussions between Jane and Branwen about Craig-y-Nos' history. They worked all this history out through words but if they hadn't it wouldn't have been a problem – I'd have worked it out through SMELLS!

The castle was built in the mid 1800s and, in 1878, it captured the imagination of the most famous opera singer of the day, Adelina Patti. She added a theatre, where she could perform. I am not a big fan of opera – those high notes hurt us dogs' ears, as they're triple-hundred-ed in volume and pitch for us.

Later the castle became a TB hospital. So lots of its history is quite sad, even though there are many happy aspects to it now and, for a dog, aspects that bring us JOY. Walk for one minute and there are woods – lots of woods. The castle

has its own and then, next door, there are more woods – in Craig-y-Nos Country Park – with a lake and a river and an open meadow and trees so tall that even I would struggle to leap up one to catch a squirrel.

Craig-y-Nos Country Park also has a dog-friendly cafe, which brought Jane JOY because, when she ordered a coffee, it arrived with a MINI WELSH CAKE, about the size of a 20 pence piece, on the side. (Forget

Craig-y-Nos Castle

the wonders of nature – for Jane a MINI WELSH CAKE is the main object of wonderment of the day.)

Craig-y-Nos is in the middle of the Beacons Way so there is lots more joy for dogs to be had there; every dog I met when we stayed – and there were a fair few – was barking about how brilliant Craig-y-Nos was with the walks and the woods and the fact that we choose our own bed for the night from the bar and transport it to our bedroom. This was, for the discerning dog like me, a nice touch.

In the late afternoon sun, in the walled garden to the right of the castle, with freshly mown grass and white metal tables and chairs set out for afternoon tea, I made chums with two dogs from the north of England, called Flip and Nudge.

Flip and Nudge had big news because their humans had got engaged that very day in that very garden and, even though we dogs don't really understand what get engaged is, we know it is BIG NEWS for humans. Given we dogs have so much to be excited about – smells and squirrels – and humans have so little – television and MINI WELSH CAKES – we pretend we are excited about their 'get engaged', for their sakes.

So that is all the JOY and during the day, when the sun is shining, Craig-y-Nos is the best spot for dogs in the whole world.

Top and Centre, Attlee and Flip;
Bottom, Nudge

Craig-y-Nos Country Park

But, when it grows dark the atmosphere changes and the humans, all eating dinner in the bar, share ghost stories. Craig-Y-Nos is supposed to be haunted – because of some of the sadnesses that have happened here – and there are ghost tours, which Jane and Branwen were too a'feart to sign up to. Indeed, after a couple of glasses of wine and much sharing of ghost stories with the other guests, Jane had to walk down some silent corridors past the deserted theatre to the loo and she made me go with her. I was certain that, if we did see a ghost, I would bravely unmask it and it would turn out to have been the pesky janitor all along.

But, much later at night, something strange did happen that made even me – fearless Phileas – shudder and the hairs on the back of my coat stand up. The strange happening occurred when Jane took me for my late night pee, in the enclosed garden at the side of Craig-y-Nos, leading down to the woods. We heard, dear reader, children's voices coming from those dark woods – happy children, playing. Which would have been all well and good except it was 10pm at night and pitch black and Craig-y-Nos is in the middle of the countryside so where had these children – and it sounded like there were a few of them – all come from?

 122

Jane stood stock still and listened and I stood stock still and listened and we were both listening and wondering: who were these ghostly, spirit voices? *Perhaps the voices of the children who were patients at Craig-y-Nos, when they were poorly?*

Then we turned tail because it was unsettling to listen to those voices and think about them and what they meant for too long. When we returned to the bar and mentioned it to Beth, who lives at Craig-y-Nos and manages it with her husband Simon, she frowned and said she had never felt a ghostly presence at the castle. But I know what I heard and Jane knows what she heard. What Jane believes and I do too is that if there were ghosts of children in those woods, they were having a lovely time. They were laughing and cheering and running about in the sheer exhilaration of all that countryside, just like I had been, during the day. So they were

"Even a squirrel couldn't climb that tree!"

happy. And that is comforting rather than creepy.

Next morning the sun was shining and the woods were beckoning and Craig-y-Nos was grand again – faded grand, with on-going renovations and patching up of one area while another falls into disrepair – but grand nonetheless.

If your humans and you are the sort of family who would find discovering the television in the hotel room doesn't work even more horrifying than discovering a ghost, Craig-y-Nos is not going to be your cup of tea or your bowl of water. But, if your humans are like Jane and you're like me, you will find Craig-y-Nos a magical, mysterious experience and the voices of those children in the woods will stay with you long after you've checked out.

123

PHILEAS PHACTS: Craig-y-Nos, Brecon Beacons

CRAIG-Y-NOS CASTLE

Brecon Road, Penycae, Powys, SA9 1GL:
01639 731167;
www.craigynoscastle.com and
www.dogfriendlywales.com 🐾
Price: starts at £63 for a twin room.
Ask for Theatre Ground Left (TGL) or
Theatre Ground Right (TGR) which open
directly onto the enclosed garden.
Or, in the former nurses' block,
a double room with a shared toilet
is £30 a night.
Charge for dogs: no
Extras for dogs: choose your own dog bed

for the night; biscuits in the bar; water
bowls; walks with the resident dogs
and ghost tours!
Access all areas: not in the dining
room but meals can be taken in the bar
Number of dogs: no maximum
Late night pee: enclosed garden
Owner's Dogs: Pepper, a German
Shepherd Collie Cross, owned by Beth
and Simon who run Craig-y-Nos; Jack,
a Golden Retriever, and Sheeba, a
white Alsatian, the owner's dogs and
Corgi Bryn (below)who visits most
days

Crickhowell, Mid-Wales, with Mojo the Spaniel

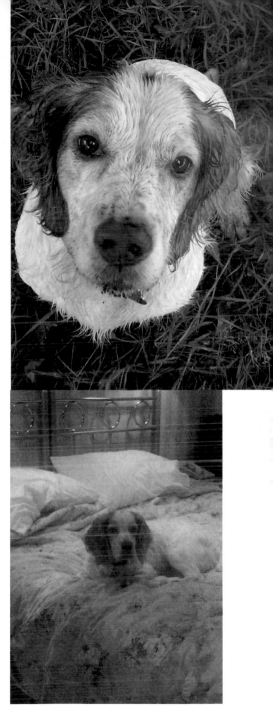

My name is Mojo and I'm a Spaniel and my human is Hudson Human. My Rover Report is on The Bear Hotel, a dog-friendly (very dog-friendly) pub and hotel in Crickhowell in the middle of Brecon Beacons National Park. Thankfully there aren't any bears as we turn the car into the cobbled forecourt – that had been troubling me a little. Even better, when we check in the receptionist gives me a dog treat. Food is my main thing – I am not called Mojo the Marauder for nowt – so, chomping on my treat, I have to conclude the holiday is, so far, very good.

The reception dog biscuit lady shows us to our room – one of the coach house rooms across the hotel forecourt – and explains that dogs are allowed everywhere apart from the dining room. I unpack my doggy biscuits and immediately head out for a walk along the River Usk, as the lady has recommended it. It's started to rain and is quite windy too but I don't care as I am exploring new territory. I meet lots of other curious canines out on the sniff and everyone, although soaking wet, is friendly.

After a couple of hours we make our way back to the hotel to dry off. We walk into the low-beamed bar (the building dates back to 1432) to

When the Spaniel met the Bear

be greeted by my fellow canine chums, all sitting under tables relaxing. Hudson Human orders a drink and we find a table so a waitress can take her food order. Then, AMAZEMENT – the waitress takes Mojo's food order!

Would I like a bowl of chicken? I'm Mojo the Marauder – of course I would. I forget my manners and jump on the table, unable to contain my glee. The other humans didn't mind that I was exuberant, but Hudson Human thought it best I returned to the room to calm down. An hour later, she appeared with the spoils – all the better for the waiting. Then I promptly fell asleep.

The next morning, I'm up early, ready for a walk before breakfast. We were planning to drive to Sugar Loaf Mountain – a bit like the mountain in Brazil, but smaller – but the weather's still poor. So we cross a road from The Bear and find a lovely little church and lots of fields with horses. After an hour, it brightens up and I can see the yellow thing in the sky. But I'm ravenous now and it's SAUSAGES and bacon for breakfast so I don't want to miss out.

After breakfast, though, as the yellow thing in the sky is still shining, we relax in the hotel's gardens. I don't want to check out. Being a Rover Reporter is fun when there's chicken, bacon and SAUSAGES involved.

PHILEAS PHACTS: Crickhowell

THE BEAR HOTEL
Crickhowell, Powys, NP8 1BW:
01873 810408;
www.bearhotel.co.uk
Price: from £95
Charge for dogs: no
Extras for dogs: every canine visitor is presented with a bowl of chicken
Access all areas: in the bar but not in restaurant
Number of dogs: check at time of booking
Late night pee: a park a couple of minutes away

Happy donkeys on the hill!

Happy Donkey Hill, Ceredigion

I wasn't convinced when Jane booked us a room at Happy Donkey Hill B&B in Ceredigion. Happy donkeys are all well and good, but, surely the whole point of MY book is that we are researching hills for happy hounds?

But, Jane assured me, Happy Donkey Hill catered for dogs too and, she reckoned, in fine style. So we high hoofed and high pawed it there – and what a high hoof and high paw it was. Single track roads all the way after Carmarthen, which Jane's mum Branwen, who was driving, did not care for one bit.

When we arrived in Llandysul – a quiet town that appears sleepy but probably isn't – Jane, dashed into the pet shop on the main street for further directions. She returned to the car without a treat for me – an aberration given that she'd been inside a pet shop – but full of chat about the cute photographs of Corgi puppies for sale on the pet shop notice board. I gave her a hard stare. We have no need of a Corgi puppy.

There was worse to come. When we arrived at the remote farmhouse, indeed atop a hill, to be met by proprietor Katie, Jane immediately said: 'Where are the donkeys? It's my dream to own a donkey.'

Agatha won't give up her top spot in the kitchen

I gave her another hard stare. We have no need of a Corgi puppy nor a donkey.

When Katie ushered us inside the B&B's cheerful farmyard kitchen and closed the front door, she said to Jane: 'You can let Attlee off the lead now.' Now this was BIG news. I was to have the run of not just our bedroom but the kitchen too? And what a welcoming kitchen it was, with rugs thrown on a flagstone floor, a Welsh dresser boasting an enamel dog treats container and a commanding Aga-style oven. Unfortunately, when Katie, at Jane's request, ushered her three dogs – Bull Mastiff Agatha and Jack Russells Porridge and Pope – into the kitchen, Agatha stole pride of place in front of the oven, even though I politely pointed out that, as a guest, I should have priority.

Then it was time for the introduction to the donkeys in the stables, during which I was left in the bedroom – charmed, I'm sure. But – fear not – I know all about the introduction as Jane returned full of it.

The earlier revelation about how she wants a donkey paled in comparison to the post-meeting-the-happy-donkeys-on-the-hill dream. Now Jane isn't going to be content with just one donkey. Oh no – she desires, in fact, the exact style of smallholding that Donkey Hill comprises. That is: 11 donkeys and one rescue pony; five cats; two pigs; goats – oh, and just for good measure, chickens. Not just any old chickens either – chickens that have been saved from batteries.

I attempt to give Jane the hardest hard stare I had ever given her in my life. *We have no need of Corgi puppies; or 11 donkeys; or one rescue pony; or five cats; or two pigs; or goats, or chickens that have been saved from batteries. We have no need of them at all.*

It is very hard to convey all this in one hard stare but I try my damnedest. Quite how Jane imagines she will care for all this livestock, given that, on occasion – QUITE OFTEN – she forgets to buy food for me and Doger (Jane's cat) and has to nip to the shop on the corner late at night, I'm not sure.

Furthermore, the five cats resident at Happy Donkey Hill – all black with evil, flashing-green eyes – are not the sort of cats I wish to share a living environment with. This smallholding is a terrible idea and, should Jane continue with it, I will be on the phone to the RSPCA, pronto. Thank Dog when it was time for the distraction of dinner. Katie recommended a dog-friendly pub called The Daffodil, a mile away. But could we find The Daffodil on those Ceredigion roads at dusk? We could not. We gave up and stopped at a pub we'd passed about five times in our Daffodil endeavours – The Gwarcefel Arms. When we walked in, everybody was talking Welsh – even the dogs. Some dogs in Wales have a reputation for speaking English but, when English dogs approach, switching to Welsh to make the point that they are bilingual and thus superior. But this was not the case in The Gwarcefel. The dogs were happy to chin-WAG – and the people too – with us tourists. Alun, who is 86 years of age (Alun is a person, not a dog) told us that he is still up at 6am every morning to run his farm and still has the energy to head out to the local for a beer in the evening.

Alun was diverting but still, the following morning at breakfast, my SAUSAGE snaffling did not hold its usual thrill. I was in a state of trepidation should, as we prepared for departure, a horse box be attached to our car and a veritable Noah's Ark of animals be ushered in, to commence a new life in our garden in Camberwell. As soon as the car door was opened, I leapt in and indicated that I was in a tremendous hurry to carry on with my researches and, when I glanced out of the back window, I was relieved to see we were not being followed.

Two months on, I am happy to report that our Camberwell mini-menagerie still only has two residents – myself and Dodger. Dodger is one too many but, given what could have been, I'm not complaining.

Some more canine guests check in at Happy Donkey Hill

PHILEAS PHACTS: Happy Donkey Hill

HAPPY DONKEY HILL

Faerdre Fach, Prengwyn Road, Llandysul, Ceredigion, SA44 4EG: 01559 364766; www.happydonkeyhill.co.uk 🐾

Price: from £70 B&B and from £375 a week in one of the three self-catering cottages

Charge for dogs: no charge for the first dog but the second is £5 a night in the B&B; in the cottages, £20 a week charge

Extras for dogs: big tin of treats in the kitchen; dog beds

Access all areas: everywhere except the hot tub

Number of dogs: confirm when booking

Late night pee: a little, enclosed paddock

Owner's dogs: yes – three

GWARCEFEL ARMS

Prengwyn, Llandysul, Ceredigion, SA44 4LU: 01559 363126

Postcard from Wales, by Anubis the Basenji

I'm Anubis the Barkless Dog and it's fair to say I'm well-travelled. I've been all the way up north to the Highlands, far to the south in Provence, east to Switzerland and bang in the centre of it all in London. *I now live in Hollywood – I'm a showbiz dog!*

But the place I've travelled more than any other is Wales. I was only three months old when I felt the sand beneath my paws for the very first time at Freshwater West in Pembrokeshire. Since then, I've spent a whole month in the Brecon Beacons while I worked on a movie. I've done woodland too, at Symonds Yat Rock, a forest where I ran for hours and admired views over the River Wye. (Technically this is in England, but who's counting?)

As for castles and ruins – well, if there's one thing I love it's sniffing old stones. Luckily, in Wales, there are plenty around – for example Tintern Abbey, the ruins of a 12th century monastery in a beautiful setting. Another day, we visited the ruins at the Three Castles – White, Skenfrith and Grosmont – where medieval dogs and their humans lived. They're fun to climb and explore and are surrounded with enclosed fields where I had an impromptu game of chase with a fellow tourist, a Rhodesian Ridgeback.

My humans use the Blaentrothy agency when we're in Wales – we've rented three cottages through them. Each was unique, beautiful, isolated, comfortable, and most importantly, dog-friendly (though for some reason I wasn't allowed upstairs.) Of the three, my favourite was called Paradise. It was the prettiest and

Anubis at Tintern Abbey

had a big enclosed garden for me.

Two tips for Wales: firstly, it is crawling with sheep. So if, like us Basenjis, you might give in to the temptation of chasing, stay on the leash in fields and find forests and woods to run free. Secondly, weather in Wales is notoriously changeable – they say if you don't like it, wait five minutes. I don't care for the cold and wet – if you're the same bring a coat, whatever the season.

PHILEAS PHACTS: Anubis in Wales

BLAENTROTHY COTTAGES
Blaentrothy Farm, Grosmont, Abergavenny, Monmouthshire, NP7 8HN:
01873 890190;
www.cottage-holiday-wales.co.uk

The beach at Freshwater West is dog-friendly all year round.

Anubis on the beach when she was three months old

THE GOWER PENINSULA

Glower at the Gower! It is a very beautiful place undoubtedly but, for me, a very annoying place. We start our Gower researches with a visit to Rhossili Bay, which *The Times* of London has stated is Britain's dog-friendliest beach. And a fine beach it is too – miles and miles of it, and, when we reach it, after mountain goat-ing down a steep cliff with lots of SHEEPS on it, I am the only dog on the whole stretch of soft toffee-coloured sand. Rhossili is, I would have to concur, stunning.

But Britain's dog-friendliest beach? I would like to know how this title is conferred. There are no bones being handed out to dogs upon arrival, nor tennis balls provided should our hapless humans have forgotten ours. What, in my hound's opinion, is really peculiar about this astonishing accolade the Glower – sorry, the Gower – has been gifted, however, is that neither the cafe nor the pub at the top of the path leading to Rhossili allow dogs. So if Rhossili is Britain's dog-friendliest beach, why are we not welcome to use its amenities?

We are grudgingly allowed to sit outside the cafe – The Bay Bistro and Coffee House. Of course, on a summer's day, sitting outside is perfectly acceptable but on the day I visited it was drizzling and sitting outside is no fun. And the chap in charge was very cool towards me – he clearly didn't like the cut of my jib. Grumph – the ANTI-MUTTRIACHRY are out in force. Ditto The Worm's Head Hotel and

Sheep have right of way on The Gower

133

pub – to use the little Welsh I've learnt, Dim Cwm, meaning No Dogs.

Thank Dog, then, for the nice lady who runs Coastal Surf and Gifts at Rhossili. She only had one table inside her rather stuffed shop – normally she serves coffees and teas outside in a little courtyard – but she allowed us inside to shelter from the inclement weather.

After the joy of the beautiful beach and the crushing disappointment of the dog-UN-friendly atmosphere at Rhossili, we went for a drive to try to understand if Rhossili is the exception or the rule to the Gower's attitude to dogs. Well, the Gower is all single-track country lanes along which, it appears, sheeps and horses have the right to walk. Why do they have the right to use the roads – inferior beasts that they are – and we dogs not have the right to use the pubs? It doesn't make sense.

Jane liked the appearance of The King Arthur Hotel, a stately-looking pad on the village square in Reynoldston – but, alas, dogs are not allowed. In the past, she's stayed at the upmarket Fairyhill Hotel, also in Reynoldston, and she wonders if we'll be welcome there for coffee and cake. But, no – while dogs are allowed to stay in some of the bedrooms, we are not allowed in Fairyhill's public areas.

Jane and I are not giver-uppers, though – especially not when hungry – and my fine nose leads us to Oxwich Bay, a hamlet on the beach. Six dogs are sitting with their owners in the gardens of the Oxwich Bay Hotel – all sitting very quietly too and not a reprobate among them, Mr Bay Cafe and Mrs Worm's Head – so

Facing page, Oxwich Bay (top) and Rhossili (bottom); inset Rhossili. Below, Rhossili.

Jane ventures inside with hope in her heart. Surely an establishment that has the patronage of six dogs outside will not turn us away inside? And Howl-ell-ujah! The ANTI-MUTTRIARCHY is vanquished, because she is told: yes, dogs are welcome inside some of the public areas of the Oxwich Bay Hotel and also to stay the night.

I chat to some of the chaps outside and one dog barks that he is staying at a dog-friendly cottage – The Old Court House. Things are looking up – until he mentions that it's owned by a vet. Another has news of a dog-friendly pub called The Greyhound, where greyhounds are welcome – and the rest of us too. Finally, I am tipped off about a dog-friendly campsite, at Nicholaston Farm, with a walk through the woods to the beach.

Afterwards we have a walk on Oxwich Bay and I'm starting to GLOWER less at the Gower. I do wish Rhossili wouldn't be so silly, though. It truly is an amazing beach. But Jane wants a slice of cake and a cup of tea with her amazing beaches. And she wants to sit in a cafe or a pub, with ME, to enjoy it.

Boomerang in Aberdovey, Snowdonia

I was very alarmed on a recent trip to the Aberdovey area of Snowdonia when we arrived at a sign announcing 'sheepdog trials'. What? I don't want to have to herd those stupid animals around all afternoon.

But, thank Dog, the chap said that, as I don't have any training with sheep, I am not, technically, a sheepdog and, therefore, not eligible to enter the trials. Good thing too – it looked bloody hard work for the 40 dogs competing. They had six to eight minutes to herd the sheep. And they had to keep them in a straight line too – no squiggly sheep allowed. As for the commands – I'd need a dog-ree to understand them. All I know is that come-by *means herd the sheep clockwise;* away *means herd them anti-clockwise.*

No – this sheepdog malarkey isn't for me. Far better to be a beach dog, romping along Aberdovey sands, and then a pub dog, snoozing under the table at The Penhelig Arms waiting for scraps of ham sandwich to fall under the table.

COASTAL SURF AND GIFTS
Bayview, Rhossili, The Gower, SA3 1PN

FAIRYHILL HOTEL
Reynoldston, The Gower, SA3 1BS:
01792 390139;
www.fairyhill.net
Price: £190 for a standard double and up
Charge for dogs: £10 per room, however many dogs
Extras for dogs: no
Access all areas: in the bedrooms but not anywhere else
Number of dogs: check when booking
Late night pee: 24 acres of grounds

THE OXWICH BAY HOTEL
Oxwich, The Gower, SA3 1LS:
01792 390329;
www.oxwichbayhotel.co.uk
Price: cottage rooms start at £85; hiring a static caravan starts at £300.
Charge for dogs: £5 per dog
Extras for dogs: no
Access all areas: in the snug and the small bar
Number of dogs: maximum five
Late night pee: the hotel is on the beach

THE OLD COURT HOUSE
Cwm Ivy, Llanmadoc, The Gower, SA3 1DJ
Email: dafyddstephenroberts@yahoo.co.uk;
www.the-gower.com
Sleeps: four
Price: starts at £300 for five nights
Charge for dogs: £20 per week per dog
Extras for dogs: bowls; throws for settees, and towels
Access all areas: yes
Number of dogs: four maximum
Late night pee: 20 yards to a nature reserve

THE GREYHOUND
Oldwalls, Llanrhidian, The Gower, SA3 1HA:
01792 391027;
www.thegreyhoundinnoldwalls.co.uk

NICHOLASTON FARM CAMPSITE
Penmaen, The Gower, SA3 2HL: 01792 371209;
www.nicholastonfarm.co.uk
Price: starting at £14 per tent; £20 per caravan or motorhome
Charge for dogs: no
Extras for dogs: no
Access all areas: yes
Number of dogs: two maximum
Late night pee: 13 acres
Owner's dogs: working Sheepdog Boyo

Rhossili Bay is dog-friendly all year round. Oxwich Bay is dog-friendly all year round but dogs must be on a lead if there are children on the beach.

THE PENHELIG ARMS
27-29 Terrace Road, Aberdovey, Gwynedd, LL35 0LT: 01654 767215;
www.penheligarms.com
Price: From £75
Charge for dogs: £10 per dog
Extras for dogs: no
Access all areas: in the bar and cocktail lounge but not in the restaurant
Number of dogs: check when booking
Late night pee: 75 yards to a little park.

Aberdovey beach is dog-friendly all year round, although there are some restrictions in certain parts over the summer

WALES DIRECTORY

BLUE BOAR INN

Castle Street, Hay-on-Wye, Powys, HR3 5DF:
01497 820884

There's a genial greeting towards dogs in this unspoilt boozer, where the barmaid happily admitted to us that she prefers them to people!

THE BOAT INN

Erbistock, Clwyd, LL13 0DL:
01978 780666;
www.boatondee.com

This traditional 17th Century inn is in a lovely setting, on the banks of the River Dee – your dog's nose will be twitching at the prospect of otters on the opposite shore. The Boat doesn't have berths, sadly – perhaps because guests would never leave – but it does operate a campsite in the neighbouring field if booked in advance (and if overnighters drink or dine at the pub.) Price: pitches start at £15 per tent, campervan or caravan

Pancake pushes The Boat out

Charge for dogs: no
Extras for dogs: ham for the regulars
Access all areas: yes
Number of dogs: no limits
Late night pee: a riverside walk
Owner's dogs: plans are in place to install a Pug!

BRYNKIR TOWER

Garndolbenmaen, Gwynedd, LL51 9AQ
Book at 01248 430258 or at
www.menaiholidays.co.uk

It's no folly to enjoy a break at this unique little property in Snowdonia – in fact, it's one of the most memorable holiday lets around. A Gothic folly built in the 1820's, the tower has massive arched windows from which your dog will love peering out at the surrounding countryside and six floors – each with just one room. That's a long way down the spiral staircase if you need a wee in the middle of the night, though!

A folly fit for Fido

Sleeps: four

Price: starts at £385 per week

Charge for dogs: £20 per week

Extras for dogs: information pack with local walks

Access all areas: not allowed in the bedrooms or on furniture

Number of dogs: two maximum

Late night pee: out of the door into the countryside

CAER BERIS MANOR

Builth Wells, Powys, LD2 3NP:
01982 552601;
www.caerberis.com

Your hound can be Lord of the Manor in this Grade II listed building – or, with the former butler's pantry and servants' hall now converted into bedrooms, he can be more of a 'downstairs' sort of dog. With 27 acres of grounds to explore, though, he won't be complaining if he does have a few pairs of boots to polish beforehand.

Price: £137.90

Charge for dogs: £10 per dog

Extras for dogs: fleece blankets in the bedrooms and an outside dog wash

Access all areas: dogs are allowed in the bar and conservatory but not the restaurant

Number of dogs: depends on size – Caer Beris has hosted every breed from Chihuahuas to Great Danes

Late night pee: 27 acres of grounds – river walks and woodland

Owner's dogs: Poodle Florric

DOLGETHIN GUEST HOUSE

Holyhead Road, Betws-y-Coed, Conwy, LL24 0BN:
01690 710241;
www.dolgethinguesthouse.co.uk

The village of Betws-y-Coed is as pretty as its name suggests, nestled in the Conwy valley among the mountains of the Snowdonia National Park, and the Dolgethin, a 150-year-old detached grey stone home, offers good-sized clean bedrooms and a hearty breakfast. What more could the mountaineering mutt ask for?

Price: from £70

Charge for dogs: £5 per dog

Extras for dogs: sausages at breakfast

Access all areas: except the dining room

Number of dogs: maximum two

Late night pee: woodland walks

Owner's dogs: Black Labrador Ebony

FALCONDALE HOTEL

Falcondale Drive, Lampeter, Ceredigion, SA48 7RX:
01570 422910;
www.thefalcondale.co.uk 🐾

The Brechfa Forest offers 18,000 acres of woodland for your dog to bounce through and the Falcondale, just ten minutes' drive away, is the place for him to sleep off his exertions. Its 'croeso' to canines is one of the most genuine around – it even offers day (or longer if necessary) training courses for unruly mutts. If they scrub up well you can take them for some fine dining in the conservatory, relaxed in the knowledge they'll know to use their cutlery correctly!

Price: £140

Charge for dogs: £10 however many dogs

Pudgeley, Maitre Dog at the Falcondale

Extras for dogs: tap, bucket and sponge to clean mucky paws; blankets; towels; throws for the beds; homemade dog biscuits at reception

Access all areas: not the dining room but meals can be taken in the conservatory

Number of dogs: maximum three

Late night pee: 14 acres of gardens and woodlands – take a torch

Owner's dogs: Pudgeley (previous page) and Major

THE FELIN FACH GRIFFIN

Felin Fach, Brecon, LD3 0UB:
01874 620111;
www.eatdrinksleep.ltd.uk
Highly recommended by Fenn from Camberwell, your dog really will be VIP pup at the Felin Fach Griffin, a dining pub with rooms. Not comfortable lying on the slate floor of the bar, sir? The waiter will fetch a blanket. Want to sleep on the chair in your bedroom? A throw is provided for that.

Price: from £175 dinner, bed and breakfast

Charge for dogs: no

Extras for dogs: bowls, towels, mats, blankets and throws

Access all areas: in the bar and part of the restaurant

Number of dogs: ask when booking

Owner's dogs: Max

KITCHEN TABLE COFFEE SHOP AND RESTAURANT

626 Mumbles Road, Mumbles, Swansea, SA3 4EA:
01792 367616;
www.thekitchentablemumbles.wordpress.com
The Kitchen Table is a small, cosy cafe with wooden benches, homemade cake for an afternoon snack and proper hearty food in the evenings, when it swaps coffee for wine. What's more, it's opposite Swansea Bay so perfect to pop into after a stroll along the promenade.

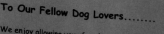

To Our Fellow Dog Lovers........

We enjoy allowing your four legged friends into the cafe, however if you are bringing a dog with you please respect the following.
Thank You! The K.T. Team

- Dogs are now only allowed in the bottom section of the cafe.
- Do not feed your dog at the table. Go outside if you wish to feed your pet.
(There is already a water bowl outside for you)
- Please try to keep your dog on a lead, underneath the table, or out of the path of others.

THANK YOU for your consideration of other customers, we want to continue to allow your lovely, well-behaved pooches into the cafe!

LITTLE DUMPLEDALE

Ashdale Lane, Sardis, Haverfordwest, Pembrokeshire, SA62 4NT:
01646 602754;
www.littledumpledale.co.uk
Twenty-two is the record for the number of dogs Little Dumpledale has hosted in one party – there really are no limits here. The self-catering accommodation on offer consists of a caravan, three cottages and a five bedroom house, all set within five acres of safe and secure farmland. (It's arable so there are no concerns about livestock.) Resident Deerhound Cross Waljan blogs about life on the farm if your dog wants an idea of the adventures to be had before checking in but, believe us, this truly is a pups' playground.

Sleeps: caravan sleeps four; the smallest cottage sleeps eight and there's room for ten in the five-bedroom house

Price: starting at £250 for the caravan, £300 for the smallest cottage and £400 for the house a week

Charge for dogs: no

Extras for dogs: Flyball training sessions

Waljan: a dog with a blog

Access all areas: yes – even in the beds!
Number of dogs: 22 maximum
Late night pee: each property has an enclosed garden
Owner's dogs: three Deerhound Crosses, Waljan, Blitzen and Donna; Fly, the Whippet, Pip the Whippet cross; Phoebe the Lurcher, and Poppy the Jack Russell

LLANCAYO WINDMILL

Llancayo, near Usk, Monmouthshire:
Book through Rural Retreats on 01386 701177 or at
www.ruralretreats.co.uk
A recently renovated windmill over five storeys, this is the perfect spot for a birthday with a zero in it – and your dog's invited to share the cake!
Sleeps: 12
Price: starting from £1592 for three nights
Charge for dogs: £25 per stay
Extras for dogs: no
Access all areas: dogs are only allowed on the ground floor, where the kitchen and dining room are
Number of dogs: one
Late night pee: the windmill is floodlit after dark, so you won't get lost.

MINER'S COTTAGE

9 Glynllifon Street, Blaenau Ffestiniog, Gwynedd, LL41 3AF:
Book through North Wales Holiday Cottages on 01492 582492 or at
www.northwalesholidaycottages.co.uk 🐾
This pretty miner's cottage in the mountains takes the business of having dogs as guests very seriously. There's a pet pantry in the kitchen, with dog bowls, treats, a brush, shampoo – basically more kit than most dogs have at home – and an area of the enclosed courtyard garden has been planted with grass so your dog can undertake any nocturnal toilettes in comfort.
Sleeps: three
Price: starting from £255 for a three-night break
Charge for dogs: no
Extras for dogs: pets' pantry
Access all areas: not in bedrooms or on furniture
Number of dogs: two maximum

NOLTON CROSS CARAVAN PARK AND CAMP SITE

Nolton Cross, Haverfordwest, Pembrokeshire, SA62 3NP:
01437 710701;
www.noltoncross-holidays.co.uk
This little campsite, with 15 hook-ups for tourers and tents and eight static caravans for rent, has its own fishing lake. Resident Russells Rosie and Patch enjoy fanning themselves in the pampas grass on sunny days.
Price: from £8 for two people per caravan or tent; £210 to hire a static for a week, sleeping six
Charge for dogs: no
Extras for dogs: no
Access all areas: yes
Number of dogs: two
Late night pee: walk down to the fishing lake
Owner's dogs: Rosie and Patch

I'm Irie, pub princess at the Ty Coch Inn, recently named as the third best beach bar in the WORLD. I play on the sand every day and receive lots of titbits from our lovely customers. Life is goooooooooood!

TY COCH INN, Porthdinllaen, Morfa Nefyn, Gwynedd, LL53 6DB: 01758 720498; **www.tycoch.co.uk**

THE OLD STABLES TEA ROOM

Bear Street, Hay-on-Wye, Powys, HR3 5AN:
07796 484766

Very dog-friendly and cosy tea rooms tucked away in Hay-on-Wye, with the focus firmly on Welsh produce.

PEMBROKESHIRE SHEEPDOGS

Tremynydd Fach Farm, St Davids,
Pembrokeshire, SA62 6DB:
01437 721677;

www.sheepdogtraining.co.uk

Visit Tremynydd Farm for the afternoon to watch a sheepdog demonstration or stay overnight in the B&B or self-catering accommodation. Beware if your dog is a chaser, though – this is a working sheep farm.

Sleeps: self-catering accommodation ranges from a Shepherd's Hut sleeping two adults to a four-bedroom farmhouse sleeping eight

Price: £60 B&B; the farmhouse starts at £600 a week

Charge for dogs: no

Anubis' favourite bookshop in Hay-on-Wye is Murder and Mayhem on Lion Street – with the Hound of the Baskervilles lurking outside . . .

The Old Stables Tearoom, left

Extras for dogs: sheepdog and puppy training classes
Access all areas: in the bedrooms in the B&B but not in public areas; not in the bedrooms in the self-catering accommodation
Number of dogs: no maximum
Late night pee: two enclosed paddocks
Owner's dogs: 25 sheepdogs!

PORTHCLAIS FARM CAMPSITE

St Davids, Pembrokeshire, SA62 6RR:
07970 439310;
www.porthclais-farm-campsite.co.uk
Laidback campsite with 100 pitches for tents, campers and caravans set in 24 acres of fields. Your dog (and you) can unzip your tent in the morning and be in the sea in two minutes!
Price: from £7 per adult in a tent or caravan
Charge for dogs: £2 per dog

Extras for dogs: no

Access all areas: yes

Number of dogs: no maximum

Late night pee: 24 acres of fields

THE QUEENS

10 Queen Street, Carmarthen,
Carmarthenshire, SA31 1JR:
01267 231800
Our dog-friendly saviours on a day out in
Carmarthenshire – pretty pub pup Jess reigns here.

SHELL ISLAND

Llanbedr, Gwynedd, North Wales, LL45 2PJ:
01341 241453;
www.shellisland.co.uk
Shell Island is quite back to basics – it's a pitch-up-
where-you-fancy place with loos and showers that
some people complain can become a bit 'Glastonbury'
at the end of a long summer's day. But the situation, a
400-acre peninsula (300 acres of which are set aside

Jess, Queen of The Queens

*I'm Lilly and I know I'll strike gold if
I keep digging on my favourite beach
– Newton Bay in my hometown of
Porthcawl.*

for camping) with three dog-friendly bathing beaches
and views all the way down to Pembrokeshire, is
glorious if you don't mind ruffing it occasionally.

Price: from £6.25 per person in a tent

Charge for dogs: £2 per dog

Extras for dogs: no

Access all areas: it's a shame dogs aren't allowed in
the on-site pubs

Number of dogs: three per booking

Late night pee: 400 acres!

WENDY THE ABERPORTH EXPRESS

Coastal Footpath, Ceredigion, Wales:
Book through Under the Thatch on 0844 5005 101 or at
www.underthethatch.co.uk
Wendy started life as a sleeper carriage in 1905 and is
named after the character in Peter Pan. There's a Peter
Pan quality to Wendy too – she's in brilliant nick, for a
centenarian. Maybe it's the cool, fresh air that keeps
her so young, or the fact she's so far away from frenetic
modern life, tucked away on the Ceredigion Coastal

Path with only dolphins in the bay and rabbits in the fields for company.

Sleeps: five

Price: short breaks start at £282

Charge for dogs: £15 for first dog and £5 for second

Extras for dogs: no

Access all areas: yes

Number of dogs: two

Late night pee: garden with a picket fence

WIND IN THE WILLOWS

Skirrid, Black Mountains of Monmouthshire, Wales: Book through Under the Thatch on 0844 5005 101 or at **www.underthethatch.co.uk**

Gypsy caravans are becoming popular holiday lets but, usually, don't allow dogs – Wind in the Willows, built to star in the film of the book, is the exception. It's set in splendid isolation in the Black Mountains. Beep beep, cried Toad – let's go!

Sleeps: two

Price: short breaks from £181

Charge for dogs: £15 for first dog; £5 for second (per break)

Extras for dogs: no

Access all areas: yes

Number of dogs: two maximum

Late night pee: there's a meadow just outside the door. (Leads on though, as there are sheep.)

A Rural Retreat for Rover

IRONBRIDGE, SHROPSHIRE

Shropshire is the county where Jane and I went on our first holiday together – just the two of us – in June 2011. At the time, she said that depression was lurking around South-East London, waiting to pounce. So she decided to catch the train to Shropshire to hide from it. She says Winston Churchill, a former prime minister, like me, Clement Attlee, described depression as a black dog following the sufferer around. I've never noticed any black dogs following Jane around – I follow her around but I am white and black and brindle. And sometimes I don't follow her around at all, even though she tells me to!

When we arrived at Telford Station, Colin, who we were renting Victoria Cottage from for a week, picked us up and drove us to Ironbridge, where our cottage was. Jane said this was very kind of Colin – beyond the call of duty.

The cottage had a patio garden with a pub at the end of it. This made for great fun, because I could go to the bottom of the garden and bark at the pub's customers.

On our first evening in Victoria Cottage we went to the pub, the Golden Ball Inn – imagine that; a golden ball! Jane had a glass of dry white wine and scampi and chips and read her book in the beer garden. The portions were big and Jane fed me lots of chips – underneath the table. Normally I am not allowed to sit underneath tables and beg for food – that's a thing dogs aren't allowed to do. But, on holiday apparently, it's okay.

Chipping Campden in the Cotswolds

Attlee the Shropshire Lad in Ironbridge (with Jane)

Everyone in the Golden Ball Inn rubbed my ears and told Jane how good looking I was.

'Thanks,' Jane said, as if they were telling her she was good looking.

The next day, a builder who was working on the house next to Victoria Cottage told us about a book that a dog had written about all the lovely walks in the Ironbridge area.

'A dog which has written a book,' he scoffed, as if it was ridiculous.

So Jane and I walked down the hill to Ironbridge and bought the book, *Walking with Boomerang: Dog-friendly Walks around Ironbridge and Coalbrookdale*, in a shop called Eleys Pies. Jane bought a pork pie and gave me half. I'd never eaten a pork pie before and I guzzled it all in one big gulp. Then we set off on one of the walks Boomerang suggests, which was very exciting, because it meant walking across the IRON BRIDGE. The iron bridge in Ironbridge is the oldest bridge in the world made of cast iron. But, to me, it was the bridge to a whole new world.

We tried a walk recommended by Boomerang called The Pork Pie Run. There were squirrels to chase and hills to climb and woods to explore and a field full of wild poppies to race through. I was so exhilarated with it all that I nearly caused an avalanche of mud and rocks in my eagerness to find out what was around the next brow of the hill and the next bend in the path. Dogs always know there is something amazing around the next bend in the path. I sometimes wish humans, like Jane, did.

Every day, for the rest of the week, we undertook one of Boomerang's walks. First Jane would have a cup of tea and a scone in the courtyard at The Tea

 148

Emporium. Watching Jane drink tea was very boring. I wanted her to hurry up so we could cross the iron bridge and reach the woods.

One morning, Jane nipped into the Post Office and left me tied to a metal table outside the Tea Emporium. But I was so impatient to run across the iron bridge that I escaped the metal table and, with my red lead flying behind me, charged across the street towards it. This caused quite a commotion as all the traffic had to stop and Jane and all the waitresses from The Tea Emporium had to chase me.

I darted across the iron bridge but, when, after about five minutes, I heard Jane calling my name, her voice sounding all strangled and sad, I stopped because I remembered why we'd come and well . . . I can be a *naughty* dog but I'm not a bad dog. (After that escapade, for the rest of our stay in Ironbridge, people kept asking Jane: 'Is that the dog that ran away across the iron bridge?' I was quite the celebrity!)

Since that first holiday in Ironbridge, Jane and I have often returned. We have hiked up the Wrekin – a big hill made by a giant with a spadeful of soil. (It's quite a climb but there's a cafe halfway up.) We have walked along the banks of the Severn to the village of Jackfield and beyond. We have caught the bus to Shrewsbury and mooched around the charity shops. We have even met the famous Boomerang – and his owner Karen – in Boomer's favourite cafe, Deli Dale, in Coalbrookdale, which has a covered area outside for dogs. Jane and Karen swapped stories about what it's like having a dog who is a writer in the family. If only Mr Builder could see us now!

The Iron Bridge, built in 1779, is part of a World Heritage Site

PHILEAS PHACTS: Ironbridge

VICTORIA COTTAGE
Wesley Road, Ironbridge,
Shropshire, TF8 7PF
Book at www.victoria-cottage.net
Sleeps: three
Price: starts at £185 for a weekend
Charge for dogs: £15 per stay
Extras for dogs: no
Access all areas: not upstairs
Number of dogs: check when booking
Late night pee: a lane down the hill
from the cottage leads into countryside

GOLDEN BALL INN
New Bridge Road, Ironbridge,
Shropshire, TF8 7BA:
01952 432179;
www.goldenballironbridge.co.uk
Price: £120 for the dog-friendly room
Charge for dogs: £15 one-off cleaning
charge
Extras for dogs: treats behind the bar
Access all areas: one bedroom at The
Golden Ball is dog-friendly – a self-
contained flat with twin beds. Dogs are
allowed in the bar but not the dining
room
Number of dogs: check at time of
booking
Late night pee: cross the road and
you're in a park
Owner's dogs: a Staffie Cross, Diesel

HORSE AND JOCKEY
15 Jockey Bank, Ironbridge, Shropshire, TF8
7PD:
01952 433798;
www.horseandjockeyironbridge.com
Dog-friendly and just up the road from
Victoria Cottage.

THE TEA EMPORIUM
9 The Square, Ironbridge, Shropshire,
TF8 7AQ:
01952 433302

DELI-DALE
Dale End, Coalbrookdale, Ironbridge,
Shropshire, TF8 7DS:
01952 432508

Boomerang's books of walks in Shropshire,
Staffordshire and London are available at
www.bestdogwalksuk.com

CHIPPING CAMPDEN, THE COTSWOLDS

I'd heard the Cotswolds is one of the most celebrity-filled areas of England, outside London, so, keen to meet an A-list amigo, I persuaded Jane we had to visit. My nose was twitching at the prospect of sniffing a better class of bottom than is available in South-East London . . .

Jane arranged a trip with her friend Maria and Maria's Boston Terrier Joan, who

could have been a celebrity dog herself as, apparently, an A-lister wanted to buy her when she was a pup. I'm not sure I believe this, however, and think it's just one of Joan's attempts to appear superior. Well, I'm superior in barking and squirrel chasing, Joan.

We booked into a pub with rooms – The Noel Arms – in Chipping Campden, a little market town. Was the Noel Arms a haunt for celebrity Noels? Maybe I'd be in luck and meet Noel Gallagher or, at the very least, Noel Edmonds and Mr Blobby, as I do so love to bark at humans dressed in ridiculous pink suits with white splodges on

The first thing that I, observant travel newshound that I am, noticed about all the Cotswolds villages and towns was the colour of the buildings. (I may be slightly colour blind but I can see the shades I need to for the benefit of my reports. As for my olfactory observations – well, they are deserving of a Pulitzer Prize!) Anyway, most the buildings in the Cotswolds – even the bus stops – are a honey-ish hue. Lots of them are very old but even the modern houses are honey coloured. (I lifted my leg against a couple to check they were, in fact, stone and not soft honey and I can confirm this is the case. Thank Dog or we'd have been in rather a sticky situation.)

Exploring the Cotswolds

Comfy beds and countryside: pawfect!

The Noel Arms is hewn from honey stone, of course, and overlooks Chipping Campden town square. It is such an important focal point in the town that the bus stop is right outside. I believe this is so the famous Noels don't have to walk far if they decide to use public transport to ferry them around instead of helicopter.

There is a cafe – dogs welcome – inside the Noel that all the Chipping Campden locals frequent. It sells homemade Battenburg – Jane's favourite cake. There is also a bar, where dogs are allowed, and a restaurant, where dogs aren't. Maybe this is where the Noels are as I haven't spotted any yet – and I've got my pawtograph book ready.

In the Noel Arms' sister hotel across the road – Cotswold House – there is a Spar, which Jane and Maria slope off to visit, leaving Joan and I confined to the room. I spent a pleasant few hours, watching the square from our bedroom window. A word of warning for humans, though – the bathroom window overlooks the square too. So don't forget to draw the curtains when lifting your leg or any passing Noels may get a shock.

When Jane returns from the SPAR I remind her that I am ready for a walk. What is the point of being bang in the middle of some of the finest countryside in England if we're not going to utilise it? Chipping Campden is at the start (or end) of the Cotswold Way – 102 miles to Bath – and also at the start (or end) of the Heart of England Way, 100 miles long. That's a lot of miles but we only managed three as Joan, well-bred lady that she is, walks at a very sedate pace. Luckily Jane and I tried another walk the following day and that was much longer and lustier – the SHEEP were prime for chasing. But, for that reason, I was on the boring lead for much of it.

And, at the end of it, still no Noels. Jane and I nipped into the tourist office before we caught the bus home to enquire about the local celebrities – and were informed that the most famous local is Jeremy Clarkson. So not a Noel at all – what a SWIZZ!

PHILEAS PHACTS: Chipping Campden

NOEL ARMS

High Street, Chipping Campden,
Gloucestershire, GL55 6AT:
01386 840317;
www.noelarmshotel.com
Price: from £105
Charge for dogs: £15 per dog per stay
Extras for dogs: booklet of local walks
Access all areas: apart from the
restaurant – but breakfast can be
taken in the conservatory, cafe and
lounge
Number of dogs: maximum two
Late night pee: a public footpath
through fields

COTSWOLD HOUSE HOTEL AND SPA

The Square, Chipping Campden,
Gloucestershire, GL55 6AN:
01386 840330;
www.cotswoldhouse.com
Price: starting at £180 in the five dog-
friendly rooms – some with hot tubs!
Charge for dogs: £25 per dog per stay
Extras for dogs: dog beds in rooms
Access all areas: dog-friendly bedrooms
only
Number of dogs: maximum two
Late night pee: a walk down Chipping
Campden's high street

Blockley, The Cotswolds, with Boomerang the Kelpie Collie cross

I'm Boomerang and I write books of walks in my home county of Shropshire and beyond. With my doggie bag jangling with pocket money from all my sales, I decided to treat the humans to a weekend away in the Cotswolds – I'd heard there were some good walks there. I booked The Crown Inn, in a village called Blockley, as there was a special offer on. Well, I have to be careful with my earnings. The Crown Inn dates back to 1575 and our bedroom was small but satisfactory. Anyway, we didn't need a massive room as I was allowed in the bar and that's where we spent most of our time.

As well as The Crown, Blockley has another dog-friendly inn – The Great Western Arms – and I checked that out too, being a conscientious Rover Reporter. I'm happy to report that the landlady greeted me with a handful of dog biscuits.

Blockley is a good central point for walks – there's an hour-long one through the woods, and a four-mile one along the Heart of England Way.

But the best place of all in the

Winchcombe welcomes walkers – and waggers!

Cotswolds is the little town of Winchcombe. It has an annual walking festival and its logo is Winchcombe Welcomes Walkers. As I'm a walker, that must mean Winchcombe Welcomes Me. Sure enough, as soon as I set paw outside the car, a friendly local greeted me with a dog biscuit. What a welcome, Winchcombe!

The Cotswold Way passes through Winchcombe and we walked, in a circle, through beautiful countryside to Sudeley Castle and back. Unfortunately, while Winchcombe may welcome walkers, Sudeley Castle does not – not even in the grounds. Oh well – The White Hart in Winchcombe had no such pretensions. We retired there after our hike for SAUSAGES and mash and, in my case, a good long nap.

PHILEAS PHACTS: Boomer in the Cotswolds

THE CROWN INN AND HOTEL

High Street, Blockley, near Broadway, Gloucestershire, GL56 9EX: 01386 700245;
www.crownhotelblockley.co.uk
Price: £89
Charge for dogs: £10 per dog
Extras for dogs: biscuits behind the bar
Access all areas: not in the restaurant
Number of dogs: one large or two small
Late night pee: dog-friendly rooms have doors direct onto the drive.

THE GREAT WESTERN ARMS

Station Road, Blockley, Gloucestershire, GL56 9DT:
01386 700362

THE WHITE HART INN

High Street, Winchcombe, Gloucestershire, GL54 5LJ: 01242 602359;
www.whitehartwinchcombe.co.uk
Price: from £49
Charge for dogs: no
Extras for dogs: no
Access all areas: everywhere except the restaurant
Number of dogs: two
Late night pee: two-minute walk to the fields

THE PEAK DISTRICT

It's 8.30am on a Wednesday morn in the Peak District and I am feeling decidedly peaky, having been stung by a wasp walking down the street with Jane to buy a breakfast newspaper. Sneaky little blighter, in its early autumn death throes but still deciding to have a go – ah well. We are in the Peaks, I suppose, so we have to experience a few troughs as well.

The base for our Peak District sojourn is just on the edge of the Peak District National Park, in Matlock Bath. It is a very confuse-bones big village (or little town) as, with its fish and chip shops and amusement arcades, it should be by the sea. But it isn't. It is book-ended by the River Derwent, on one side, and a huge bank of mountains (perhaps they're hills but they're pretty high) on the other. Lord Byron described Matlock Bath, according to a quote on the bus stop, as just like Switzerland. (The exact quote is more poetic but I can't remember it bark-for-bark.)

Jane and I are staying in Hodgkinson's, which is a small-in-scale but grand-in-design hotel on the main street. It is a tall, narrow Georgian building and bowls and blankets are laid out for my arrival. At breakfast, even though I am not allowed in the dining room, I am not forgotten as a SAUSAGE is wrapped for me, Christmas-cracker style, in tinfoil. I'm welcome in the sitting room but there

---

A brush with a fox at Hodgkinson's

is a ruff character under one of the chairs. I bark and rage at him, telling him to get stuffed. And – grrrr-huzzah – he is!

In its day, Matlock Bath was a grand Spar town – no, Jane is correcting me – a grand spa town. Now it has a faded charm and comes ALIVE at weekends when bikers visit, and in the summer. (I hope the wily rogue under the armchair doesn't come alive at weekends and in the summer.) Every September and October illuminated boats sail along the river and this, apparently, is quite the spectacle. But, when we visit, there are no bikers or illuminations and we have the walks by the river and in the woods and up the hills all to ourselves.

The barman in the County and Station pub describes the town as: 'an old tart who hibernates during winter but puts on her make-up and stockings and scrubs herself up every summer.'

Anyway, the County and Station is our favourite pub in Matlock Bath because when we arrive and ask if it's dog-friendly, the chap frowns and says: 'only where the carpet is green.' And when we peer in, the whole carpet is green apart from one little patch of red and this is BOL funny!

Four dogs reside at the County and Station – Poppy and her three puppies (now grown-up) – and Poppy sits on a bar stool and oversees events. (On our visit, she actually fell off the bar stool, which I wasn't supposed to find amusing, but I did. I'm a dog – not a saint.) The bar lady asked if I'd like a treat and served me a whole bowl of Bakers. I scoffed that and Jane's left-over steak and ale pie.

County and Station pub dog Poppy

Indeed, I ate like a King of Canines in Matlock Bath. When we popped into Flavours Coffee Shop, just up the road from our hotel, I was given a slice of bacon. While in Flavours – or outside, on the terrace, to be exact – Jane and I performed a conversion, as if we were missionaries for dog travel, touring Britain and preaching the benefits of allowing dogs inside to establishments. Flavours is not currently dog-friendly inside – although most of Matlock Bath's pup-ulation stop at the door for a slice of cheese when out on walks. But, when Jane explained the law about dogs in cafes to the couple who run Flavours, they say they will open their doors to dogs henceforth. Howl-ellujah!

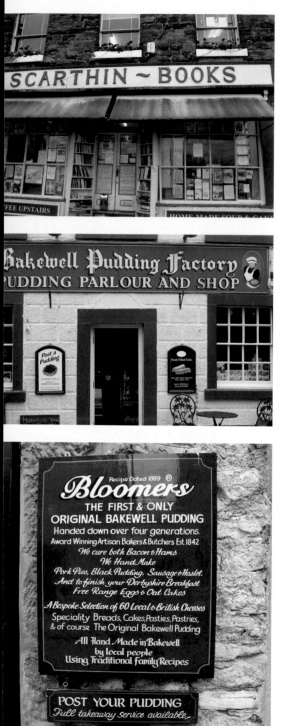

If only the cafe in Scarthin Books in Cromford, a village about half-an-hour's walk from Matlock Bath, was dog-friendly. (Something called the Industrial Revolution was born in Cromford but it must have moved because we didn't meet it!) Anyway, Jane ate a cheese scone in Scarthin Books about five years ago and the memory of the brilliance of that scone has remained with her since and been the bar against which all cheese scones are now measured – a bar that has never been met.

So, within half an hour of checking into Hodgkinson's, we were hot-footing and hot-pawing it to Scarthins, a narrow old bookshop with shelves stacked up against each other and so many ancient books that it's a smorgasbord of scents from all the bookworms who have read them over the years. But, alas, there was a sign on the door saying that, while dogs are allowed in the shop, we are not allowed in the cafe. The cheese scone dream was dashed. I took out my frustration with a jolly good bark at the ducks in the pond opposite. Out damn scone!

The next day, we visited Bakewell – half an hour on the bus from Matlock Bath – and our thoughts were not of scones but of Bakewell tarts and puddings and where, in the town, they originated. Every coffee shop

Cafe society in the Peak District

and tea room claimed their provenance! The woman in the Tourist Information wouldn't nail her colours to a particular mast and neither would the lady in the pet shop, because, she said, the cafe owners were all her customers and it would be unfair to give one the accolade of the 'Eureka – I have invented the Bakewell tart' moment.

Where did the Tart start?

I couldn't give a stuffed fox about it all but Jane wanted to be sure she was eating her Bakewell tart in the place where they were born. Finally, after much trudging, the man in Bakewell News tells us that the pudding was invented not in a cafe but in a pub – the Rutland Arms. (Obviously the cafe owners are not all customers of the man in Bakewell News!) But, he said, after it had been invented, a woman who lived in the cottage that is now The Old Original Bakewell Pudding Shop started manufacturing the puddings in vast quantities for sale so that has a claim.

Jane was happy with that explanation so we trotted off to The Old Original Bakewell Pudding Shop. But, after all this investigation, dogs weren't allowed inside. Of course – finding a dog-friendly cafe is difficult enough, never mind one with a Bakewell pudding thrown in! We had to sit in the courtyard, where, heartily sick of Bakewell puddings by now, I chomped on a bone instead.

Afterwards we had a tramp along the Monsal Trail, which can be picked up in Bakewell and follows an old railway line nearly all the way to Buxton. The Peak District countryside was stunning – VIEWS – but there were an awful lot of cyclists in my way. If only I'd stocked up on Bakewell tarts to throw at them!

CHATSWORTH HOUSE
Chatsworth, Bakewell, Derbyshire, DE45 1PP
www.chatsworth.org
The grounds of Chatsworth House – Pemberley in the 2005 film adaptation of Pride and Prejudice – are dog-friendly, making them a perfect day out for Border Terriers Jodie and Jenna.

Phileas Phacts: The Peak District

HODGKINSON'S HOTEL

150 South Parade, Matlock Bath, Derbyshire, DE4 3NR: 01629 582170; **www.hodgkinsons-hotel.co.uk**
Price: starting at £93
Charge for dogs: £10 per stay
Extras for dogs: dog bowls and beds in the rooms and sausages for breakfast
Access all areas: apart from the restaurant
Number of dogs: check when booking.
Late night pee: cross a little footbridge to Lovers' Walk, a pretty path along the River Derwent

COUNTY AND STATION

258-260 Dale Road, Matlock Bath, Derbyshire, DE4 3NT: 01629 580802

FLAVOURS COFFEE SHOP

190 South Parade, Matlock Bath, Derbyshire, DE4 3NR: 01629 580845

SCARTHIN BOOKS,

The Promenade, Scarthin, Cromford, Derbyshire, DE4 3QF: 01629 823272; **www.scarthinbooks.com**

THE BOAT INN

Scarthin, Cromford, Derbyshire, DE4 3QF: 01629 258083; **www.the-boat-inn.co.uk**

THE GREYHOUND

Market Place, Cromford, Derbyshire, DE4 3QE: 01629 822551;
www.greyhoundhotelcromford.co.uk
Price: double rooms from £85
Charge for dogs: no
Extras for dogs: no
Access all areas: everywhere except the restaurant
Number of dogs: two big or three small
Late night pee: step out on to Cromford square
Owner's dogs: Radley, the Yorkshire Terrier

RUTLAND ARMS HOTEL

The Square, Bakewell, Derbyshire, DE45 1BT: 01629 812812;
www.rutlandarmsbakewell.co.uk
Price: from £70
Charge for dogs: £10 per stay
Extras for dogs: no
Access all areas: dogs are allowed in the bar and the lounge
Number of dogs: two per room
Late night pee: up the hill and you're in the countryside

THE OLD ORIGINAL BAKEWELL PUDDING SHOP

The Square, Bakewell, Derbyshire, DE45 1BT: 01629 812193;
www.bakewellpuddingshop.co.uk

THE RED LION

The Square, Bakewell, Derbyshire, DE45 1BT: 01629 812054;
www.red-lion-bakewell.co.uk
Lovely traditional pub – it's just a shame that, while dogs are allowed in the bar, they're not allowed to stay over.

Canal Boating in Shropshire with Willow the Coton de Tulear

Greetings landlubbers – it's Rover Reporter Willow the Coton de Tulear here to tell you about my holiday on a narrow boat on the Llangollen Canal. I wasn't even five months old and didn't know what a boat was when Hannah, her family and I first went onboard the Queen Victoria – I'm sure we were given a regal boat due to my connections as the royal dog of Madagascar. I thought it was just another house, albeit a strange, long and narrow one.

It had a kitchen and a shower room and a comfy seat that I picked out straight away. *Just like a house. . .* It had three bedrooms. *Just like a house. . .*

But, suddenly, it roared and started rocking. Not like a house at all. . .

I didn't panic, even though – pull my tail – our holiday home was floating down the canal. So a boat is a house that moves on water? Now I understood.

Well, this was just super-doggy-duper! I stood with my paws on the sides of the boat as we passed fields and trees – it was like a walk in fast-forward, with new smells and places to see flashing in front of my nose and eyes every second with constant, changing information about our surroundings.

I saw – and smelt – lots of bigger, dirtier versions of me in a field. Apparently these are sheep!

People walking on the towpath smiled and waved. I must have looked so cute – a fluffy ship's figurehead. Sometimes passing dogs tried to keep level with me by running along the towpath, barking. But they were no match for Willow the Water-Pup as I was chauffeured past on my very own Royal Barge!

I liked this boating lark – until Hannah tried to make me wear a life jacket. It was an ugly object – luminous orange and bulky – and there was no way on Dog's green earth I would wear such an item. As if I needed one – hundreds of years ago my Coton ancestors jumped from pirate ships and swam ashore to Madagascar. So swimming is in my genes.

Fashion crisis averted, I concentrated on the important business of relaxing – gliding along and mooring up for a stroll along the tow path. Every time I stepped ashore a whole new world awaited me.

The first night we moored the boat near a village called Chirk Bank, which smelt of that forbidden treat – chocolate. Apparently there's a Cadbury's factory nearby. We ate in a dog-friendly pub called the Bridge Inn, a short walk from the canal. I was only allowed in the tiled bar area and there wasn't much room but

Hannah says the food was good and I met a friendly Jack Russell.

It was fun staying on the canal overnight although pitch black on the towpath – no problem for my keen eyesight but tell your humans to carry a torch. (Just to warn any scaredy-dogs out there, the boat occasionally bangs against the side of the canal in the night and wakes you up.)

Chirk Bank is in England but, the next day, we crossed an aqueduck and were in WALES! (We crossed another aqueduck on our trip too – at Pontcysyllte. We were suspended 70 foot in the air, on a boat but, really, up in the sky like that, we should have been on a plane!)

Anyway, WALES – a whole new country to explore. We visited Llangollen, a tourist town with shops and restaurants and boats pulled by horses on the canal. Poor horses – they don't sail in style, like us dogs.

The Chain Bridge Hotel in Llangollen is dog-friendly and I heard good barks about it from local dogs. We ate at the Telford Inn at Trevor. I didn't figure out who Trevor is but he certainly knows how to make a waggy, welcoming pub: I was given lots of fuss and lay in front of the fire while my humans tucked into some lovely food. (I'm guessing it was lovely as there were no scraps left for me.)

Back in England, we went to another town called Ellesmere but I'm sad to report that it was NOT a dog-friendly town and there was nowhere for the humans to eat that would let me in. Do they not do CUTE? We had to take a Chinese takeaway back to the boat.

Eventually we had to turn around – we couldn't keep tootling along the canal forever – and, on our last night, we ate at the Jack Mytton in Oswestry, not far from our boatyard. Inside, there were lots of interesting things on the walls and the landlord gave me a dog treat. I was sorry the pub dog wasn't there – apparently he looks like me but is ten times my size.

Oh well – next time. And there will be a next time because I have taken to the nautical life like a duck to water.

PHILEAS PHACTS: Narrow Boating in Shropshire and Wales

MAESTERMYN AND WELSH LADY CRUISERS

Ellesmere Road, Whittington, Shropshire, SY11 4NU:
01691 662424;
www.maestermyn.co.uk
Price: short breaks from £459 for four people
Charge for dogs: £35 per dog per trip
Extras for dogs: no
Access all areas: yes, apart from the furniture
Late night pee: the banks of the canal

THE CHAIN BRIDGE HOTEL

Llangollen, Denbighshire, LL20 8BS:
01978 860215;
www.chainbridgehotel.com
Price: from £79.95
Charge for dogs: £10 per dog
Extras for dogs: no
Access all areas: four ground floor rooms are dog-friendly and the bar and lounge.
Late night pee: canal towpath

THE JACK MYTTON INN

Hindford, Whittington, Oswestry, Shropshire, SY11 4NL:
01691 679861;
www.jack-mytton.co.uk

BRIDGE INN

Chirk Bank, Shropshire, LL14 5BU:
01691 773213

THE TELFORD INN

Station Road, Trevor, LL20 7TT:
01978 820469

LUDLOW, SHROPSHIRE

Ludlow is one of the finest little towns I have stumbled across in my travels. It is very ancient with narrow streets and medieval buildings and a castle which used to govern all the land. We dogs are allowed in the castle grounds to sniff the ruins and imagine the lives of the noble hounds – our fore-dogs – who once roamed these parts. The only time we're not allowed in the grounds is during Ludlow Food Festival, every September. This is very annoying as that is the time I would most like to be allowed in. I have visited during Food Festival week

Attlee at Deli-Dale cafe in Coalbrookdale

and stood at the castle gates, peering in at all the stalls selling SAUSAGES and doing my best Oliver Twist impression. Alas – to no avail.

Ludlow is a fiercely independent little town – fierce and independent being qualities it shares with ME. and does not appreciate chains of shops and restaurants opening on its cobbled streets. So there are lots of independent shops and tea rooms – many with wooden tree trunks on the front of their white painted walls to signify how HISTORIC they are. These buildings are called Listed and Ludlow has over 500 of them. Even the bank has a tree trunk on the front. It is a BRANCH.

The Feathers Hotel in Ludlow, is bedecked with branches. It is very OLDE. It's supposed to be haunted but there was no indication of any ghostly presence during my stay. There was, however, a frightful creaking sound at about 9pm

The bath is in the bedroom!

one evening. This frightful creak, it transpired, was the sound of the lift juddering to a halt halfway between two floors with some unfortunate chap inside. This caused quite the commotion. The vertiginous victim was finally liberated after half an hour but, from all accounts, required a stiff whisky to steady his nerves.

I have also stayed at Fishmore Hall in Ludlow. From the outside it is a smart, cream-coloured Georgian house but, inside, it is the height – and a very tall height at that – of modern. Prick up your ears dogs and listen to this – the bath was in the bedroom! Forget the ghosts at The Feathers – this was really terrifying. I don't like baths – the bathroom is the one room in my home I never venture inside – and yet, here I was, with the bath in the room with me at all times. The horror!

When Jane went for dinner in the Fishmore restaurant, leaving me alone in the room, it had an evil glint in its taps, as if threatening that, at any second, it would fill with water and I'd be plunged in.

Thank Dog the bed in the room was so big that I could hide from the bath on it. I know sleeping on beds in hotels is ILLEGAL but Jane could see how shaken up I was by the tub of terror so she allowed me. Please accept our humble apologies, Mr and Mrs Fishmore.

PHILEAS PHACTS: Ludlow

THE FEATHERS HOTEL

Bull Ring, Ludlow, Shropshire,
SY8 1AA: 01584 875261;
www.feathersatludlow.co.uk
Price: from £115
Charge for dogs: no
Extras for dogs: no
Access all areas: not in the restaurant but in the lounge, where meals can be eaten
Number of dogs: check at time of booking
Late night pee: car park out the back

FISHMORE HALL

Fishmore Road, Ludlow,
Shropshire,
SY8 3DP:
01584 875148;
www.fishmorehall.co.uk
Price: from £150
Charge for dogs: £30 per stay
Extras for dogs: bowls and mats
Access all areas: not in the restaurant but in the lounge and the bar
Number of dogs: maximum two
Late night pee: hotel gardens at the side

Resident Rover: Zip in the National Forest

I am a very lucky dog. I live bang in the National Forest, where loads and loads of trees are being planted in the Midlands to create a wonderful wooded area for dogs (and humans) – eight million new trees already and growing! Lots of the trees are still small so I run through them, pretending I'm in the weaving-through-poles event at Crufts.

My favourite sort of afternoon in the forest is spent around Dead Dane's Bottom, in Derbyshire, darting into the deep woods, chasing RABBITS and then taking a great long run up Cadborough Hill, where I flop down and wait for my family to catch up. The forest is all MINE.

Or so I believed. But, recently, my folks returned home one day, not with biscuits for me, as usual – but with a puppy!

Why – I ask you? WHY?

I was not impressed with this roly-poly bundle of red Fox Lab called Scrubs. I barely budged from my bed all weekend. Sulked.

But – ha – the incomer has to stay indoors for now so the forest is still all MINE.

My heart is softening towards Scrubs, though. He looks out of our windows at all the trees and I know that he wants to be out in them. What a shame to be able to see all that FOREST and not to be able to be in the middle of it. I'll let him share, I've decided. It's just as well the forest is big enough for both of us.

Resident Rover: Boomerang's Top Pub in the Midlands

THE WHITE HORSE

The Square, Clun, Shropshire, SY7 8JA:
01588 640305;
www.whi-clun.co.uk
This is my birthplace – the town, not the pub – and if you want to visit Clun to pay homage check into The White Horse, which wins plaudits for its locally sourced food and microbrewery.

Price: from £60
Charge for dogs: no
Extras for dogs: snacks behind the bar
Access all areas: apart from the dining room but breakfast can be eaten in the bar
Number of dogs: maximum three
Late night pee: two minutes' walk to the castle grounds
Owner's dogs: Tilly, a Jack Russell cross

HEART OF ENGLAND DIRECTORY

ALTON STATION

Alton, Staffordshire, ST10 4BU:
Book through Landmark Trust on 01628 825925
or at **www.landmarktrust.org.uk**
About two thirds of Landmark Trust buildings are
dog-friendly and this converted little station in
Staffordshire is first class. Its Italianate design makes
it Railway Children cute and, inside, all its original
features have been retained. The station master's
house has hardly changed while the ticket office has
become a bedroom; the ladies' waiting room a kitchen
and the porters' room a shower room. Dogs will love
chugging along the old railway line for their morning
constitutional.

Sleeps: up to eight
Price: from £514 for three nights
Charge for dogs: no
Extras for dogs: no
Access all areas: not on furniture
Number of dogs: two
Late night pee: the railway line

THE BOAT INN

209 Ferry Road, Jackfield, Ironbridge,
Shropshire, TF8 7LS:
01952 884483;
www.boatinnjackfield.com
Really attractive little 18th Century pub on the banks of
the river — prone to flooding so you might be arriving at
the boat by, ahem, boat.

THE COTSWOLD FARM PARK CAMPSITE

Bemborough Farm, Guiting Power,
Gloucestershire, GL54 5UG:
01451 850307;
www.cotswoldfarmpark.co.uk
However exotic a creature your dog might reckon he
is, he'll be put in his place by a stay at the campsite
on this rare breeds farm — there are Highland cattle,
Gloucester Old Spot pigs and, apparently, a type of
goat that's as rare as a panda. You're on a hill, with
the Cotswolds laid out before you — and the walks start
when donkeys Ivy and Tinsel wake you at dawn with
their braying.

Price: starting at £14 per standard pitch (tent or
tourer) for two people
Charge for dogs: no
Extras for dogs: no
Access all areas: dogs aren't allowed in to the farm
itself
Number of dogs: check when booking
Late night pee: two-miles-long wildlife walk

THE DIRTY DUCK

Waterside, Stratford-upon-Avon,
Warwickshire, CV37 6BA
The Dirty Duck, aka the Black Swan — the only pub in
the UK with two names — is a Stratford institution and

170

over the years many luminaries, and their dogs, have graced its bar stools.

FIELDWAYS

12 Chapel Lane, Cold Aston, Gloucestershire, GL54 3BJ: 01451 810659;
www.fieldways.com

At Fieldways, dogs are treated as equally important guests as their owners – even the two Burmese cats Motty and Paddington have grown used to holidaying hounds checking in. Inside, the house is as welcoming as its toffee-colour exterior suggests and proprietor Alan goes the extra mile, be that preparing Pimms on a sunny evening or mulled wine for late arrivals on a winter's night.

Price: from £90

Charge for dogs: £5 per dog

Extras for dogs: treats; bowls and towels

Access all areas: not the dining room but people can eat in the conservatory with their dogs

Number of dogs: maximum two

Late night pee: spacious fenced garden with donkeys to greet in the neighbouring field

THE GRANARY TEAROOMS,

6 South Street, Leominster, Herefordshire, HR6 8JB: 01568 614290

A find for Fido in Leominster – a dog-friendly cafe, selling homemade bone-shaped dog biscuits. Owner Norrie is an artist and often finds inspiration from among her canine clientele like the wee Westie, below left.

THE GUEST HOUSE AT MANOR COTTAGE

Bagendon, Cirencester, Gloucestershire, GL7 7DU: 01285 831417;
www.cotswoldguesthouse.co.uk

Wiggy the Deerhound will be delighted to welcome you and your dogs to the self-contained timber framed Guest House in the grounds of Manor Cottage. (Her two terrier friends Sonic and Piper aren't as young as they once were so she's always seeking new playmates.) Pop to Manor Cottage for breakfast where Sue will cook you a full English and you can chat dogs and life in front of the AGA.

Sleeps: two

Price: from £130 a night

Charge for dogs: no

FIELD HOUSE
Minchinhampton, Gloucestershire
Book through
Landmark Trust on 01628 825925 or at
www.landmarktrust.org.uk

*Former working gun dog handsome Thorn
stayed at handsome Field House, a gabled
stone farmhouse Landmark Trust property
in the Cotswolds. He enjoyed the huge
gardens and the orchard; walks at nearby
Minchinhampton Common and, most of all,
the dog treats stall at Stroud market.*

Sleeps: six
Price: from £589 for a three-night stay
Charge for dogs: no
Extras for dogs: no
Access all areas: not on furniture
Number of dogs: two
Late night pee: a massive walled 'garden'

Extras for dogs: Sue will dog sit for the day
Access all areas: yes
Number of dogs: no maximum as long as they're
sheep proof – Sue doesn't want to fall out with her
neighbours!
Late night pee: two-acre fenced garden
Owner's dogs: Wiggy, Sonic and Piper

HAWKSTONE PARK HOTEL,
Weston-under-Redcastle, Shrewsbury,
Shropshire, SY4 5UY:
01948 841700;
www.hawkstoneparkweston.co.uk
A Grade I listed landscape, your dog won't just
be walking through some of the most dramatic
countryside in England at Hawkstone Park Follies –
he'll be walking through 100 acres of history too! The
parks were laid out in the 18th Century but, later,
abandoned and neglected until, in the late 1980s,
they were rediscovered, brushed up and opened to the
public. Now trails along cliffs lead to glorious grottos
and hidden caves with all of Shropshire laid out before
you. Hawkstone Park Hotel is the closest kip – just a
mile away.

Price: doubles start at £79
Charge for dogs: £10 per dog
Extras for dogs: no
Access all areas: not in the dining area or bar but
they're allowed in the lounge
Number of dogs: two per room
Late night pee: plenty of grassy areas

THE LAKESIDE YURT

Beckford, near Tewkesbury,
Gloucestershire, GL20 7AU:
Book through Sykes Cottages on 01244 356666 or at
www.sykescottages.co.uk
This place does what it says on the tin – it's a yurt,
at the side of a lake! It's open-plan inside, with a roll
top bath, a coal effect gas fire, a big double bed and a
terraced dining area looking out over the lake. You even
have your own hot tub thrown in. Perfect for a romantic
retreat – are you really sure you want to take the dog
along?
Price: from £368
Charge for dogs: no
Extras for dogs: no
Access all areas: yes
Number of dogs: one small, well-behaved dog
Late night pee: there's an enclosed field

THE MONTPELLIER CHAPTER

Bayshill Road, Montpellier,
Cheltenham,
Gloucestershire, GL50 3AS:
01242 527788;
www.themontpellierchapterhotel.com
Dogs with a bookish bent can check into The

Montpellier Chapter during the Cheltenham Literature
Festival and be book-ended in luxury, with a comfy bed
and some literature all of their own – a list of local
walks and dog-friendly attractions stored on an iPod on
arrival. There's even a library where dogs can browse
the works of J.K. Growling and Nancy Muttford.
Price: from £125
Charge for dogs: no
Extras for dogs: designer dog beds; walks on the iPod;
leads and bowls and dog biscuits in the bar
Access all areas: everywhere but the restaurant
Number of dogs: two maximum
Late night pee: Montpellier Gardens is a three-minute
walk away

OLD HALL HOTEL

The Square, Buxton, Derbyshire, SK17 6BD:
01298 22841;

www.oldhallhotelbuxton.co.uk

Old Hall Hotel is, as the name suggests, pretty old – in fact, it's England's oldest hotel and Mary Queen of Scots slept here. (She was a dog lover – indeed, one of her dogs hid under her skirts as she was beheaded – so it's highly possible her dogs slept here too!)

Price: £89 up

Charge for dogs: no

Extras for dogs: no

Access all areas: in the lounges and the back bar but not in the restaurant or wine bar

Number of dogs: maximum three

Late night pee: the hotel is directly opposite Pavilion Gardens, 23 acres of parkland

THE OLD LOCK-UP,

North End, Wirksworth, Nr. Matlock,
Derbyshire, DE4 4FG:
01629 826272;

www.theoldlockup.co.uk

Put your canine in the clink – The Old Lock-Up in the Derbyshire town of Wirksworth began life as a police station back in the 1850s and, over the next century, many a miscreant spent a night under its roof. These days proprietor Tim will read you your rights – truffles on arrival, a Jacuzzi, evening meals with any special dietary requirements met and a fry-up in the morning. In fact the only villain these days is Moriati the cat – and even she's pretty friendly.

Price: starting at £90 for the first night and £80 thereafter

Charge for dogs: £10 per stay, however many dogs

Extras for dogs: no

Access all areas: not in the breakfast room but welcome in the bar and lounge

Number of dogs: enquire when booking

Late night pee: fields and woods within five-minutes walk

Owner's dogs: no

THE OLD POETS' CORNER

1 Butts Road, Ashover, Chesterfield,
Derbyshire, S45 0EW:
01246 590888;

www.oldpoets.co.uk

It might have a mock Tudor frontage but in fact The Old Poets' Corner has been around since the 1700's, when it was a coaching inn. And there's nothing mock about the ale – it's real all the way with The Old Poets' a CAMRA favourite. Ashover is in the middle of some beautiful countryside with many circular walks starting, and finishing, with a pint at the Poets'.

Price: starts at £75

Charge for dogs: £5 per dog

Extras for dogs: dog bowls

Access all areas: yes

Number of dogs: no limit

Late night pee: fields at the back of the pub

Owner's dogs: no, but there's always a muttley crew of locals assembled of an evening

THE PEACOCK AT ROWSLEY

Bakewell Road, Rowsley, Derbyshire, DE4 2EB:
01629 733518;

www.thepeacockatrowsley.com

The Peacock at Rowsley started life in the 17th Century as dower house to Haddon Hall – now it's displaying its fine plumage throughout its 16 bedrooms. Lots of walks start from the front door, through woods, along the River Derwent and past Chatsworth House and the Haddon Estate.

Price: starting at £160

Charge for dogs: £10 per dog

SAMUEL BARLOW,

Alvecote Marina, Robeys Lane, Alvecote, near Tamworth, Staffordshire B78 1AS: 01827 898175;

www.samuelbarlow.co.uk 🐾

And the award for Britain's dog-friendliest pub goes to . . . the Samuel Barlow, on the canal in Alvecote, a couple of miles from Tamworth. Although unprepossessing upon arrival – a red brick box with a car park in front – its beer garden, with sofas and tables and chairs looking out at the barges moored on the canal, is pretty and inside a friendly atmosphere prevails.

It scores on all the points that make a pub dog-friendly – water bowls throughout, treats behind the bar – and earns extra points in the shape of a Mutts' Menu. (It changes every day but on our visit Attlee was treated to chicken and gravy. Patrons pay what they wish and all proceeds go to the RSPCA.)

But what really clinches the prize is that the Samuel Barlow actually holds events for our canine companions with its annual charity Sunday roast for dogs – 100-plus usually attend – and organised dog walks starting from the door.

Proprietor Paul tells us that, on a Sunday morning, he opens up to find that at least a couple of members of the local pups' parade have slipped off from their morning walks to visit the Barlow. And, should a dog go missing in the Alvecote area, Paul's number is the first that owners call.

The Peacock at Rowsley

Extras for dogs: a treat during turndown!
Access all areas: not in the dining areas but in the lounge where meals can be taken
Number of dogs: ask when booking
Late night pee: gardens leading to the river

POOH HALL COTTAGES

Pooh Hall, Woodside, Clun, Shropshire, SY7 0JB:
01588 640075;
www.pooh-hallcottages.co.uk
Highly recommended by Phileas readers, this cluster of three cottages, two of which are dog-friendly, perched high in the Shropshire hills offers a relaxing rural retreat – if you really want to chill out, there's a menu of home cooked meals that can be delivered to your door.
Sleeps: two
Price: three-nights starts at £295
Charge for dogs: no
Extras for dogs: hot and cold dog shower; spare leads and bowls and throws
Access all areas: not on the furniture
Number of dogs: two per cottage
Late night pee: you're on a bridle path
Owner's dogs: Bryher, a working Italian Spinone

THE RED LION

Main Street, Long Compton, Warwickshire, CV36 5JS:
01608 684221;
www.redlion-longcompton.co.uk
It's clear who the real landlady is in this traditional Cotswolds pub – Chocolate Labrador Cocoa, who is always at the centre of things. (Her skills with the old paw up and eyes wide trick can melt even the hardest of hearts!) Dating back to 1748, the pub has recently been refurbished with a blend of traditional and contemporary design but it retains its place at the hub of the local community.
Price: from £90
Charge for dogs: no

Cocoa at The Red Lion, left and Rosa at The Severn Trow, right

Extras for dogs: pigs' ears behind the bar

Access all areas: yes

Number of dogs: maximum two

Late night pee: an acre of land

Owner's dogs: charming Cocoa

THE SEVERN TROW B&B

Church Road, Jackfield, Shropshire, TF8 7ND:
01952 883551;

www.severntrow.co.uk 🐾

Over the years, this four-bedroom B&B, built in
1671, has played home to a church, a brothel, a
soldiers' billet and a skittles alley. Now it's one of the
dog-friendliest B&B's around, with proprietor Sara
considering, rather than charging for dogs, giving
their owners a discount as they are, she says, the most
pleasant guests to have around.

Price: from £70

Charge for dogs: no

Extras for dogs: breakfast of sausage, bacon and three
homemade dog biscuits

Access all areas: yes

Number of dogs: no maximum

Late night pee: on the quiet road outside

Owner's dogs: Buster, an Airedale/Labrador cross (with
a touch of the Captain Mainwaring way about him) and
Rosa the Dalmatian

SHERWOOD FOREST CABINS

My Forest Holidays, Sherwood Pines Forest Park,
Edwinstowe, Nottinghamshire, NG21 9JH:
0845 130 8223;

www.forestholidays.co.uk

Rover Hound and his merry mutts can stay in a wooden
cabin in the middle of Sherwood Forest – a luxury
wooden cabin at that – at the My Forest Holidays
site in Nottinghamshire, part-owned by the Forestry
Commission and bang in the middle of 3,300 acres
of woodland. Take one of the trails through the forest
and then, while Rover naps, relax in the hot tub on the

Resident Rover: Tilly in the Peak District

My Mum edits www.dogfriendlypeakdistrict.co.uk (which lists the best cafes and pubs for a biscuit and destinations for days out) and I'm chief researcher. My favourite place in the Peaks is Goyt Valley, where I whizz around the woods, sniffing out squirrels and rabbits.

terrace or with an 'in-cabin' massage or spa treatment

Sleeps: four

Price: you won't need to rob the rich – prices start at £215 for three-nights

Charge for dogs: £10 per dog

Extras for dogs: treats for sale in the on-site shop; beds and bowls in the cabins

Access all areas: all of the forest is dog-friendly although leads on in the area next to the cabins

Number of dogs: three maximum

Late night pee: 3,300 acres of forest

WIRKSWORTH CHAPEL

Wirksworth, Derbyshire:

Book through Under the Thatch at 0844 5005101 or at **www.underthethatch.co.uk**

Pack your garlic if you're kipping at this little Gothic chapel in the middle of a cemetery in Wirksworth, Derbyshire – you're working the graveyard shift. Actually, eerie as it might sound, the chapel is light and airy inside with fresh white sheets and a cosy feel – nothing spine-tingling about it at all.

Sleeps: two

Price: from £164 for two nights

Charge for dogs: no

Extras for dogs: no

Access all areas: yes

Number of dogs: one

Attlee and Jane at the top of the Wrekin in Shropshire

THE **EAST OF ENGLAND**

SOUTHWOLD, SUFFOLK

My Dog but dogs love to holiday in Southwold!

'It's like Crufts in Southwold today,' the bus driver says when Jane and I board the bus at the train station in Halesworth to visit the town. He's a bit wrong there, because I wouldn't be going to Crufts, seeing as I'm a MONGREL. But when we step off the bus at Southwold High Street, I can see what he's getting at.

Big dogs; little dogs; friendly dogs and snooty dogs; friendly dogs and snooty owners – they're all in Southwold. Sniffing around, basking on the beach, browsing in the shops and eating fish and chips on the promenade – it takes me (and therefore Jane) five minutes to walk a few hundred yards because I'm so busy smelling the pavements, finding out the NEWS of who's been where and done what and lifting my leg to ticker tape some bulletins of my own.

Our kip is a self-catering cottage – bang on the High Street and very bijou and Bohemian, with driftwood floors and framed 1950's advertising posters. The tasselled lime-green cushions are an attraction to me but probably not an attraction in the way the cottage owners would like, so Jane moves them out of the way of my sharp terrier teeth.

Southwold is a quaint little seaside town with beach huts and a lighthouse and

Windmill, Norfolk Broads

Top: Southwold: a dog-friendly little town

a pier, which, unlike most piers, we dogs are actually allowed on! I am rather disturbed, however, in the arcade – the Under the Pier show, a collection of off-the-wall, homemade machines – to find a contraption that is attempting to put us dogs out of business. The Rent-a-Dog machine is a mechanical dog that humans can take for a walk along a treadmill – it even has a red lead like me. Where does this Rent-a-Dog get off?

Attlee's nemesis: Rent-a-Dog, left; Mrs T's chippie, right

I stare at it, hard, and it stares back at me, hard. We are involved in a stare-off.

'You've won Attlee,' Jane informs me after half an hour and we depart. Take that mechanical mutt!

Jane rewards me for telling Rent-a-Dog off with fish and chips. The best fish and chips in Southwold is supposed to be at Mrs T's, in a fisherman's hut down at the harbour. It's a good walk along the beach – about a mile. But, when we reach Mrs T's, it's shut. We could cross the water and go to the Bell Inn in Walberswick, highly recommended in the visitors' book at our cottage. But, instead, we walk back to town through the sand dunes. There are RABBITS to smell and RABBIT HOLES to stick my snout into.

'You wouldn't get this level of excitement walking on a treadmill with Rent-a-Dog,' I tell Jane as we pick up fish and chips from Mark's – a proper chippie where queues commence at 5pm and remain all evening.

There are lots of amaze-bones walks around Southwold but there is also lots of sitting on the beach to do and drinking cups of tea in the Adnams Cellar and Kitchen Cafe (where there are posh blue metal bowls for dogs) to do and drinking glasses of wine (Jane) and eating steak pie (Jane and me) in the Lord Nelson, a fine traditional boozer, to do.

For breakfast of a morn, we repair to Cafe 51. The lady who runs it is originally from Camberwell – like us. There is also a cafe that sells meringues the size of dog bowls – the Two Magpies – which is recommended to us by Sox, a cheerful and chatty terrier we encounter on the beach. (When we meet Sox, she's guarding

Sox – defender of beach huts, left; pie and a pint in the Lord Nelson, right

PHILEAS PHACTS: Southwold

THE OLD HOUSE COTTAGE
49 High Street, Southwold, Suffolk,
IP18 6DJ
Book at Best of Suffolk on
01728 553070 or at
www.bestofsuffolk.co.uk
Sleeps: two
Price: start at £244 for a short break.
Charge for dogs: no
Extras for dogs: no
Access all areas: yes
Number of dogs: two small dogs
Late night pee: you're bang on Southwold High Street

THE BELL INN
Ferry Road, Walberswick, Suffolk,
IP18 6TN:
01502 723109;
www.bellinnwalberswick.co.uk
Price: from £90
Charge for dogs: £5
Extras for dogs: biscuits behind the bar
Access all areas: dogs are allowed everywhere except the dining room but breakfast can be taken in the bar
Number of dogs: one
Late night pee: green in front of the pub.

MRS T's FISH AND CHIPS
The Harbour, Southwold, Suffolk,
IP18 6TA:
01502 724709

ADNAMS CELLAR AND KITCHEN STORE CAFE
4 Drayman's Square, Victoria Street,
Southwold,
Suffolk, IP18 6GB:
01502 725612;
www.cellarandkitchen.adnams.co.uk

MARK'S FISH AND CHIPS
32 High Street, Southwold, Suffolk,
IP18 6AE:
01502 723585

THE LORD NELSON
East Street, Southwold, Suffolk,
IP18 6EJ:
01502 722079;
www.thelordnelsonsouthwold.co.uk

CAFE 51
51 High Street, Southwold, Suffolk,
IP18 6DJ:
01502 726157

TWO MAGPIES BAKERY
88 High Street, Southwold, Suffolk,
IP18 6DP:
01502 726120;
www.twomagpiesbakery.co.uk

Areas of Southwold beach are dog-friendly all year round.

BRANCASTER, NORFOLK

I had never been to Norfolk before our trip to Brancaster and I was not in a happy frame of mind as we journeyed there, having had a fight with a fox that morning. When the vile vulpine hadn't fled my garden at the first note of my blast of barks, I saw red. Floating like a butterfly and stinging like a bee, I'd scored a couple of direct hits but, as he fled, the fox lashed out at my nose, causing a deep gash, a lot of pain, a stream of pumping blood and a visit to the vet's.

'Will Attlee be able to run on the beaches?' Jane asked the V.E.T. as she prescribed antibiotics. 'We're going to North Norfolk today.'

'Keep him on his lead,' the V.E.T. advised. 'The wound could flare up if it gets silicon from the sand in it.'

I was so depressed I thought my little stump of a tail would never wag again. I'd kept our garden clear of the orange menace and this was my repayment – not to be allowed to run free, as DOG intended, on the beach.

Still, I brightened as Tim, our official photographer for the trip, drove us through North Norfolk. The buildings – traditional stone and flint – felt far away from London and that feckless fox. Our hotel – Titchwell Manor – was on the coast road with views of the marshes leading to the BEACH and, when the sea air hit my lungs, I was rejuvenated.

I was well looked after at Titchwell, which cheered me up too. Inside our room, there was a big metal bowl, a bag of biscuits and a dog bed. The bed was a bit flowery for my taste but I'm not going to split hairs.

Ted and his sidekick Wilf are the literary lads who run Southwold's bookshop – Wells Photo. Dogs are welcome inside and there's a picture of Ted on the door reassuring passing hounds of this.

WELLS PHOTO
4–6 Queen Street,
Southwold,
Suffolk, IP18 6EQ:
01502 723906

Bed and basket at Titchwell Manor

What I liked best about Titchwell Manor was the big wooden kennel filled with comfy sofas in the walled garden. How thoughtful – the proprietors had organised a private space, just for me. But, Jane said, it wasn't a kennel for dogs – it was a summer house, for PEOPLE.

Titchwell Manor is in a titchy hamlet called Titchwell – with a post box. But Brancaster, a metropolis with a couple of pubs and a shop, is 20 minutes' walk away. We went for a drink at The Ship, which has lights made from driftwood. *Silly use for driftwood – much better to be thrown across the sand, to chase . . .*

And, the next day, I was chasing driftwood on Brancaster beach. When we arrived at all those miles and miles of sand with a shipwreck out to sea and dunes for snuffling in, Jane couldn't bear to keep me on the lead so she set me free. (Keep this under your hats, hounds. I wouldn't want her to be in trouble with the V.E.T. and she cleaned my wound straight afterwards.)

I sprinted and circled and jumped and sprinted and circled some more, enjoying the sand, instead of the grubby old pavements of South-East London, beneath my paws. Birds wheeled overhead and I chased them. Jane ran in front

The beach at Brancaster

of me and I chased her.

But, after our walk, trouble – Jane had lost my lead. It had fallen out of her coat pocket when we were running, she reckoned, and so we had to scour the beach for it, because it was made by someone called Cath Kidston and thus very special. I was pleased because we retraced our steps and walked the beach all over again. Jane wasn't pleased because we didn't have a spare lead or any rope so she'd have to carry me or bend double holding my collar until we found a pet shop.

But, as we departed Brancaster beach with Jane bending down and holding me by the collar in an ungainly fashion, a couple with two dogs asked if she was okay. She explained our troubles and the couple gave us their spare lead. A blue, Flexi extender one it was too – not any cheap rubbish. This couple and their organisational skills in packing a spare lead had saved our BACON and there's a lesson there that Jane would do well to learn.

Lucky I had the new lead too because there was so much still to do on the North Norfolk Coast. There was the Orange Tree in Thornham to visit, which had been highly recommended by a number of my Phileas Phollowing as it has its own doggie menu.

There was Holkham beach, about a 20-minute drive from Brancaster, where

Beach huts, Wells-next-the-Sea

we parked in a forest leading to the beach. We walked along the beach and, at the end, Wells-next-the-Sea appears, with its kennels on stilts – all right, beach huts – on the sand. Just behind the kennels on stilts is the Beach Cafe, which has a special VIP area for dogs, called the K9 club.

After I'd networked, Jane and I walked back to Holkham through the woods, which are part of a nature reserve and an important site for twitchers – twitchers as in humans who like bird watching, not twitchers as in dogs with twitchy noses who can smell over 1,000 SMELLS at one time.

Back in the hotel, I slept like a puppy in the FLOWERY dog bed without it offending my delicate style sensibilities, which just shows how very tired I was after a very exciting day.

PHILEAS PHACTS: North Norfolk

TITCHWELL MANOR
Titchwell, near Brancaster, Norfolk,
PE31 8BB:
01485 210221;
www.titchwellmanor.com
Price: from £95
Charge for dogs: £8 a night
Extras for dogs: Basket, bowl, biscuits,
poo bags, map and list of rules for dogs
Access all areas: everywhere except the
conservatory/restaurant
Number of dogs: two maximum
Late night pee: car park with bins

THE SHIP
Main Road, Brancaster, Norfolk,
PE31 8AP:
01485 210333;
www.shiphotelnorfolk.co.uk
Price: from £100
Charge for dogs: £10 per dog per stay
Extras for dogs: beds, towel and treats
Access all areas: in the bedrooms and
bar, where people can breakfast

Number of dogs: no restrictions
Late night pee: massive car park round
the back

THE ORANGE TREE
High Street, Thornham, Norfolk, PE36 6LY:
01485 512213;
www.theorangetreethornham.co.uk
Price: starts at £89
Charge for dogs: no
Extras for dogs: menu for mutts!
Access all areas: yes – in the bar, where
breakfast is served
Number of dogs: as many as will fit in the
bedroom!
Late night pee: big car park

BEACH CAFE
Beach Road, Wells-next-the-Sea, Norfolk,
NR23 1DR: 01328 713055;
www.holkham.co.uk

Dogs are allowed on parts of Brancaster
and Holkham beaches all year round.

Resident Rover: Basil the Boston, from Brentwood

Hi, my name is Basil Barkarama. When I'm not pre-occupied being handsome, I earn my doggie biscuits as chief reviewer and roving re-pawter for pup culture and modern dog lifestyle website www.barkarama.co.uk.

For a social chap like myself, my hometown of Brentwood has it all. One day it's glitz and glamour – the next it's cutting loose in beautiful countryside. So if your paws should carry you this way, here's my woof guide . . .

Coffee, Cocktails & Celeb Spotting

Well-behaved and compact dogs like me are allowed to join their humans for drinks and a bite to eat in the courtyard cafe of Essex's most famous nightclub, Sugar Hut. Dog Mum and I cosy up next to the oriental style aviary, listening to the birds' chirps and watching the glamorous patrons.

Boutique Shopping

Just off Brentwood's High Street is the cobble stoned Crown Street – the place for stylish boutiques, beauty salons and cafes. Most are dog-friendly but the friendliest is Fusey, owned by fellow handsome chap Joey Essex. The Fusey pack know how to make a four-legged guy feel welcome and let me sit behind the counter while my pet parent browses the rails.

Soaking Up the Scenery

Brentwood sits atop a hill surrounded by beautiful countryside. My favourite place to blow away the cobwebs and survey my kingdom is 500-acre Weald Country Park. There's loads of open space to run, as well as forests for relaxed walks. I go to Weald once a month to hang out with my fellow squishy facers at the Meet Up Group for French & English Bulldogs, Bostons and Pugs UK.

A Pint and a Pup Nap

On the edge of Weald Country Park is the Tower Arms Country Inn & Dining Rooms – a historic yet stylish pub built in 1701. It serves great British food, real ales and fine wine but best of all dogs are welcome in both the bar and the picturesque gardens. We often swing by for a hearty, post-walk meal (sausage and mash, please) or for a mighty roast dinner. Dogs are allowed to stay overnight too, in the Abbott room.

PHILEAS PHACTS: Brentwood

SUGAR HUT

Sugar Hut Village, 93-95 High Street, Brentwood, Essex, CM14 4RR:
01277 235060;
www.sugarhutbrentwood.com

FUSEY,

20 Crown Street, Brentwood, Essex, CM14 4BA:
01277 217888;
www.fuseyofficial.com

TOWER ARMS COUNTRY INN & DINING ROOMS

Weald Road, South Weald, Brentwood, Essex, CM14 5QJ:
01277 210266;
Price: starts at £70 for the Abbott, a double room
Charge for dogs: no
Extras for dogs: bed; biscuits; bowls on request
Access all areas: everywhere except the restaurant
Number of dogs: two small dogs
Late night pee: three acres of grounds
Owner's dogs: Alfie and Charlie, Bichon Frises

THAXTED, ESSEX

I'm the dandy highway dog / Stand and deliver / Some biscuits or your life!

A little Adam Ant there, bitches and gentle dogs, to celebrate the fact that, today, we are in Thaxted, Essex – supposed home of the great highwayman himself, Dick Turpin.

Thaxted is just eight miles from Stansted Airport yet a world away if you contrast the space-age airport terminal, of which my friends with passports have spoken, to the old fashioned village. There is a big building that is six centuries old called the Guildhall. It is huge and white, timber-framed and appears too hefty for the seven wooden pillars that support it at the front. *I won't be standing under that for a pee.*

And there is a traditional butchers', selling Thaxted SAUSAGES.

Thaxted's main street runs up a hill to the cathedral-sized parish church at the top and opposite is our kip for the night – The Swan Hotel, part of the Old English Inns chain. Dogs are welcome in all Old English Inns at no extra charge. High Paw!

When we sit down for dinner, next to a coal fire, the menu is all PIES – and, in the morning at breakfast, the menu is all SAUSAGES. Rover Result!

After SAUSAGE-O-CLOCK, Jane and I go on a walk, called Turpin's Trail. I'm on his trail all right, the dastardly highwayman – or else he can recruit me as his trusty highway hound and I'll assist in his dastardliness in exchange for SAUSAGES.

The walk takes us past alms houses, which Jane won't allow me to lift my leg against as they're too pretty, and a windmill called John Webb's Windmill, also too pretty to pee against apparently. Still, there are hedgerows to stick my

snout in and wide open fields to sprint in and a river so I can rummage in the reeds. I believe I smell trouble – aha, Dick Turpin. We're on to him!

Alas, no – Jane puts me on the lead as we have to cross a busy road and I lose the scent.

I'm depressed by this turn

Thaxted's main street, left;
Almshouses, Thaxted, opposite

of events but, back in Thaxted, on the main street, we find that rarest of things – a dog-friendly restaurant. Parrishes is a licensed restaurant where we dogs are welcomed of an evening. It is laid out like a French bistro with candles and linen tablecloths and this is appropriate because in France, according to Phileas Dogg's foreign correspondent Monty Spaniel, dogs arc allowed in every restaurant in the land. Why more eateries in Britain cannot adopt this *très jolie* attitude I do not know. So grrrrrr-huzzah for Thaxted for leading the way!

PHILEAS PHACTS: Thaxted

THE SWAN HOTEL
Bullring, Thaxted, Essex, CM6 2PL:
01371 830321;
www.oldenglishinns.co.uk/thaxted
Price: from £45 for a double
Charge for dogs: no
Extras for dogs: no
Access all areas: yes, in the bedrooms and bar
Number of dogs: check at time of booking.
Late night pee: step out on to the main street
Owner's dogs: no

PARRISHES RESTAURANT,
36 Town Street, Thaxted, Essex, CM6 2LA:
01371 830482;
www.parrishes.co.uk

WOODHALL SPA, LINCOLNSHIRE

It's the first morning of our trip to Woodhall Spa, a friendly village in Lincolnshire, and Jane and I have struck dog travel GOLD.

The previous evening, after we'd checked into our guesthouse, The Vale, and had chicken, leek and ham pie in the Mall public house, we'd noticed, on our perambulations, some interesting certificates in the windows of Woodhall Spa cafes and shops. On these certificates were hand-drawn pictures of a Border Terrier and, underneath, the words – The Rosie Awards.

'This unique award,' the small print read, 'is given to establishments which welcome dogs on leads at the discretion of the management. Dog owners and dog lovers are grateful for all such places and the Rosie Award is recognition of this much needed facility.'

This Rosie sounded like a kindred canine so, after breakfast, we set out to find her – first stop, Archie's Coffee House on the main street, which had a Rosie Award proudly displayed in the window.

'Do you know where we could find the person who gives out these Rosie awards?' Jane asked at the counter.

'Yes,' the lady replied. 'He's sitting right behind you.'

And so it came about that Jane and I were introduced to Edward Mayor – one half of the team behind the Rosie Awards. But Rosie herself – the inspiration – had passed away a few weeks earlier. This was sad news but, Edward, a retired art historian, assured us that her eponymous awards would live on.

'I always carry a copy of the law regarding dogs in restaurants,' Edward informed us. 'Places that don't allow dogs claim they don't allow them because of health and

194

safety legislation. But that's nonsense. The law says that dogs are allowed in any restaurant as long as they don't enter the kitchen.'

Hear hear Edward! Bark bark!

'It's demeaning for a dog to wait in the car,' Edward said. 'They're part of the family.'

Well, I'm presenting Edward with an award – the Phileas Dogg Award for Services to Caninekind. I've just invented the award but Edward seems pleased, nonetheless.

To be honest, Edward has done my work for me in Woodhall and Jane thinks we can relax. But I am nothing if not thorough. So I lead her on a research trip through Woodhall Spa's woods. Hidden

among them is a KINEMA – the Kinema in the Woods. A kinema is the same as a cinema except the films are projected back to front. Or front to back? I don't know – I'm a dog.

Next stop is the Petwood Hotel, which has a Rosie Award and was the squadron headquarters of the Dambusters in the Second World War. I want to visit simply because it has the word PET in its title. It's very posh but very PET-friendly with sumptuous grounds – a bit too highly manicured and squirrel-free for my liking, however. Squirrels don't do topiary.

We mooch along to Woodhall Spa's Cottage Museum. Dogs allowed – yes, it has a Rosie Award, thank you very much.

Next morning, it's back to Archie's, where we're reunited with the locals we met the previous day. Jane sits down with a coffee and her laptop so I can dictate my findings to her, just as a coachload of tourists arrive.

'Lots of tourists today,' someone remarks and Jane smiles, assuming she's included in that statement.

Coffee shop owner Josh shakes his head.

'You're a local now,' he says. 'You were in yesterday.'

The Vale, where Jane and I stay in Woodhall Spa, is exceptional for many reasons. First and foremost, it doesn't have a garden. Instead it has a lake – a natural lake, not a man-made one – with geese who, just like tourists, arrive at the start of summer and then fly off to warmer climes in autumn. There are ducks, too, which the bossy geese chase. It's a damn shame Jane won't let me off the lead because I'd chase those bossy geese and show them what it's like to be picked on by the bigger chap.

The second reason The Vale is exceptional is because of the proprietors – John and Margot. John is 91, ancient in dog years, and went to the same school as my noble namesake, Clement Attlee. Margot is a young'un, though – just 73. John is full of stories rivalling even mine in drama – and he refuses to give up work, even though he's a nonagenarian, as he enjoys meeting guests.

THE VALE GUEST HOUSE

50 Tor 'o' Moor Road, Woodhall Spa, Lincs, LN10 6SB:
01526 353022;
Price: from £50, single occupancy
Charge for dogs: no
Extras for dogs: sausages at breakfast
Access all areas: yes
Number of dogs: ask at time of booking
Late night pee: the lake
Owner's Dogs: John and Margot have always had dogs but feel they're too old for the responsibility so love meeting holidaying hounds

PHILEAS PHACTS: Woodhall Spa

THE MALL
High Street/Broadway, Woodhall Spa,
Lincs, LN10 6QL:
01526 352342;

ARCHIE'S
12 Station Road, Woodhall Spa, Lincs,
LN10 6QL:
01526 354775 🐾

KINEMA IN THE WOODS
Coronation Road, Woodhall Spa, Lincs,
LN10 6QD:
01526 352166;
www.thekinemainthewoods.co.uk

PETWOOD HOTEL
Stixwould Road, Woodhall Spa, Lincs,
LN10 6QG:
01526 352411;
www.petwood.co.uk
Price: £100
Charge for dogs: £20 however many
dogs
Extras for dogs: presents at Christmas!
Access all areas: not in function rooms
or restaurant
Number of dogs: check at time of
booking
Late night pee: massive grounds

Petwood Hotel, left; Kinema, right

Lincoln, with Willow the Coton de Tulear

It's me – little Willow, the Coton de Tulear from Yorkshire – on a day out in Lincoln. First stop is, of course, breakfast. We stumble upon the Wig and Mitre, a quaint pub situated at the top of the aptly named Steep Hill. The landlady's friendly and is interested in learning all about the proud history of us Coton de Tulears. She also serves up a fabulous full English.

Then it's time for the obligatory cultural walk all around the Cathedral Quarter, passing Lincoln Castle. The castle's origins can be traced back to 1068, and it's now home to the Lincoln Magna Carta. (I have no idea what this is and, as dogs aren't allowed inside the castle, I'm not able to find out.)

We wander around the grounds of the Cathedral, too – apparently one of the finest Gothic buildings in Europe – but, again, dogs aren't allowed inside. I prefer walking outdoors to being cooped up indoors anyway. I find a statue of a man called Tennyson – he must have been a fine human being because he shares his statue with his dog!

Then we visit the Arboretum PARK. Forget culture and history – this is more like it! It's full of fountains, ponds and statues, including one of a lion, which I don't reckon much to. Why couldn't they take a leaf out of Tennyson's book and have had a big dog instead of a big cat?

I thought that was doggie paradise but there's more – somewhere called West Common – a huge green field stretching as far as my nose could smell. Ever the diligent Rover Reporter, I trot boldly up to a passing Springer Spaniel to quiz him on the Common. Well, he barked, this area is known as Common Land, which means that every Lincoln resident has the right to keep livestock on it for a fee of around £30 a year.

There were quite a few horses on the Common – pretty harrogant horses too, if you ask me, grazing on the playing fields and the archaeological sites of the Common where they're not actually supposed to be. But, obviously, it's a horse's life in Lincoln – and, for a day trip, it's a dog's life too.

Willow, the Lincoln Imp in the Cathedral Quarter

PHILEAS PHACTS: Lincoln

WHITE HART HOTEL
Bailgate, Lincoln, LN1 3AR:
01522 526222;
www.whitehart-lincoln.co.uk
If Willow has inspired you to visit Lincoln, The White Hart, bang in the historic centre of the city with views of the castle and Cathedral, comes highly recommended.
Price: from £120
Charge for dogs: £10 per dog

Extras for dogs: no
Access all areas: in the rooms and in the bar
Number of dogs: check when booking
Late night pee: the ancient streets

WIG AND MITRE
30 Steep Hill, Lincoln, LN2 1LU:
01522 535190;
www.wigandmitre.com

Resident Rover: Jessie at Brackenborough Hall, near Louth, Lincolnshire

'There are lots of great walks around our Grade II listed moated manor house and plenty of space to run, sticks to chase and stones to pick up. Often new dogs come to play with me, staying in one of our three self-catering apartments, and I love having visitors. Sometimes they return and tell me about their days out to the nearby beaches. Me — I prefer to stay home and watch the tractors on the farm.'

BRACKENBOROUGH HALL FARM COACH HOUSE HOLIDAYS,
Brackenborough, Louth, Lincs, LN11 0NS:
01507 603193;
www.brackenboroughhall.com
Sleeps: three to eight
Price: £136 per apartment and up
Charge for dogs: £20 per dog per stay
Extras for dogs: spare leads; bowls; towels and throws so spoilt dogs can sit on sofas
Access all areas: not on beds
Number of dogs: four per apartment
Late night pee: loads of countryside
Owner's dogs: lovely Jessie!

NORFOLK BROADS

The Norfolk Broads and not a Broad in sight – none of my favourite broads anyway, like Skye and Plum and Fenn. This is all very boring-bones and not what I'd imagined when Jane said we were visiting the Broads for a few days.

Walks, I think, trying to cheer myself – we are in the countryside so there will be lots of WALKS. Alas, no – instead of walking, we are sailing. Sailing on a vessel

Meandering along at 6mph

called a pleasure cruiser, which is like a caravan except it travels on water instead of on road. Our cruiser is Concerto 4 – and a very appropriate name too as it makes a right racket when it starts up. It has a kitchen/lounge, two bedrooms and a bathroom, all along one corridor, and a prow out front, where passengers can sit and have a prow-wow (or, in my case, a bow-wow).

After a few hours on the water, I have my sea paws and venture out to the prow. Jane is lounging there, drinking wine, and not doing anything to keep the evil swans away. They're gliding up close and peering in as if they're pirates about to board and steal our silver. A couple of barks from me and I've seen them off!

The broads looked just like rivers to me, with reeds and marsh land on the banks leading to forest behind. But apparently broads are waterways that were formed hundreds of years ago when Norfolk was the busiest place in the world and people dug up peat from the ground for fuel. (The history books say people but I reckon that dogs probably undertook the brunt of this labour. We are much better diggers than humans – Gizmo nearly reached Australia.)

Dogs at The Dog

'If you fancy a budget trip to the Broads, without getting your paws wet, the well-named The Dog Inn in Ludham has a campsite in the field next to it. The Dog has been voted Norfolk's dog-friendliest pub several times and the barman told me: 'This pub's called The Dog so it would be a bit rotten not to let you lot in.' Quite right too, mate. Over the summer months, the pub hosts the local Morris dancing troupe and there's a regular meat raffle.'

THE DOG INN

Johnsons Street, Ludham,
Norfolk, NR29 5NY:
01692 630321
Price: £8 per pitch
Charge for dogs: no
Extras for dogs: no
Access all areas: yes
Number of dogs: no limit
Late night pee: two fields
Owner's dogs: Giblot, a free-range Jack Russell

In about the 14th Century, the pits, where there had once been peat, filled up with water – up and up – and connected to local rivers. Now the Norfolk Broads have more than 200 square kilometres of navigable waterways. That's a lot of facts I've dug up with my own fair paws!

The reason people find boat trips on the broads so relaxing is because you chug along at your own pace – maximum 6mph – finding pretty spots to moor up for the night. (In our case, selection of spots was determined more by proximity to a pub than aesthetic appeal.)

However, I didn't find it very relaxing at all – I had to be on 24/7 swan alert; Jane was forever shouting WINDMILL and there was the

"Paws on shore, thank Dog!"

constant worry that she'd decide to drive. (Under Jane's command, the boat ricocheted from one side of the broad to the other like a squirrel racing around the park to find a tree to climb to escape my attentions.) I prefer my paws safely on Terrier Firma so my favourite part of the trip was mooring at the pubs. Broads folk seem pretty companionable to canines and I'd hardly started my Bisto-kid nose-in-the-air routine (Royal Academy of Canine Drama, 2010 alumni) before well-wishers were clustering round, offering chips.

PHILEAS PHACTS: The Norfolk Broads

RICHARDSONS HOLIDAYS

The Staithe, Stalham, Norfolk, NR12 9BX:
01692 582277;
www.richardsonsgroup.net
Price: starting at £280 for a four berth boat.
Charge for dogs: £35 per dog per trip
Extras for dogs: no
Access all areas: yes
Number of dogs: two
Late night pee: grassy banks of the Broads

WAYFORD BRIDGE INN

near Stalham, Norfolk, NR12 9LL:
01692 582414;
www.norfolkbroadsinns.co.uk/ wayford-bridge-inn
Price: starting at £75 for a double
Charge for dogs: £6 per dog
Extras for dogs: sausages for breakfast.
Access all areas: dogs aren't allowed in the restaurant.
Number of dogs: three maximum
Late night pee: 30 seconds to the banks of the Broads

SUTTON STAITHE HOTEL

Sutton, Stalham, Norfolk, NR12 9QS:
01692 580244;
www.suttonstaithehotel.co.uk
Price: £59 for a double up
Charge for dogs: £5 per dog.
Extras for dogs: bowls in the bar
Access all areas: in the bar but not the restaurant
Number of dogs: check when booking
Late night pee: 100 yards from the Broads

WAYFARERS CAFE,

Ludham Bridge, Ludham, Norfolk, NR29 5NX:
01692 630322

DEDHAM VALE AND CONSTABLE COUNTRY

What is this I smell before me?

Jane has been out for dinner and now she's unwrapping something from tinfoil and waving it tantalisingly in front of my eyes. I make a grab – this is good stuff. A succulent cut of meat, the juiciest I've ever tasted. More!

I'm told that I'm feasting on chateaubriand, the finest and most tender cut of beef there is. £60 a pop, it's cost. Jane often brings home doggie bags, as she calls them – usually a square of leathery lasagne or a couple of lumps of grey scampi. *But this chateaubriand – this is the Mulberry of doggie bags!*

Jane and I are staying in a hotel called Maison Talbooth, in a converted Victorian rectory in Essex. Various celebrities have kipped here – Simon Cowell, Olly Murs and now me!

It's not just the nosh that's posh – the room is super-pizzazz. The lampshades are made of gold discs. I stick my snout in the bathroom and am temporarily blinded by the gleam coming from the marble floor. And the huge, sunken bath – no way am I going anywhere near that. On the terrace outside there's another bath – a tall, fat,

wooden one. When Jane pulls the lid off and pushes some buttons spurts of water fizz like fireworks. A hot tub, Jane calls it. It's terrifying.

As for the bed, it's big enough for 20 dogs – more if they're Chihuahua's. There are about 150 pillows and cushions – too many for even a sharp-toothed fellow like me to chomp through. I sleep on a thick brown faux fur throw and pretend it's the hide of a great bear I've killed with my own gnashers in a forest in Canada.

The next morning, after Jane has snaffled SAUSAGES for me from breakfast, we visit a pretty village called Dedham, a mile away. All the houses and shops are brightly painted and the locals use wicker baskets for their purchases instead of Morrisons carrier bags, like people in Camberwell. We have lunch in

Flatford, Dedham Vale

a pub with butter-coloured walls, called The Sun, and then walk, through somewhere called Dedham Vale, to Flatford.

The skies are big and full of SMELLS but, for a lot of the walk, I'm on the lead because there are cows and SHEEPS around. And horrible smug swans . . .

In Flatford, there's a river with a big barn on one side and, on the other, a white-painted cottage. Jane is intent on taking a photo of me in front of the cottage. She says it's the exact spot where a famous picture called The Hay Wain was painted and, if I stand still, I can be in The Hay Wain too. A very grand dog I am now, feasting on chateaubriand and appearing in the one of the world's most famous paintings. That's something to bark about back in Camberwell!

PHILEAS PHACTS: Constable Country

MAISON TALBOOTH
Stratford Road, Dedham, Colchester,
Essex, CO7 6HN:
01206 322367;
www.milsomhotels.com
Price: start at £215 for a double
Charge for dogs: no
Extras for dogs: no
Access all areas: ask for the
Shakespeare room as it has a huge
hall area where dogs can be left with a
bowl of water while guests go to dine
at Le Talbooth the hotel restaurant, five
minutes by courtesy car away
Number of dogs: two
Late night pee: the grounds are lit at
night

Charge for dogs: no
Extras for dogs: no
Access all areas: allowed in the bar and
the bedrooms
Number of dogs: maximum two small.
Late night pee: a meander around
Dedham

THE SUN INN,
High Street, Dedham, Essex, CO7 6DF:
01206 323351;
www.thesuninndedham.com
Price: £110

DUNWICH, SUFFOLK

Inspired by Evie, Phileas Dogg's camping correspondent, we are going camping. I'm glad because Evie is always barking on in the park about what great fun camping is and so are Fenn and Skye. I don't like to be the only one who hasn't done something.

We're camping at Cliff House, near Dunwich – a big site with wooden cabins and caravans and static homes. The pitches for the tents are next to the CLIFFS. There are lots of trees between our pitch and the cliffs, I try to tell myself. Well, ten trees anyway . . .

Down a steep set of wooden steps on the CLIFF side is the longest beach I have ever seen. It goes on and on and in the distance we can see Southwold but it's so far away I could never run there, even with my sturdy little legs. This beach is Dunwich and the sea here has a great secret below the waves – a hidden town. In 1286 there was a fierce storm and the town was swept into the sea – houses, churches and windmills. *Other dogs may mock me for being tentative around the sea but a story like this proves my point.*

The beach at Dunwich

Legend says that, if you listen hard on the beach, you can hear the bells of the lost churches ringing beneath the water.

I'm Rohan the Border Terrier and I favour Felixstowe!

Now there's a village called Dunwich with a pub, The Ship, with rooms. But no rooms above a pub for us – we are camping, thank you very much.

Jane has read Evie's top tips for terriers in tents and bought a stake for £3 in an outdoors shop for me to be tethered to when the people are having a pow wow around the campfire and Jerome is entertaining the group with songs he learnt with Ipswich Boy Scouts. It makes for a pleasant evening but, while I'd like to say I wouldn't have sprinted off without the stake, I can't lie – I would. There are rabbits on the heath.

I could not settle down to sleep in the tent, though. It was cold. It was

PHILEAS PHACTS: Dunwich

CLIFF HOUSE HOLIDAY PARK
Minsmere, Dunwich, Saxmundham, Suffolk, IP17 3DQ:
01728 648282;
www.cliffhouseholidays.co.uk
Price: from £18 per pitch based on two people; lodges from £234 for three nights
Charge for dogs: from £1.50 off peak a night to £2.90 peak
Extras for dogs: no
Access all areas: dogs are allowed in the on-site bar, 12 Lost Churches
Number of dogs: check at time of booking
Late night pee: pathways through the trees and heath

THE SHIP AT DUNWICH
St James Street, Dunwich, Suffolk, IP17 3DT:
01728 648219;
www.shipatdunwich.co.uk
Price: £97.50
Charge for dogs: £5.
Extras for dogs: dog biscuits and SAUSAGES at breakfast.
Access all areas: yes.
Number of dogs: ask at time of booking.
Late night pee: 200 yards to the beach.
Owner's dogs: Chocolate Sprocker Spaniel Elmo.

Dunwich beach is dog-friendly all year round.

uncomfortable, especially when the airbed I was fighting Jane for room on deflated at 1am. The sea sounded so close with its big roaring waves that I feared we'd blown down the cliff and swept away. And when the birds woke at dawn – what a racket!

'We're awake,' they squawked. *Such arrogance – announcing that they have risen to the world. We don't need to know. Just go quietly about your business, birds.*

The blimin' birds woke Jane too, who was so cold she had to go for three showers to warm up.

This is not fun. I don't know what Evie, Fenn and Skye are barking on about. I am not a happy camper. I want to stay in the Ship at Dunwich and not in a tent.

Resident Rover: Millie the National Trust Norfolk Coast office dog

For the past 11 years Millie, as well as helping with general administration duties in the National Trust Norfolk Coast office, has travelled in the NT Land Rover with the rangers, keeping check on the bluebells at Bullfer Grove (her favourite spot in spring) and visiting Blakeney Point after the breeding bird season.

LONG MELFORD, SUFFOLK

I have visited Long Melford in Suffolk a hundred times – or three at least. It has lots of old houses with wooden beams that humans make a fuss over and it reminds Jane, she says, of a bygone age when people said hello to each other in the street. Dogs still say hello to each other in the street, even if humans have lost the art, and

Lord Little Melford of Long Melford

of this I am proud. And what a street Long Melford boasts – the longest in Suffolk! There are always lots of dogs to sniff bottoms with.

The best place to stay in Long Melford, because it's right on the village green, is The Black Lion Hotel. When we're in residence, we ask for the room with the window seat, overlooking the green. I am probably not supposed to sit on this window seat to

observe the canine comings and goings in the village, but, when I'm in the room alone, I do. Little Melford, the Black Lion Labradoodle, has told me to desist but, as I've witnessed him sleeping on a sofa in the public areas of the hotel, he can keep his nose out of it.

PHILEAS PHACTS: Long Melford

THE BLACK LION HOTEL
The Green, Long Melford, Suffolk, CO10 9DN:
01787 312356;
www.blacklionhotel.net
Price: £125 room
Charge for dogs: no
Extras for dogs: no
Access all areas: everywhere except the restaurant

Number of dogs: one
Late night pee: the village green
Owner's Dogs: Melford the Labradoodle

TIFFINS TEA EMPORIUM
Drury House, Hall Street, Long Melford, Suffolk, CO10 9JT: 07854 355098;
www.tiffins-tea-emporium.co.uk 🐾

Mucky Paws Guest House for Dogs

In the course of our research Jane and I have stayed in lots of dog-friendly establishments but Mucky Paws in the village of Great Cressingham, 11 miles from Thetford, is the only one we've found actually named in honour of holidaying hounds.

(Horses can stay too, in a field behind the red-tiled and white-painted cottage, but it isn't named in their honour. If it was, it would be called Mucky Hooves.)

Inside, too, all the rooms are named especially for dogs. I am in Mutley's room, which is appropriate because Jane can be Dastardly on occasion, when I know she has treats but, however hard I stare, trying to melt her bag with my laser vision so they fall out, she refuses to hand one over.

Our room is comfortable – white walls and dark beams and a homey feel. The bathroom, boasts a massive white metal claw-footed bath, which I wouldn't go near, no matter how mucky my paws were. (And they could be quite mucky, as we are on the Peddars Way, a path through some of Norfolk's finest woodland, heath and coastland.)

Three very fortunate dogs are full-time residents at Mucky Paws – Milo, Millie and Tia. They've landed on their paws.

The breakfast room – oak beams and white stone walls – is a veritable dog library with all manner of dog-related books on the shelves. There's also a little lounge on the landing just for dogs, with a basket and a bowl of water. This hits quite the right note for the weary canine traveller.

We only have one night at Mucky Paws so we don't have time to pop into The Olde Windmill, the pub in Great Cressingham, for dinner. Apparently it's super-dog friendly, though. Also nearby is Red Wing's Horse Sanctuary, which has won lots of dog-friendly awards, although why any right-minded hound would want to visit a load of old nags is beyond me. Oh well – there's nowt so queer as Fido.

MUCKY PAWS (THE VINES),

The Street, Great Cressingham, Norfolk, IP25 6NL: 01760 756303;
www.muckypawsretreat.co.uk 🐾
Price: starts at £64 for a double
Charge for dogs: £5 for one dog; £8 for two and £10 for three
Extras for dogs: treats at reception; towels in the rooms; little sitting area on the landing; baskets and bowls; cage on request and toys
Access all areas: yes
Number of dogs: check at time of booking
Late night pee: a huge open field about three minutes' walk away
Owner's dogs: Milo, Millie and Tia

EAST OF ENGLAND DIRECTORY

BARTLES LODGE

Church Street, Elsing, Dereham, Norfolk, NR20 3EA:
01362 637177;

www.bartleslodge.co.uk

Bartles is tucked away in the sleepy little village of Elsing, deep in rural Norfolk. It offers B&B accommodation in a converted stables or pitch up in your own caravan or tent (Caravan Club members only) in the 11 acres of grounds, complete with three fishing lakes.

Price: £70

Charge for dogs: £4

Extras for dogs: no

Access all areas: not in the licensed dining room

Number of dogs: one

Late night pee: 11 acres of grounds

BLACK PRINCE CANAL BOATS

Ely, Cambridgeshire, CB7 4DY
To book telephone: 01527 575115;

www.black-prince.com

Take in the views of the cathedral city of Ely from the deck of a dog-friendly narrow boat or cruise down to Cambridge through the Fens.

Sleeps: two and up

Price: starts at £412

Charge for dogs: £30 per dog per holiday

Extras for dogs: no

Access all areas: not on the beds

Number of dogs: two maximum

Late night pee: moor up and take your pick

THE BLUE BOAR

Silver Street, Maldon, Essex, CM9 4QE:
01621 855888;

www.blueboarhotel.com

Jack Russell Pupsy is the star at the Blue Boar – a traditional coaching inn in Maldon – and even has a beer named after her in the microbrewery, Farmer's Ales, attached to the pub.

Price: £85

Charge for dogs: no

Extras for dogs: sausages at breakfast

Access all areas: yes

Number of dogs: one

Late night pee: car park out the back

Owner's dogs: Jack Russell Pupsy

BOUNCERS FARM CAMPSITE

Wickham Hall Lane, Wickham Bishops,
Essex, CM8 3JJ:
01621 894112;

www.operaintheorchard.co.uk/
about-bouncers-farm-campsite.html

Pretty, little campsite in an orchard with space for a few tents alongside the site's two permanent gypsy caravans. Be aware, though – the shower cubicle is powered by wood so hot water can be a little unpredictable at times.

Price: from £12 per tent, including one adult; £4 for each additional adult

Charge for dogs: £1

Extras for dogs: no

Access all areas: on leads at all times
Number of dogs: discuss when booking
Late night pee: you're in the middle of an orchard
Owner's dogs: yes – they're friendly but will have a nose in your dog's bowl for titbits

BRUDENELL

The Parade, Aldeburgh, Suffolk, IP15 5BU:
01728 452071;
www.brudenellhotel.co.uk

Bang on Aldeburgh's dramatic shingle beach, the Brudenell is the perfect pad for Rover to rest after a run and a whirl in the waves – it's just a shame that dogs aren't allowed anywhere in the hotel other than the bedrooms. Oh well – ask for a room with a sea view at the front of the hotel and you'll probably be happy enough to order room service and gaze out the window at that big Suffolk sea and sky

Price: from £150
Charge for dogs: £10 per dog
Extras for dogs: no
Access all areas: bedrooms only
Number of dogs: two maximum
Late night pee: the beach
Owner's dogs: none

CRAGG SISTERS TEA ROOM,

110 High Street, Aldeburgh, Suffolk, IP15 5AB:
07813 552181;
www.craggsisters.co.uk

Very dog-friendly Aldeburgh tea rooms, with an amazing collection of knitted tea cosies for sale

DARWOOD HOUSE FARM CARAVAN PARK,

Old Woodhall, Horncastle, Lincs, LN9 5SA:
01526 353228;
www.darwoodhousefarm.co.uk

Sarah and David at Darwood House Farm are real dog lovers and, along with their red Patterdale Teddy, promise a warm welcome to all caravanning canines. The 12-acre site has a shepherd's hut (sadly not dog-friendly) and walks in ancient woodland on the doorstep.

Price: £13 per caravan but you must be a Caravan Club member to stay.
Charge for dogs: no
Extras for dogs: no
Access all areas: 12 acres to explore.
Number of dogs: one lady turned up with six Cocker Spaniels
Late night pee: walk to the end of drive and you're deep in the woods
Owner's dogs: Teddy, a red Patterdale

DIVA DOGS, PET BOUTIQUE AND GROOMING PARLOUR

42 New Street, Chelmsford, CM1 1PH: 01245 496644;
www.divadogs.co.uk
Diva Dogs is where the stars of The Only Way Is Essex take their dogs to be groomed and, as well as a beauty parlour, has a shop where all manner of pup paraphernalia is available for purchase. Chihuahua Tallulah from Kent picked up a couple of pink frocks.

THE GEORGE HOTEL

High Street, Cley-next-the-Sea, Holt, Norfolk, NR25 7RN: 01263 740652;
www.thegeorgehotelatcley.co.uk
One of Norfolk's prettiest villages, built in traditional red brick and flint, Cley-next-the-Sea boasts Norfolk's most photographed windmill.
Price: start at £80
Charge for dogs: £10
Extras for dogs: treats behind the bar
Access all areas: in the bar and in the front part of restaurant
Number of dogs: two maximum
Late night pee: the pub garden

THE GEORGE HOTEL OF STAMFORD

71 St Martin's, Stamford, Lincs, PE9 2LB:
01780 750750;
www.georgehotelofstamford.com
Famous coaching inn in picturesque Stamford, recently voted Britain's finest town in *The Times*.
Price: from £160 for a double
Charge for dogs: no
Extras for dogs: welcome pack including treats and a blanket
Access all areas: everywhere except restaurant
Number of dogs: check at time of booking
Late night pee: 500 yards from Stamford's top spot for dog walkers, The Meadows
Owner's dogs: two cats Sooty and Sweep

THE HOSTE

Market Place, Burnham Market, King's Lynn,
Norfolk, PE31 8HD:
01328 738777;
www.thehoste.com
The Burnham's are some of the prettiest villages in North Norfolk and the Hoste is a 17th century coaching inn with a spa attached (humans only) in the centre of Burnham Market. Stay in one of the individually designed rooms, choosing between a tartan four-poster and a leather sleigh bed, or opt for the dog-friendly railway carriage just down

the road.

Price: £63 per person based on two sharing the railway carriage

Charge for dogs: £15 per stay

Extras for dogs: rugs to sling on beds so Rover can kip at his master's feet

Access all areas: everywhere apart from the restaurant but dogs are welcome in the bar and the conservatory

Number of dogs: maximum two

Late night pee: a stroll around Burnham

HOTEL DU VIN

15–19 Trumpington Street, Cambridge, CB2 1QA.
084473 64253;
www.hotelduvin.com/locations/cambridge

All Hotel du Vin's are dog-friendly and this one, bang in Cambridge's historic centre and housed in a former university building on the fantastically named Trumpington Street, is full of charm. As a city, though, Cambridge could work on its dog-friendliness as, when Attlee and Jane visited, finding a pub that allowed dogs inside seemed as much of a struggle as acquiring a degree in Astrophysics.

Price: from £169, not including breakfast

Charge for dogs: £10 per dog

Extras for dogs: bowls and beds

Access all areas: everywhere except the main restaurant

Number of dogs: maximum two

Late night pee: Trumpington Street!

MARTELLO TOWER

Aldeburgh, Suffolk, IP15 5NA.
Book through Landmark Trust on 01628 825925 or at
www.landmarktrust.org.uk

Your dog would defend you against attack and Martello towers were built to defend our nation against attack (from Napoleon) so there's a very tenuous connection here. The tower is a stub, stocky little affair where you, and your dog, can relax feeling safe as houses.

Sleeps: four

Price: from £678 for three-nights

Charge for dogs: no

Extras for dogs: no

Access all areas: not on furniture

Number of dogs: two

Late night pee: on the beach outside front door

THE OLD STABLES COFFEE SHOP

Market Place, Horncastle, Lincs, LN9 5H:
01507 523253;
www.theoldstables-horncastle.com
Highly recommended by Edward Mayor and recipient of a
Rosie Award – the owner has three Pugs.

THE OLDE WINDMILL INN

Water End, Great Cressingham, Watton, Norfolk,
IP25 6NN:
01760 756232;
www.oldwindmillinn.co.uk
The Olde Windmill has eight en-suite bedrooms as well
as a camping and caravan site with five pitches in the
paddocks behind the building
Price: starting at £80 in the Inn; £10.50 per
campervan; no charge for tents
Charge for dogs: £5 per dog in the bedrooms; no
charge in campsite
Extras for dogs: no
Access all areas: in the bar and in the conservatory
but not in the restaurants
Number of dogs: maximum two
Late night pee: in the paddocks

SARA'S TEA ROOM

64 High Street, Leigh-on-Sea, Essex, SS9 2EP:
01702 477315
Ask any dog owner in the South-East or East Anglia about
their favourite dog-friendly places and Sara's Tea Garden
will probably be mentioned. It's a little gem in the pretty,
old part of Leigh-on-Sea and super-cute, with a picket
fenced garden out front. A photograph of owner, Sara's
Golden Lab Flossie sits atop the counter. Flossie died a
couple of years ago but she'll be wagging her tail in the
sky to know her memory lives on in such a warm and
welcoming place.

THE SWAN HOTEL

Lavenham, Suffolk, CO10 9QA:
01787 247477;
www.theswanatlavenham.co.uk
The Swan, with its white and timber framed frontage, has
to be the prettiest hotel in Suffolk – and it's in one of the
county's prettiest towns. Dating from the 15th Century,
inside it's a maze of nooks and crannies and your dog's
nose may prove useful in sniffing out your bedroom at
night as, up wooden stairs and along crooked corridors, it's
easy to become lost after a wine or two with dinner.
Price: from £195
Charge for dogs: £10 per dog
Extras for dogs: no
Access all areas: everywhere apart from the Gallery
Restaurant and Brasserie
Number of dogs: two maximum
Late night pee: courtyard gardens
Owner's dogs: no

TOWER WINDMILL

Tower Road, Burnham Overy Staithe,
King's Lynn, Norfolk, PE31 8JB:
For a brochure or to book telephone: 01263 740241;
www.nationaltrust.org.uk
Rent your very own windmill for the weekend – Tower
Windmill, between Brancaster and Wells-next-the-Sea, is
the property of the National Trust and available to hire for
groups of up to 20. The mill, which stands proud and alone

Room service for Rover at The William Cecil

looking out over the North Norfolk coastline, is six-storeys high with an attached cottage and outhouse.

Price: from £430 for a weekend

Charge for dogs: no

Extras for dogs: no

Access all areas: yes

Number of dogs: two

Late night pee: the windmill is in own enclosed grounds

WEYBOURNE FOREST LODGES

Sandy Hill Lane, Weybourne,

Norfolk, NR25 7HW:

01263 588440;

www.weybourneforestlodges.co.uk

What better hang-out for a hound than bang in the middle of a 100-acre forest glade? The wooden self-catering lodges are all individually designed – we favour the three-bedroom Toblerone-shaped Squirrel Lodges – which look like they should be nestled on the side of a Swiss mountain. The site runs a breeding programme for red squirrels, though, so keep your dogs on leads.

Sleeps: two to six

Price: from £190 for a short break in a two-person lodge

Charge for dogs: £25 a week per dog

Extras for dogs: no

Access all areas: not in bedrooms

Number of dogs: two

Late night pee: the forest

THE WILLIAM CECIL

St Martins, Stamford, Lincs, PE9 2LJ:

01780 750 070;

www.thewilliamcecil.co.uk

Rover can order room service at the William Cecil – £4.50 for a bowl of Bakers or £14 for Sirloin steak. It's a classy kip for canines – and humans too – set in the middle of prime dog-walking country.

Price: doubles from £100

Charge for dogs: £20 per dog per room

Extras for dogs: lots – dog sitting on request; mutts' menu; room service for Rover and beds and bowls

Access all areas: everywhere except the restaurant

Number of dogs: two

Late night pee: the hotel's on the edge of the Burghley estate – acres of grounds

Owner's dogs: no

A PUPS' PUB (AND PARK) CRAWL AROUND LONDON

Hurrah – I am the Resident Rover as we're in my home hood of London and, to celebrate, my pack and I are presenting a grand pub and park crawl of the capital. We'll see you around London as easily as the little Scottie on the Monopoly board with Lady Luck rolling the dice!

Since I'm safely on home turf and among friends, I have an admission to make. On occasion, Jane dresses me up. Jane's friend Annie makes outfits for dogs and often requires a model. As I am a patient, helpful sort of chap, I'm the only member of my park's muttley crew willing to fulfil this role. I am, quite literally, the tailor's dummy.

One of my favourite ways to spend an afternoon in London is to walk by the canals. Normally I stroll along happily, barking at ducks. During the Angel Canal Festival, however, my walks by the canal become rather murky. This is because, to add to the carnival atmosphere of the Angel Canal Festival, Jane makes me wear an OUTFIT!

Oh how everybody clapped and cheered when the Pearly Dog met the Pearly King and Queen. Oh how a little bit of me scrunched up and died inside. Thank Dog for the dog-friendly Narrow Boat pub, where I repaired afterwards for a swift bowl of water to forget the shame of it all.

I'm much safer at home in South-East London's trendy and bohemian Camberwell. (That's how estate agents describe it anyway.) Jane doesn't make me

Costume drama for Attlee, Angel Canal Festival, September 2012

dress up around my hood. Even she can see that would be going too far.

I know the watering holes of South-East London like the back of my paw, being the booze hound that I am. My favourite Camberwell pub is the Hermit's Cave – I went there on my first evening with Jane, having graduated from Battersea School for Dogs that very morning. It's no-nonsense; no food except crisps and nuts (paw out for some of those) and no music so I don't have to listen to the barmaid's awful mix tapes. It is just a traditional boozer with coal fires in winter, seats on the street for smokers and real ales. A hermit would hate it, though – it's very friendly.

Then there's The Bishop in East Dulwich. It has a pub dog – a Weimaraner – but as far as I can tell he sleeps all the time. If I was a pub dog I'd be awake, on the snout for scraps.

Greenwich is just two buses away from us and Greenwich Park has the most squirrels of any park I know. It's interesting for people too, because the Royal Observatory is there and that's where time is made. But dogs have no concept of time so I have no concept of what the Royal Observatory is. SQUIRRELS!

Brockwell Park, in Herne Hill, is just one bus journey away. It is on a hill and at the top there's a mansion. The dogs of Brockwell Park tend to be of a superior class so Jane doesn't worry about me falling in with the wrong crowd there. After the park, we pop into Herne Hill Books, where I am welcomed as a dog of letters, and then have a coffee in The Commercial Hotel. (Commercial Break – The Commercial Hotel is very dog-friendly!)

When I do cross the river to go north, it's usually to have a run on Hampstead Heath. Afterwards, we head to The Bull and Last, where there are

Making a pig's ear of it . . .

pigs' ears behind the bar for the Hounds of Hampstead Heath. I am an Honorary Hound of Hampstead Heath so I am allowed a pig's ear too.

The one place we will never, ever venture again is Epping Forest. We went there once. I was so excited by the smells and the denseness of the trees and the promise of rabbits that I dashed off to explore. Deeper and deeper into the trees I dashed; fainter and fainter Jane's shouts of 'Attlee' became. The adventure only seemed to last a few minutes but, when I followed my nose and returned to the spot where I'd left Jane, she was crying and crumpled, crouched on a tree. Apparently my adventure had lasted a whole hour and Jane thought that I'd fallen down a big hole in the ground and been swallowed up. I have had my Epping Forest passport revoked.

PHILEAS PHACTS: Attlee's London

THE ANGEL CANAL FESTIVAL
www.angelcanalfestival.org

THE NARROW BOAT
119 St Peters Street, Islington, London, N1 8PZ: 0207 400 6003; www.thenarrowboatpub.com

THE HERMIT'S CAVE
28 Camberwell Church Street, London, SE5 8QU

THE BISHOP
25-27 Lordship Lane, East Dulwich, SE22 8EW: 0208 693 3994; www.thebishopeastdulwich.com

HERNE HILL BOOKS
289 Railton Road, London, SE24 0LY: 0207 998 1673; www.hernehillbooks.com

THE COMMERCIAL HOTEL
212 Railton Road, London, SE24 0JT: 0207 733 8783; www.thecommercialhotelhernehill.co.uk

BULL AND LAST
168 Highgate Road, London, NW5 1QS: 0207 267 3641; www.thebullandlast.co.uk

Attlee at the Hermit's Cave

LONDON: PICKED BY THE PACK

I'm Roxy and my favourite pub in the city, by a country mile, is The Albion in Bethnal Green – it's the first pub I ever set paw in and I have stayed loyal since. Everyone there is so friendly – even Yogi, the pub dog, who is HUGE. It's a good place to warm up after a snowy winter walk in Victoria Park.

Roxy, above, Yogi, above right, and Molly, right

THE ALBION
94 Goldsmiths Row, London, E2 8QY:
0207 739 0185

THE CASTLE
15 Grosvenor Rise East, London,
E17 9LB:
0208 509 8095
I'm East End girl Molly the Shih-Tzu and I live in Walthamstow. My local is The Castle in Walthamstow village, where I am always presented with a bowl of water. I'm not one for long walks but I do enjoy a stroll along the disused rail tracks, close to Finsbury Park. It's just over two miles along the embankments and through the shaded cuttings where trains used to run to Highgate.

THE CADOGAN ARMS

298 King's Road, London, SW3 5UG:
0207 352 6500;
www.thecadoganarmschelsea.com
I'm STOMPY and my favourite
STOMPING ground is the King's Road,
where I can show off my designer good
looks. (I don't take the tennis ball with
me when I'm up west.)

Stompy

HOLLY AND LIL,

103 Bermondsey Street, London, SE1 3XB:
0203 287 3024;
www.hollyandlil.co.uk
I'm Holly and, even though this photograph (below) is of me on Primrose Hill, my main hang
out is London's most dog-friendly drag — Bermondsey Street. Dogs are welcome in every
shop, pub, restaurant and hotel — including MY shop, Holly and Lil. It sells the finest canine
couture in town, even if I do say so myself. Well, I am the muse for the collection!

BERMONDSEY SQUARE HOTEL

Bermondsey Square, Tower Bridge Road, London,
SE1 3UN: 0844 815 9834;
www.bespokehotels.com/bermondseysquare
Price: starts at £99
Charge for dogs: £20 per stay per dog
Extras for dogs: boutique bed in the room
Access all areas: in the bar but not the restaurant
Number of dogs: two maximum
Late night pee: a park opposite

SOHO HOUSE

40 Greek Street, London, W1D 4EB:
0207 734 5188;
www.sohohouselondon.com
I'm Clover the Beagle from the Bronx
and I lived in London for six months
while my Daddy was working in the
city — at the circus, no less! I saw all
the sights and had dinner at Soho
House, a posh Private Member's
Club. Even though dogs aren't really
allowed, an exception was made for
me! Lesser dogs might have been
fazed but I took it in my stride — as a
New Yawker, I've seen it all before!

THE CLOCKHOUSE

196a Peckham Rye, London, SE22 9QA:
0208 693 2901;
www.clockhousepub.com

I'm Mitzy and my party trick is holding three
tennis balls in my mouth at once — often
performed at Peckham Rye Park and Common.
Afterwards, I pop into The Clockhouse, just across
from the Common, where there's a bar especially
for us dogs, with treats on the table and water
bowls underneath.

Attlee says: 'In October, Jane entered me in the All Dogs Matter Halloween Dog Walk on Hampstead Heath, starting at the Spaniards Inn. DRESSING UP AGAIN – Grrrrr-NOT-Huzzah! It was very embarrassing as every other dog in the competition was dressed as something frightening – and I was dressed as a beefeater.'

THE SOCIETY CLUB

12 Ingestre Place, London, W1F 0JF:
0207 437 1433; **www.thesocietyclub.com**
I'm Modesty – or am I Immodesty? Anyway,
I'm a society dog at Soho's Society Club – MY
cafe selling cakes and cocktails and books
and photographs and all manner of wonderful
wares. I work hard in the shop all day and then
have a stroll around Soho Square to hear the
tails of the city.

THE SPANIARDS INN

Spaniards Road, Hampstead, London, NW3 7JJ: 0208 731 8406;
www.thespaniardshampstead.co.uk

ALL DOGS MATTER

30 Aylmer Parade, London, N2 0PH: 0208 341 3196;
www.alldogsmatter.co.uk

223

KINGSTON UPON THAMES, SURREY

London isn't every dog's bowl of biscuits. I spent my formative months as a stray, surviving on the mean city streets, and now I live in Sarf London where I'm well known in the hood. So I can cope. But I understand how the crush of human- and canine-kind can be overwhelming for our country cousins.

Still, you can experience London by day, without actually staying in the centre of it at night, by making your kip the Chase Lodge Hotel in Kingston upon Thames,

Hampton Court, a stroll from Kingston Upon Thames

half an hour from Waterloo on the train and home of an 'art installation' of red telephone boxes toppling on each other like dominoes – great to lift your leg against!

I checked out the Chase Lodge and can report that it is a comfy bolt hole from the metropolis, just the right side of chintzy. The staff are friendly and the road it's on is quiet so you can sleep without being interrupted by the sirens and cat calls of the central London streets. My only complaint would be the breakfasts – no SAUSAGES. Apparently the breakfast at the Chase Lodge is something called continental. Well, the poor dogs on the continent have my sympathy as there's no fry in their fruhstuck – just toast, croissant, yoghurts and fruit. I threw my slice of toast across the room in disgust!

We headed for a walk afterwards so I could clear my head of this outrage – Kingston is a half-hour's stroll from Hampton Court, where dogs are allowed in most of the grounds, but, sadly, not the maze. I'd have loved to get in there and follow my nose to work out the exit route – I'm sure I'd have done it in record time.

Phone box dominoes – perfect for dogs to pee against!

PHILEAS PHACTS: Kingston upon Thames

CHASE LODGE HOTEL
10 Park Road, Hampton Wick,
Kingston Upon Thames, Surrey, KT1 4AS:
0208 943 1862;
www.chaselodgehotel.com
Price: starts at £85 for a small double.

Access all areas: not in the breakfast room
Extras for dogs: no
Charge for dogs: no
Number of dogs: maximum two
Late night pee: the quiet street

THE BELL, TICEHURST, SUSSEX

In the course of my researches for this book, I have stumbled across many establishments that provide extras for dogs – thoughtful little touches that make our stay that bit more comfortable. But The Bell, in Ticehurst, Sussex, excels itself for, dear Rover, it provides a tree in every bedroom. A Silver Birch tree, indeed!

When we walked into our room and I was faced with this marvel, my immediate reaction was to lift my leg. Jane is always provided with an en-suite and here was I, provided with an en-tree.

Tower of books

 226

Ajax at The Bell

But: 'No Attlee,' Jane said. 'The tree is for decoration. Not weeing against.'

What's the point of that? I was baffled. But the en-suite tree, is, it seems, just a quirky design touch and of no function whatsoever. It's one of many quirks at The Bell – top hats as lampshades; televisions disguised as gilt-framed mirrors; a yurt in the back garden There's a tower of books reaching from floor to ceiling in the restaurant – again, major leg-lift potential. Again – leg-lift forbidden. Very frustrating – thank Dog there was a lamp post outside or I'd have been in trouble! (It must have been ruddy torture for regular Ajax. Little wonder he placed himself next to the massive hearth in the bar and didn't budge all evening.)

Ah well, the friendly staff, access all areas welcome to dogs and hearty breakfast did make up for the fact my bladder was in a constant state of tension.

PHILEAS PHACTS: The Bell, Ticehurst, Sussex

THE BELL INN
High Street, Ticehurst, Sussex, TN5 7AS:
01580 200234;
www.thebellinticehurst.com
Price: £90 and up

Charge for dogs: no
Extras for dogs: SAUSAGES at breakfast
Access all areas: yes
Number of dogs: ask when booking
Late night pee: country lanes

Resident Rover: Ted's Guide to Kent

I'm Ted – hound on the ground in Kent. My favourite things are surfing, chasing squirrels and being a celebrity. I've been on television, in the newspapers and am often recognised when I'm out and about in Dover, where I live, and asked for my paw-tograph. Fun!

Dover Castle allows dogs to roam the grounds – they even hand out poo bags at the entrance. But we're not allowed inside, which is a pity because I'd like to sniff out one of the six ghosts who haunt the building.

Connaught Park in Dover is a great place for dogs all year round. Winter is best as I love romping around in the snow!

My favourite hostelry in Dover is the Cricketers in River, opposite Dover Athletic football ground. It's access all area for dogs and in the summer there are barbecues in the garden, where I practise the old 'tilt of the head and lift of the paw' routine.

If my human Karol and I are feeling energetic, we walk all the way to St Margaret's Bay and The Coastguard pub and restaurant – it's friendly to dogs and serves delicious home-cooked meals for humans. And it's right next to the Channel, if you fancy dipping an adventurous paw in the water. Oooh la la!

Cultured canines, such as myself, should visit Margate. Sadly we're not allowed

---

Ted finds some art at his level in Margate

'I'm on Broadstairs beach: beam me up Scotty!'

Free Comic Book Day: not for the faint-hearted Fido

in Turner Contemporary but we can sit in the cafe outside and the part of the beach behind the Turner is dog-friendly all year round. Some of the smaller galleries let dogs in, including my favourite, the Pie Factory. And I dipped my creative paw into the art world by taking part in a Star Trek installation at the Substation Project Space with my humans!

If you want some cuisine with your culture, I recommend the Great British Pizza Company on Marine Drive – a Great Dane called Henry is maitre d'og and will usher you to your table and present you with FREE bones and biscuits.

Barking about ART, I must mention Folkestone, where there is an art installation just for us dogs. It's called Barking Rocks and is all tree trunks for us to snuffle and snout in so we can exercise our minds and our paws at the same time!

Next up in my tail-wagging tour of Kent is Broadstairs. The beach is barking brilliant – it's just a shame it's not dog-friendly all year round. So I go at the start of October when there's also a Food Fair on the promenade – SAUSAGES!

Whitstable beach is dog friendly all year round – it's where I learnt to surf. The Old Neptune is on the sand and, in the summer, there are barbecues – perfect for a handsome fellow like me to pick up some SAUSAGES. And the off-licence in

Ted and Bagpuss

Whitstable has a big jar of dog biscuits on the counter for us booze hounds!

Kent's capital, Canterbury, is full of strange and scary things for dogs – witness this giant pink cat I spotted on a billboard outside Canterbury Museum!

Whatever Comics in Canterbury welcomes canine customers with biscuits so, in return, I give out free comics on Free Comic Book Day. There are some rather unpleasant characters around but I try to be bold.

For Kentish countryside, I favour Molash, eight miles from Canterbury. It's a small village with 90 houses, a church and a pub, the George Inn. The church is so old that there are yew trees in the grounds that have split into two. I sit in between the split bit and pretend I'm a SQUIRREL, perching in a tree!

I love the walks through King's Wood, next to Molash – it's great for chasing squirrels as there are so many trees for them to scurry around in. I point my head towards the sky, waiting for one to fall out. There's an art project in King's Wood called SuperKingdom – lots of different homes for animals have been built among the trees. I thought about checking into one of these little homes and staying in the woods forevah but we're going home via the George Inn and SAUSAGES and I don't want to miss out. Perfick, as they say in Kent.

PHILEAS PHACTS: Kent

THE CRICKETERS
Crabble Lane, River, Dover, Kent,
CT17 0JB: 01304 206396;
www.cricketersdover.com

THE COASTGUARD
The Bay, St Margaret's Bay, Dover,
Kent, CT15 6DY: 01304 851019;
www.thecoastguard.co.uk

TURNER CONTEMPORARY
Rendezvous, Margate, Kent, CT9 1HG:
01843 233000;
www.turnercontemporary.org

PIE FACTORY
5 Broad Street, Margate, Kent, CT9 1EW
www.piefactorymargate.co.uk

SUBSTATION PROJECT SPACE
2 Bilton Street, High Street, Margate,
Kent, CT9 1EE

GREAT BRITISH PIZZA
14a Marine Drive, Margate, Kent,
CT9 1DH: 01843 297700;
www.greatbritishpizzacompany.wordpress.com

THE OLD NEPTUNE
Marine Terrace, Whitstable, Kent, CT5 1EJ:
01227 272262;
www.neppy.co.uk

THE OFFY
5 High Street, Whitstable, Kent, CT5 1AP:
01227 272114

WHATEVER COMICS
9 St. Peter's Street, High Street,
Canterbury, Kent CT1 2AT:
01227 453226;
www.whatevercomics.com

THE GEORGE INN
The Street, Molash, Canterbury,
Kent, CT4 8HE:
01233 740323;
www.thegeorgeinnmolash.co.uk

Some of the beaches in Margate are dog-friendly all year round. Dogs are not allowed on Broadstairs beach between May and September. Whitstable beach is dog-friendly all year round.

ATTLEE ON THE ISLE OF WIGHT

Everybody had told us, prior to our departure to the Isle of Wight, that many aspects of island life are stuck in the 1970s, as if this were a bad thing. Surely this could only be a goooood thing. The 1970s was a golden age for canines. Scooby Doo was at its hey-day in the '70s, before Scrappy appeared. The Littlest Hobo began in 1979 and Hobo is a hero of mine. *Maybe tomorrow, I'll want to settle down; until tomorrow, I'll just keep moving on . . .*

On arrival at Ryde, Jane, Elisa and I boarded a tube train to Shanklin, where we were staying. We don't have a tube train in Camberwell so, in this way, the Isle of Wight is ahead of SE5 in time. In fact, why doesn't the Isle of Wight gift Camberwell its tube train? We really need one.

Fancy kennels on Small Hope Beach

Our hotel – the Melbourne Ardenlea   did bear some resemblance in decor to the 1970s. I have watched Fawlty Towers, so I KNOW. However, unlike Fawlty Towers, the staff at the Melbourne Ardenlea were charming and there was no confusion when I ordered a Waldorf salad. Also, the Melbourne Ardenlea was extremely dog-friendly while in Fawlty Towers a Shih-Tzu's SAUSAGES are laced with Tabasco and chilli powder which is not very friendly at all.

Crazy golf was extremely popular in the 1970s. However I was not keen on the crazy golf on the Isle of Wight as Jane attached me to a lamp post in the middle of the course, and abandoned me in THE RUFF so she and Elisa could have a game. This really was not cricket.

The Isle of Wight's beaches were much more like it. We walked along the coast

Underground on the Isle of Wight

from Shanklin to Sandown, about two and a half miles. The best beach was Small Hope. (It's strangely named as there was Big Hope – big hope of me stealing another dog's ball; big hope of Jane buying me a sausage from the cafe). It even had brightly painted kennels especially for us dogs. Grrrr-huzzah!

In Sandown, we settled on the terrace at Daville's, looking out to sea, for curried chips – Jane – and mini Marrowbones – me – served at no charge by the friendly owner.

Jane had never heard the word Daville, which she assumed was French. But, the owner told us, Daville's is named in honour of the previous incumbent – Dave Hill. (Daville – Dave Hill. See what they have done there?) He recommended Godshill village as the prettiest place on the island so we three grockles (as they call tourists, which raised my hockles) caught the bus there.

At first it didn't look like much but that's because we'd alighted a stop too early. In fact, it is home to one of the best dog-friendly attractions I've ever visited – Godshill Model Village. Godshill Model Village does exactly what it says on the

Model SAUSAGES at the model butchers

When are my humans going to throw a blimin' stone for me to chase? Oh, I'm Pete and I'm on Sandown Beach on the Isle of Wight, by the way.

tin – it is a model of the village! It has a model pub and a model church and a model railway and a model butchers with model SAUSAGES. There was a model pub too, so I stopped in for a model pint of beer.

What really impressed me is that the village's model dogs are as big as its model humans. Its creators, 60 years ago, were obviously people of integrity and intelligence who recognised that a dog is a human's equal and decided to symbolise this equality by making model dogs and model humans the same size. Forget God – DOG himself must have created this canine Xanadu.

PHILEAS PHACTS: Isle of Wight

For travel to the Isle of Wight, log on to **www.wightlink.co.uk**

THE MELBOURNE ARDENLEA

4 6 Queen's Road, Shanklin,
Isle of Wight,
PO37 6AN:
01983 862596;
www.mahotel.co.uk 🐾
Price: doubles start at £70
Charge for dogs: £4 per dog
Extras for dogs: 'Don't Disturb the Dog' sign for the bedroom
Access all areas: everywhere except the restaurant and the swimming pool
Number of dogs: two maximum
Late night pee: small garden

CRAZY GOLF AT PIRATES COVE ADVENTURE PLAYGROUND

The Esplanade,
Shanklin, PO37 6BG

DAVE HILL'S

Belvedere Hotel, Esplanade, Sandown,
Isle of Wight, PO36 8AE

GODSHILL MODEL VILLAGE,

High Street, Godshill, Isle of Wight,
PO38 3HH:
01983 840270;
www.modelvillagegodshill.co.uk 🐾

For information about beach restrictions during the summer on the Isle of Wight, log on to **www.visitisleofwight.co.uk**

CAMPING IN THE SOUTH EAST OF ENGLAND, BY EVIE

I'm Evie and I live round the corner from Attlee in the mean streets of South-East London. We meet most mornings and he's probably as near to a friend as I have. I'm not really one for dogs.

I have two owners, Jacky and Kirsty, and I came from Battersea Dogs and Cats Home eight and a half years ago when I was a pup. I like to believe that people think I am mysterious and enigmatic because no one knows my origins. However I'm often referred to as a 'funny little dog' which doesn't suggest it's working. I'm complicated. Leave it at that.

Anyway, any old dog can stay in a cosy cottage or a posh hotel but it takes a real dog to go camping. That's why I am Phileas Dogg's camping correspondent. Here are my top three camp sites in all of England . . .

WELSUMMER CAMP SITE, KENT

This is THE best campsite. Fact. It is small and cute and there's a walk all around it through an orchard. There are pre-erected tents for lazy people or you can bring your own, like us, and camp in the woods. (Campervans and caravans aren't allowed. They are for WIMPS!)

We wanted to go to nearby Leeds Castle for a day but, despite having a Dog Collar Museum, no dogs are allowed. Pah. Instead we went to Maidstone, for a pleasant stroll around the Archbishop's Palace and All Saint's Church, which is, apparently, the grandest Perpendicular Church in all of England. Then we took a trip on the Kentish Lady – a big and rather terrifying boat. We sailed along the Medway and had ice creams and I was forced to wear a silly hat.

Evie helping pack up the tent

PHILEAS PHACTS: Welsummer Camping

WELSUMMER CAMPING

Chalk House, Lenham Road,
Harrietsham, Kent ME17 1NQ:
01622 843051;
welsummercamping.com
Price: small tents start at £20 for two
people
Charge for dogs: no
Extras for dogs: a doggie tent is available
for £5 if your dog requires privacy.
Access all areas: yes.
Number of dogs: check at time of
booking
Late night pee: the walk around the
campsite

THE KENTISH LADY

is at www.kentishlady.co.uk

BLACKBERRY WOOD, SUSSEX

Blackberry Wood is one of Kirsty's best campsite selections. Campers are given their own clearing in the woods, making it very private (although the blasted birds still find us to wake us up early every morning). Each clearing has a fire and a big metal contraption for cooking on. Meat at my level – brilliant. There's a big, long walk to the pubs in Ditchling through fields – both The Bull and the White Horse have tasty morsels for mutts. And, in the evenings, we sprawl on rugs in the fields and bark and chat until the sun goes down. There are always lots of empty bottles to clear up afterwards.

PHILEAS PHACTS: Blackberry Wood

BLACKBERRY WOOD

Streat Lane, Streat, Nr Ditchling,
Sussex, BN6 8RS: 01273 890035;
blackberrywood.com
Price: £5 per tent plus £5-£9 per person.
Charge for dogs: no
Extras for dogs: no
Access all areas: yes
Number of dogs: ask at time of booking
Late night pee: Blackberry Woods!

THE WHITE HORSE

16 West Street, Ditchling,
Sussex, BN6 8TS: 01273 842006;
www.whitehorseditchling.com

THE BULL

High Street, Ditchling, Sussex,
BN6 8TA:
01273 843147;
www.thebullditchling.com

HURST VIEW, NEW FOREST

This adventure takes us to Lymington, a market town in the New Forest. Kirsty has chosen a campsite called Hurst View, which is much bigger than our usual sites, with log cabins and caravans. But it's the only place in the New Forest that allows campfires and Kirsty loves campfires. I do not love campfires.

Anyway, we have lots of space in the tents area and there are dogs everywhere. One day I return to find a Westie in my tent. I don't like Westies.

We are camping with another dog, too – Oliver (pictured). He might be big but he is scared of everything so I keep him in line. And we participate in our favourite sport, which is competitive wee-ing. I try my best but Oliver has longer legs than me.

PHILEAS PHACTS: Hurst View

HURST VIEW CARAVAN PARK
Lower Pennington Lane, Pennington,
Lymington, Hampshire, SO41 8AL
01590 671648;
www.hurstviewleisure.co.uk
Price: from £20 for two people in a tent
Charge for dogs: no
Extras for dogs: no
Access all areas: yes
Number of dogs: check when booking
Late night pee: lots of open space

Evie's list of Canine Camping Essentials

I have my own travel bag for camping, containing:
- *poo bags.*
- *collapsible travel bowls – everyone is jealous of these.*
- *wipes in case of fox perfume.*
- *flashing disco collar for night - time adventures.*
- *bags of food and sachets of meat – DO NOT FORGET.*
- *bag of bedtime biscuits.*
- *my fleece-lined rain jacket.*
- *stake and chain to make sure I don't wander off when we are sitting around the camp fire. As if – the gossip is too interesting!*
- *spare lead and collar.*

On my travel bag dream list is:
- *a sleeping bag for dogs. – I want one.*

Searching for seaweed on Hastings Beach

HASTINGS

Oh I do like to be beside the seaside, especially when there's an abandoned ice cream cone on the pavement to snaffle – and then an abandoned bag of chips as well. Hastings – Tastings, thank you very much!

The most exciting event in Hastings prior to my arrival was a big battle, in 1066. That's a long time ago so we're safe.

Within five minutes of arriving at the modern and friendly White Rock Hotel another two hounds have checked in and I've had a bark off with a Border Terrier. Most amaze-bones of all, a dog called Rocky – the hotel dog, apparently – works behind reception.

The lady who showed us to our room said she preferred canine to human guests, because dogs don't get drunk, rowdy and have arguments. It's true – apart from the occasional bark off, I am a very polite guest.

The White Rock is bang on the sea front. Hastings beach is a very long, often pebbly beach but I can't run all the way along it because it's divided by groynes and they are too tall to leap over. Even a race horse would struggle.

Just next to the hotel, there is a shop called Collared, which had a pretend pink dog in the window. Thank Dog it's pretend because if it was real it would attract some strange comments down the park. I know how bitchy bitches can be!

The old bit of Hastings, about quarter of an hour from the beach, is called, appropriately, The Old Town. There is a shop selling old, restored bicycles and a place called The Furniture Hospital, which is like the vets, but for chairs and settees.

Rocky the White Rock receptionist (right)

Ye Olde Pumpe House is in the Olde Towne and has lots of historic beames on the outside. Inside, there are lots of nooks and crannies and I am allowed EVERYWHERE! The food is decent pub grub – big portions so lots of spare chips. A man sitting outside The Anchor Inn tells us that The Anchor is the oldest pub in Hastings. But, according to the website, it's only the second oldest. Humans lie!

The other shopping bit of Hastings, about ten minutes from our hotel, is Norman Road in St Leonards-on-Sea. There's a shop there called The Dawg's Biscuits, which, I'm guessing, sells biscuits for dawgs. But it was closed. There's also a shop called SHOP. I was allowed into SHOP – more than that, I was beckoned in, when I was standing outside. The owner was practically rolling out

*I'm Dougal, chief dog biscuit taster at the Black Dog Bakery (**www.theblackdogbakery. co.uk**). My favourite beach is West Wittering in Sussex, where I spell my name out in the sand so everyone knows who I am.*

the red carpet, even though part of SHOP was a cafe and people in cafes normally say: 'Move that scruffy mutt away from the cheese scones.'

They like capital letters on Norman Road because as well as SHOP there is a cafe called LOVE. Jane LOVED LOVE because it was a mishmash of comfy sofas and bistro tables and paintings and oddities that customers could buy – for example, a red velvet throne which would have suited me perfectly had Jane had a few hundred quid to spare. But she didn't – instead she had a fiver to spend on bubble and squeak for her and a SAUSAGE for me.

PHILEAS PHACTS: Hastings

THE WHITE ROCK HOTEL
1–10 White Rock, Hastings, Sussex, TN34 1JU: 01424 422240; www.thewhiterockhotel.com 🐾
Price: from £84
Charge for dogs: no
Extras for dogs: biscuits
Access all areas: everywhere
Number of dogs: check when booking
Late night pee: the beach
Owner's dogs: Rocky, the receptionist

COLLARED
37e Robertson Street, America Ground, Hastings, Sussex, TN34 1HT: 01424 719918; www.collareddog.co.uk

BELLS BICYCLES
4 George Street, Hastings, Sussex, TN34 3EG: 01424 716541; www.bellsbicycles.co.uk

YE OLDE PUMPE HOUSE
64 George Street, Hastings, TN34 3EE: 01424 422016; www.yeoldepumphouse.com

THE ANCHOR INN
13 George Street, Hastings, TN34 3EG: 01424 422256; www.anchorhastings.co.uk

THE DAWG'S BISCUITS
65 Norman Road, St Leonards-on-Sea, Hastings, Sussex, TN38 0EG

SHOP
32–34 Norman Road, St Leonards-on-Sea, Hastings, Sussex, TN38 0EJ

LOVE CAFE
28 Norman Road, St Leonards-on-Sea, Hastings, Sussex, TN37 6AE: 01424 717815; www.thelovecafe.me

Restrictions are in place on Hastings beach – log on to www.hastings.gov.uk

An evening stroll on Brighton beach

BRIGHTON

Brighton promenade – a perfect place for a stroll on a Saturday afternoon. Relaxing; eating an ice cream; wearing a Kiss Me Quick hat . . .

But what's this approaching? A mob of strange people, covered in blood, walking in a staccato, stumbling-sort-of fashion like Malamutes on Mogadon. There are LITERALLY millions of them.

Jane says they're zombies. Are these zombies a designer cross breed of humans, like designer cross breeds of dogs – the Cockapoo and the Labradoodle – that has gone terribly wrong? But Jane says no: zombies are the living dead, walking the earth as corpses. Howl-O-Ween!

Then we saw a Zombie DOG! This freaky fella was trying to put the fear into me, howling like a Hell Hound and putting his putrid paws up for a fight. I wasn't cowed though, despite the fact the stench of rotting flesh was making my eyes water. He was running back to his kennel in the underworld after meeting Phileas Dogg and no mistake.

I'm Brando and my favourite occupation is watching the world go by on Brighton seafront from my window seat.

After the sight of all that blood, even a carnivore like me felt queasy so we headed for some vegetarian food at The Prince George. The burrito was so massive I even forgot about zombie dog for a minute. Then we went to the Ginger Dog – woof – in Kemptown, where I was served a big bowl of water as soon as I set paw inside. I believe the good publicans of Brighton had heard of my encounter with the TERRIFYING

Not all dogs in Brighton are zombies – some are artists' muses, like Stanley Philpot. Stanley says: 'The human that belongs to me and my stepbrother Moses is Sam. She's an artist and she models many of the dogs she paints on Moses and me. Indeed, I have my very own stationery range! We live three minutes from the sea in Brighton but Sam doesn't take us to the beach often. She says we steal people's picnics! So we catch the bus to the South Downs and, after walkies, we stop in at Mr Wolfe for the best coffee in Brighton and Hove.'

Mr Wolfe, 15 Montpelier Place, Brighton, Sussex, BN1 3BH
www.mrwolfe.co.uk
Sam's work is at *www.samtoft.co.uk*

ZOMBIE DOG and were in paw of me for keeping the streets safe.

After my terrifying experience I'd have liked settle my head down for the night in a hotel – Paskins Townhouse, for example, which is dog and environment-friendly. But Jane's funds didn't stretch to that so we had to kip the night at our friend Don's. Ah well – it meant we could stop at The Gladstone, a big yellow pub near Don's flat, for a nightcap. The Gladstone is very bohoundian and full

of student-types, perfect for me being, as well as a Slayer of Zombie Dogs, something of an intellectual.

The next morning Jane wanted to visit Devil's Dyke for a good walk. But after my encounter of the previous day, I refused to go anywhere near the Devil, even if he was only ten minutes from the city centre by number 77 bus.

"Put your paws up, Zombie Dog!"

PHILEAS PHACTS: Brighton

PRINCE GEORGE
5 Trafalgar Street,
Brighton, BN1 4EQ:
01273 681055;
www.princegeorgebrighton.co.uk

THE GINGER DOG
12 College Place,
Brighton, BN2 1HN:
01273 620990;
www.thegingerdog.com

THE GLADSTONE
123 Lewes Road,
Brighton, BN2 3QB: 01273 620888;
www.thegladstonebrighton.com

PASKINS TOWNHOUSE
18/19 Charlotte Street,
Brighton, BN2 1AG:
01273 601203;
www.paskins.co.uk
Price: £100 and up
Charge for dogs: £10 per dog per stay
Extras for dogs: bowls, mats and SAUSAGES for breakfast
Access all areas: not in the dining room
Number of dogs: maximum of two
Late night pee: stroll along the street

There are dog restrictions on Brighton beaches in the summer. Log on to www.brighton-hove.gov.uk

SOUTH EAST ENGLAND DIRECTORY

THE ANGEL HOTEL

North Street, Midhurst, Sussex, GU29 9DN:
01730 812421;
www.theangelmidhurst.co.uk
In the heart of the South Downs National Park, which is a walking wonderland, The Angel is a statuesque and elegant Georgian beauty with log fires, wooden beams and a relaxed atmosphere.
Price: £130 and up
Charge for dogs: no
Extras for dogs: biscuits behind the bar
Access all areas: not in the restaurant but meals can be taken in the cosy lounge
Number of dogs: two small
Late night pee: enclosed courtyard area

FISHERMAN'S HUTS

The Harbour, Whitstable, Kent, CT5 1AB:
01227 280280;
www.whitstablefishermanshuts.com

Spend the night in a traditional wooden fisherman's hut next to the sea wall in Whitstable and be lulled to sleep by the sound of the waves – and rudely awoken by the screeching seagulls! Whitstable high street is a two-minute walk away.
Sleeps: from two to five people
Price: £75 and up
Charge for dogs: no
Extras for dogs: no
Access all areas: dogs are allowed in four of the 12 fisherman's huts
Number of dogs: two maximum
Late night pee: two metres to the sea wall

FOUR SEASONS HOTEL HAMPSHIRE

Dogmersfield Park, Chalky Lane, Dogmersfield, Hampshire, RG27 8TD:
01252 853000;
www.fourseasons.com/hampshire
Black Labrador Oliver Beckington was born with a silver bone in his mouth! He's Lord Paw of the Manor at the Four Seasons Hotel Hampshire and has a sumptuous Georgian pile to call his own, as well as 600-acres of grounds. Oliver Beckington – Ollie, to his friends – has appeared on the cover of glossy magazines; his couture collection is by top doggie designers Mungo and Maud and he has a direct route from his bed, at the concierge's desk in the hotel, down his own corridor to the kitchen to collect his daily bone. The concierge is custodian of a leather-bound tome with the words 'Oliver's Walks' embossed on the cover in gold – this is where guests can book a time to accompany Lord Paw on a stroll around 'his' estate.
Price: from £285
Charge for dogs: £35 one off charge per dog

GAUCHO

64 Heath Street, London, NW3 1DN:
0207 431 8222;
www.gauchorestaurants.co.uk
Take Fido to the flicks — Gaucho in Hampstead hold
regular dog-friendly events for charity, including a pop
up picture house. Pupcorn, anyone?

GOLDEN LION

99 Alresford Road, Winchester, Hampshire, SO23 0JZ:
01962 865512;
www.thegoldenlionwinchester.co.uk
Enjoy some al fresco alcoholic refreshment on a sunny
day in the beer garden at the Golden Lion, where the
thoughtful proprietors have fenced some off some
ground to make an enclosed play park for dogs. Just
throw him the odd crisp over the fence and he'll be
happy!

Extras for dogs: welcome treat; designer beds and
bowls; spring water in the room; a menu for dogs and
the services of a dog sitter, should Rover require some
time out from his humans

Access all areas: in all the public areas apart from
where food is served

Number of dogs: two per room

Late night pee: 600 acres of grounds

Owner's dogs: Oliver Beckington Esq

LONG ARM AND THE SHORT ARM

18 Lemsford Village, Welwyn Garden City,
Herts, AL8 7T:
01707 322401;
www.mcmullens.co.uk/longarmandshortarm
A welcome stop on Honey's walks around Brocket Hall,
the Long Arm and the Short Arm provides her long paws
and short paws with bowls of water and a selection of
chews

MALMAISON

Oxford Castle, 3 New Road, Oxford, OX1 1AY:
084469 30659;
www.malmaison.com
Oxford's Malmaison is housed in a former prison. The
old A-wing is where lags should lay their heads but,
it sleeping in what was once a cell (actually three
knocked together to form each boutique bedroom) is
a bit full-on for you, some of the hotel is in housed
what used to be the prison's administrative quarters.
Your pup's allowed in the bar for porridge and good
behaviour will be rewarded with sausages.
Price: starts from £160
Charge for dogs: £10 per dog per stay
Extras for dogs: basket, biscuits and bowls
Access all areas: not in the restaurant
Number of dogs: one small dog
Late night pee: the grounds of Oxford Castle

THE MILESTONE

1 Kensington Court, London, W8 5DL:
0207 917 1000;
www.milestonehotel.com
The Milestone's the hottest hotel for VIP hounds around
town and the service really is very important pet. Your dog
can be a proper Kensington Kanine with a hamper of treats
on arrival, custom-made cushions for kipping on and a
turndown service for tail-waggers.
Price: a Deluxe King is £402
Charge for dogs: a £1000 deposit is taken in case of
damage – refunded on departure
Extras for dogs: baskets, beds, bowls and treats
Access all areas: dogs are allowed in all the public areas
apart from where food is being served – however, the
Oratory adjoining the restaurant can be booked privately
by guests wishing to bring their dogs to dinner
Number of dogs: one per room
Late night pee: Kensington Gardens

Put your paws up at The Milestone

OLD SWAN AND MINSTER MILL

Old Minster, Minster Lovell, Witney,
Oxfordshire, OX29 0RN:
01993 774441;
www.oldswanandminstermill.com

Dogs have their own swimming pool at this pad – the River Windrush which runs through the 65-acres of grounds. The Old Swan part of the property dates back six centuries, with log fires and oak beams, while the newer Minster Mill shares the same honey-coloured Cotswold stone exterior. The pretty village of Minster Lovell is a short stroll away and booklets of local walks are handed out on arrival so you – and your dog – can really make the most of the glorious Cotswold countryside.

Price: £155 and up

Charge for dogs: £20 per dog

Extras for dogs: treats on arrival; beds, bowls, blankets and a doggie dinner of chicken and rice.

Access all areas: not in the dining rooms but meals can be taken in the bar

Number of dogs: depends on size of room

Late night pee: 65-acres of grounds

Owner's dogs: two Poms and three Chihuahuas

THE PIG

Beaulieu Road, Brockenhurst, Hampshire, SO42 7QL:
0845 0779 494;
www.thepighotel.com

Your dog will want to snout out The Pig in Brockenhurst (pictured right) – one of its bedrooms is called the 'Dog House' and has its own little ante-room for hounds with under-floor heating and a designer bed!

Price: starts at £205

Charge for dogs: no

Extras for dogs: personalised dog biscuits with their names on them

Access all areas: everywhere except for the restaurant

Number of dogs: check when booking

Late night pee: big grounds

RANVILLES FARM HOUSE B&B,

Pauncefoot Hill, Romsey, Hampshire, SO51 6AA:
02380 814481;
www.ranvilles.com

Ranvilles has been a fixture on the Fido-friendly front for years and its welcome to dogs is frippery-free – but genuine. The owners of this 15th-Century farmhouse pride themselves on their breakfasts – fill your boots and then go for a tramp through the New Forest National Park, three miles away

Price: £80 and up

Charge for dogs: first dog is free; then £3.50 per dog

Extras for dogs: bed, towels, bowls, poo bags and treats

Access all areas: everywhere but the dining room

Number of dogs: four Newfoundlands once checked in during a dog show

Late night pee: enclosed field

Owner's dogs: Black Labs Billie and Bertie

THE ROSE INN

The Green, Wickhambreaux, Kent, CT3 1RQ:
01227 721763;
www.theroseinnwickhambreaux.co.uk
This has to be one of the prettiest pubs in the country
and Barnie (pictured) is lucky enough to have it as
his local. When he's not romping through the Kent
countryside at 100mph, he's to be found curled up by
the fire in the Rose on a wintry Sunday lunchtime.

ROYAL HARBOUR HOTEL,

Nelson Crescent, Ramsgate, Kent, CT11 9JF:
01843 591514;
www.royalharbourhotel.co.uk
The Royal Harbour manages to pull off homely and
quirky yet stylish and sophisticated at the same time
from its prime position in a crescent of Georgian
houses right on Ramsgate sea front. At low tide, walk
from Ramsgate to Broadstairs, seal spotting along
the way.
Price: starts at £90
Charge for dogs: £10 per dog per stay
Extras for dogs: sausages in the morning
Access all areas: everywhere!
Number of dogs: two maximum
Late night pee: a small garden

Barnie: Canine King of Kent on a misty morn

THE RUBENS AT THE PALACE

39 Buckingham Palace Road, London, SW1W 0PS:
0207 834 6600;
www.rubenshotel.com
HRH (His Royal Hound) will be perfectly at home at
the palace, especially as it's just five minutes' stroll
from the real Buck House — bark-off with the Queen's
corgis, anyone? There's a pet concierge, who will
give your HRH advice on travelling around London; a
turndown treat; grooming services and fresh mineral
water in your buddy's bowl — replenished without him
having to ask, as in all the best hotels. If your mutt
wants to impress his mates, this is the place to hold
his birthday celebrations with a canine-canny cake!
When he checks out he'll be presented with a framed
photograph of himself taken during his stay!
Price: £323 and up
Charge for dogs: no but a deposit of £500 is required.
Extras for dogs: so many!
Access all areas: everywhere
Number of dogs: one
Late night pee: St James's Park

TOM'S ECO LODGES,

Tapnell Farm, Newport Road,
Yarmouth, Isle of Wight, PO41 0YJ:
01983 897089;

www.tomsecolodge.com

It's a dog's life for Bailey – Resident Rover at Tom's Eco
Lodge on the Isle of Wight. There are five eco-lodges
on this six-acre site, set in a glade of rolling fields
bordered by woods – prime countryside for pups. Bailey
greets all guests – human and canine. High Paw
Bailey!

Sleeps: each lodge sleeps up to six

Price: starts at £400 for four nights

Charge for dogs: £25 per stay however many dogs

Extras for dogs: no

Access all areas: dogs have to be kept on leads around
the farm

Number of dogs: three max

Late night pee: six acres of fields and woodland

Owner's dogs: Bailey (above)

Attlee in Amersham

Some scenes from Four Weddings and a Funeral *were filmed in The Crown in
Amersham which means people view it as a very romantic destination, that film being a
slush-fest and all. But I am not a Slush-Puppy and do not understand all this romance
stuff. I just go up to one of my bitches – Skye or Plum, say – and push my bottom in their
face. That works for me.*

THE CROWN,

16 High Street, Old Amersham, Bucks, HP7 0DH:
01494 721541;

www.thecrownamersham.com

Price: £105 and up

Charge for dogs: £10

Extras for dogs: no

Access all areas: apart from the restaurant

Number of dogs: two maximum

Late night pee: courtyard and fields

I'm Kipper and my name says it all – I love the sea. But, being a city dog, I have to spend most of my time keeping my human's feet warm at the Kennel Club's London offices and accompanying her on walks around inner-city parks. Still, she understands that, at heart I'm a pirate pup – I love rolling in fish guts – so, at weekends, she drives me to Camber Sands and Rye, in East Sussex, to get my fishy fix.

Camber Sands has everything a dog could wish for – dunes to roll down and a big flat beach for running full pelt. (And my human is entertained at the beach café instead of cramping my style on the sand.)

After I've worked up a thirst, it's time to head into Rye for a stroll around the shops and then a biscuit and a bowl of water at the The Ship Inn. However busy the pub is, I'm always allowed space to sprawl. The staff respect the pirate in me.

THE SHIP INN,
The Strand, Rye, East Sussex, TN31 7DB:
01797 222233;
www.theshipinnrye.co.uk
Price: £75 and up.
Charge for dogs: £10 per dog.
Extras for dogs: Bonio's and a SAUSAGE for breakfast.
Access all areas: everywhere!
Number of dogs: three little maximum.
Late night pee: Strand Quay.

I'm Monty. I was rescued from a puppy farm and found a lovely new home with Klare, who works for the RSPCA. Now I work there too but, when I have a day off, I indulge in my hobby – surfing in West Sussex.

I'm Fenn and I'm practising for the Grand National on a day out in the village of Shalford, in Surrey.

LULWORTH COVE, DORSET

My first ever holiday, a couple of weeks after Jane had the great privilege of adopting me from Battersea School for Dogs was to Dorset. Jane wanted to take me to the countryside and the sea – which, she guessed, I'd never seen before. She researched places to stay on the Internet and found a dog-friendly pub in West Lulworth, Dorset, called The Castle Inn. On its website, it had photographs of every dog who'd ever stayed and because Jane was proud of me – all shiny/scruffy and new – she thought I deserved a place on that website.

So, one frosty December morning, we caught the train with our friend Don from London Waterloo to a town called Wool. When we climbed off the train at Wool, I was quiet and didn't bark at any of the strange animals we saw – even the white ones, which looked like WOOL. (Of course I know now they are SHEEP but then I was a young pup of just six months old and everything was new and confuse-bonesing multiplied by a hundred.)

Even the invisible air I breathed was confuse-bones. It wasn't the fried chicken and exhaust fumes air of Camberwell or the disinfectant and doggie air of Battersea – it was country air, smelling of trees and SHEEP and something I didn't recognise. *Something salty . . .*

I didn't know, then, how privileged I was to be allowed everywhere at The Castle Inn, a traditional pub with a thatched roof. Dogs are allowed in the comfortable and cosy bedrooms, in the restaurant and in both the bars. Nearly everyone staying had

The coast path along the cliffs at Durdle Door on Dorset's Jurassic Coast

a dog. Over breakfast, when we dogs were served bowls of sausages by the waitress, Jane chatted to the other dog owners. It was useful for her, she said, because she'd only had me for a fortnight so she picked up lots of tips. For example – dogs like carrots. Afterwards, she was always feeding me carrots. I don't like carrots.

Jane enjoyed telling everyone I was a Battersea dog. At first, I was a bit unsure I wanted everyone to know my humble origins but within an hour I was proud to be a mongrel. The other guests and the staff at The Castle pondered my lineage. A Fox Terrier, one person said. A Jack Russell father and an Irish Wolfhound mother, said another.

Running free on Durdle Door beach

We were so lucky, Jane kept saying, because, even though it was December, the sun was shining. We went for walks from The Castle Inn to Lulworth Cove, a mile and a half along country roads. All the houses were thatched – even the bus stop – and, in Lulworth Cove village, there were fudge shops and cream tea cafes. They were closed, because it was out of season, but it didn't matter as Jane was on a diet.

At Lulworth Cove, we were meandering happily along when, suddenly, we saw it. I'd smelt it for a long time but not known what it was. Now Jane told me. This was the sea.

'You've never seen the sea before,' she cried and she pulled me towards it on my lead. It shames me to admit it now but I was terrified. The sea was white and frothy and angry. All the hairs on my back bristled and I barked and barked but, even though the sea went away, it came straight back again. I barked some more and again it returned, unabashed. Don said I was like a canine King Canute, which I didn't understand but the King bit sounded okay.

When she realised I didn't like the sea, Jane took me on a long walk in the hills around Lulworth Cove instead. I had the most fun I'd ever had in my short life. There were holes in the earth with interesting smells and I stuck my nose in them and snuffled. I chased tennis balls and ran through bushes and up hills. I was free!

But then we came across the sea again, at a beach called Durdle Door, which has a huge arch at the start of it and is made of shingle and sand. When I stood on the sand the first time I didn't like the scratchiness of it between my paws but when I ran across it, and it all sprayed up around me, it made me happy. I liked the seaweed too.

PHILEAS PHACTS: Lulworth Cove

THE CASTLE INN,
Main Road, West Lulworth,
Dorset, BH20 5RN:
01929 400311;
www.thecastleinn-lulworthcove.co.uk 🐾
Price: starting at £95
Charge for dogs: no
Extras for dogs: biscuits and sausages

Access all areas: yes
Number of dogs: no limit
Late night pee: country lanes
Owner's dogs: Tye and Tyler – two
friendly Rottweilers

Durdle Door beach is dog-friendly all
year round.

Then a man with a tripod and a camera came on to the beach, which we'd had all to ourselves, and instructed Jane to put me on the lead. He said he wanted to take a photograph of the giant arch without me running across and ruining it. He frowned at me as if I was a great nuisance. Of course I was young then, and unknown, but I am known now. I'm Phileas Dogg. Now that man would want to take my photograph instead of the giant arch.

Attlee and the Arch at Durdle Door, Dorset

The beach at Mawgan Porth

MAWGAN PORTH, CORNWALL

I am on my first voyage to Cornwallshire and it is a long way in the car from my hood in South-East London – a very long way, involving two stops at those motorway services places that don't allow dogs. Haterz!

Jane and her friend the photographer cheer when we pass a sign that says Cornwall. That means we have arrived – or nearly arrived, as we still have to drive around lots of one-lane country roads behind tractors. At last, we're over the brow of a hill and there before us is a beach the colour of a Golden Retriever and the shape of one of those shoes a horse wears on its paws. It is a perfect beach, with a cliff at the back of it, and we are at our destination – Mawgan Porth, on the north Cornwall coast.

Our cottage is called 4 Porth Farm Cottages – part of a little crescent of grey stone dwellings. The door knocker is in the shape of a wellington boot and this promises great joy because wellington boots equal WALKS.

Inside the cottage there is a big kitchen table with a picnic laid out for our arrival. Cornish tea bags, for Jane, and Cornish strawberry jam, for Jane, and Cornish dog treats, for me. *And Costa Rican coffee, which isn't Cornish at all.*

Inside a big pink fridge that has the word SMEG written on it, there are Cornish SAUSAGES and Cornish butter and Cornish bacon and Cornish eggs. We are in Cornwall.

256

My favourite thing about 4 Porth Farm Cottages is the kitchen floor, which is made up of grey slate tiles. When I lie on them, they are warm. This is something called under-floor heating – what it means is that Mother Earth is warming the tiles from deep inside her core to make them cosy for me to sprawl on. Grrrrr-HUZZAH!

Outside the cottage there's grass to roll on and a rowing boat and a tyre attached to a wire. The humans play on this but it seems a very odd game – sitting on a tyre, whizzing down a wire. Why don't they chase a stick like normal mammals?

Outside the cottage, in greater Cornwallshire, there are grand adventures to be had.

On the beach at Mawgan Porth, there are lots of dogs – some of them are even in the water with the big roaring, rearing waves. I don't like the sea but maybe these Cornish dogs, so brave in Cornwallshire, would balk at some of the rough-housing I have to deal with in the parks of South-East London.

The Beach Hut on Watergate Bay

There's a pub opposite the beach called The Merrymoor Inn. It is the only pub in Mawgan Porth but that doesn't matter because it is very merry-more and full of dogs. There is also a fish and chip shop and a restaurant, as well as a corner shop and a newsagents and a surf shop. Then there's a shop called Grand Central Disco Beads. This is a big hilaire joke because Mawgan Porth is tiny and if it had a grand central disco there would be no one to go. Dogs are allowed in Grand Central Disco Beads, which sells beads in shiny colours.

One day, we go to a beach called Watergate Bay, about a mile from Mawgan Porth across the cliffs. It is the biggest beach in the world and is made of Golden Labrador-colour sand. There are big multicoloured birds that people control on leads flying above it. Jane says these are kites and I bark at them because I don't like the way they flop to the ground and crumple before billowing up into life again.

There are also a lot of bipeds that look like humans but don't smell like humans. They smell of rubber and are clutching big white sticks of wood – too big for me, even, to fetch. They take the planks of woods into the sea – stand on them and then fall off. Jane says these people are surfers.

This is a lot for a little dog's brain to process, even though I am above average HQ (hound-telligence quotient), so we take a break at the Beach Hut, a restaurant in a fancy shed on stilts on the beach. The waitress tells us that when the tide comes in the sea reaches right up to the shed's huge glass windows. I don't want to hang around for this terrifying event so I yawn and pretend I'm tired and need to head back to the cottage for a snooze on the warm grey kitchen slates.

PHILEAS PHACTS: Mawgan Porth

4 PORTH FARM COTTAGES
Mawgan Porth, Cornwall:
Book with Beach Retreats on
01637 861005
or log on to **www.beachretreats.co.uk**
Sleeps: six in three bedrooms
Price: from £446 for three nights
Charge for dogs: £20 per dog per stay
Extras for dogs: Cornish dog treats!
Access all areas: not upstairs
Number of dogs: check at time of booking
Late night pee: a large garden but it's not enclosed

THE MERRYMOOR INN
Mawgan Porth, Cornwall, TR8 4BA:
01637 860258;
www.merrymoorinn.com
Price: starts at £70
Charge for dogs: £5 whether one dog or two
Extras for dogs: no
Access all areas: not in the breakfast room but breakfast can be taken in the bar
Number of dogs: two
Late night pee: to the beach

THE BEACH HUT
Watergate Bay, Cornwall, TR8 4AA:
01637 860877;
www.watergatebay.co.uk

Mawgan Porth beach and Watergate Bay are dog-friendly all year round.

FOWEY, CORNWALL

Meet Lady Bramble of Fowey Hall Hotel: queen of all she surveys and probably the luckiest dog I have observed in my travels. Bramble resides in an imposing country house hotel in the elegant town of Fowey, has endless walks on the beaches and country trails courtesy of the hotel guests and a constant supply of scraps from the kitchen. I am jealous.

Bramble invited me, Britain's top canine correspondent, to her grand gaffe for a visit. Being the gracious chap I am, I asked Jane to accompany me and good thing I did, because Bramble had sorted out the best room in the house for us – I would have been embarrassed to have it all to myself. Never mind a suite – it was more of a flat, with gleaming, polished dark wood furniture, huge gilt rimmed mirrors (who's that dog who keeps appearing?) and sparkling chandeliers.

There was a welcoming patchwork quilt on the bed too. Jane, for some reason, seemed to believe that this beguiling berth was hers, not mine, and I had to sleep in the front room. A bit rich but, for the sake of hound/human harmony, I let it go.

Anyway, I believe I have discovered my spiritual home among the fishermen's cottages and cliffs of Fowey. Normally it's Jane who wants to up sticks and move to every place we visit, but this time it's me who wants to pack my sticks and go.

After breakfast on the terrace overlooking the gardens with Fowey below us, we headed on the woodland path from the hotel down to Readymoney Cove. Readymoney – I like the sound of that! Because it was October the beach was dog-friendly and lots of friendly dogs were making use of it – one brave chap swam so far out to sea he was practically in Ireland.

Then we climbed a woodland trail because Jane wanted to reach a cove where there's a boathouse that's featured in a novel by someone called Daphne du Maurier. The novel, as far as I can gather, is famous because

Lady of the Manor: Bramble at Fowey Hall

Baxter, the Visit Cornwall dog

'My name's Baxter and I'm the snout of Visit Cornwall's Dogs Love Cornwall campaign. I've got my paws sandy on beaches all over Cornwall but my fave has got to be Porthmeor beach in St Ives – where I learnt to surf!'

www.visitcornwall.com/ dogslovecornwall

The South West Coast Path passes through Fowey

it has the opening line: 'Last night I dreamt I went chasing squirrels again.'

But it started to rain and then it rained even more. I have a waterproof coat but Jane doesn't and she was becoming a very wet, wet blanket. We paddled through the puddles back to Fowey and found our salvation in a dog-friendly cafe, aptly named The Lifebuoy which, for drowning woman and dog, it was. Then we headed down the steep streets of Fowey to the harbourside where we found further salvation from the rain in The King of Prussia and beer-battered fish and chips. It's a friendly pub which warmly welcomes dogs into the bar but not the bedrooms – a shame, as it occupies a good position on the harbour and those bedrooms windows would be good to harass seagulls out of. BOL!

Afterwards, as the rain continued, we sought refuge in The Lugger and then in Jo Downs Handmade Glass Shop and then in the Daphne du Maurier centre, which doubles as the Tourist Information. I was welcomed everywhere and no one raised an eyebrow when I disposed of the rainwater on my coat with a shake all over their establishment's floor.

When the rain stopped, we strolled along the harbour and met a dog with a job. I am always happy to meet dogs with jobs, as there are very few of us. (Jane says I am over-enthusiastic when I meet dogs with jobs – for example, when I bark my head off in greeting towards guide dogs and police sniffer dogs, apparently I'm distracting them from IMPORTANT work.)

Anyway, Nino is in charge of the chalet on Fowey harbour selling river trips. I asked her whether she might need an assistant – that is, me – so keen was I to remain in Fowey. She interviewed me, to see if my CV was up to scratch, and then said that I shouldn't call her on the dog and bone – she'd call me. Which I think is a PROBABLY. Woof!

PHILEAS PHACTS: Fowey

FOWEY HALL HOTEL
Hanson Drive, Fowey, Cornwall, PL23 1ET: 01726 833866;
www.foweyhallhotel.co.uk
Prioo: £170
Charge for dogs: £10 per dog
Extras for dogs: dog beds; treats; poo bins in the car park
Access all areas: not in the restaurant but everywhere else, including the morning room and in the lounge in front of the coal fire
Number of dogs: check at time of booking
Late night pee: a lovely woodland walk leads from the car park
Owner's dogs: Bramble

LIFEBUOY CAFE
8 Lostwithiel St, Fowey, PL23 1BD: 07715 075869;
www.thellfebuoycafe.co.uk

KING OF PRUSSIA
3 Town Quay, Fowey, PL23 1AT: 01726 833694;
www.kingofprussiafowey.co.uk

LUGGER INN
Fore Street, Fowey, PL23 1AH: 01726 833435

JO DOWNS GLASS
21 Fore Street, Fowey, PL23 1AH: 01726 832005,
www.jodowns.com

THE TOURIST INFORMATION AND DU MAURIER LITERARY CENTRE
5 South Street, Fowey, PL23 1AR: 01726 833616;
www.fowey.co.uk

Readymoney Cove has a seasonal dog ban over the summer months.

Resident Rover: Monty Spaniel in Cranborne, Dorset

I'm in Cranborne – a pretty village in the middle of Thomas Hardy country – for the weekend. It's right on the Thomas Hardy Way, a path stretching for 212 miles and covering many Hardy-related locations, such as his birthplace. I'd assumed it would be crowded with local squires and milkmaids eating strawberries so I'm surprised when we don't meet a solitary soul on our walks. Oh well – I pose outside Cranborne Manor, which dates back to the 12th Century, instead. Maybe if the squire's at home he'll invite me in for a cuppa!

The scenery around here – milkmaids or not – is stunning. Golden fields fall to each side, bordered with bands of trees in the distance. Uncut wheat fields are edged with late scarlet poppies. (My powers of describing the Dorset countryside rival Tom Hardy's himself!)

The Close – the local name for the fields at the back of Cranborne Manor – is like a canine social club. I meet several other dogs, including a Collie, a couple of Labradors and some Spaniels, including another TRI-COLOURED Spaniel.

We're rare, you know.

Be careful though – lots of the fields are grazed by White Park cattle. They're almost pure white, with black markings around the eyes, nose and mouth and HUGE horns. I give them a wide berth.

We take a stroll into the village to visit the recently refurbished 17th Century inn at Cranborne and are introduced to Mikey – the pub dog. A dog with his own pub – now there's an idea I could get behind.

PHILEAS PHACTS: Cranborne, Dorset

THE INN AT CRANBORNE
Cranborne, Wimborne, Dorset, BH21 5PP:
01725 551249;
www.theinnatcranborne.co.uk
Price: starting from £85
Charge for dogs: £15 per dog
Extras for dogs: breakfast – sausages and bacon

Access all areas: yes
Number of dogs: maximum two
Late night pee: grass across from the car park
Owner's dogs: Mikey, the Jack Russell

Fistral beach, Newquay

THE LEWINNICK LODGE, NEWQUAY, CORNWALL

We are off to Cornwall, on the 10.14am train from London Paddington to Par, so Jane can report on The Lewinnick Lodge in Newquay for a newspaper. I relax in our first-class seats – we're doing this in style – and take advantage of the complimentary biscuits while dreaming of the lovely Cornish beaches on which I'll soon be racing. I haven't even packed my quill and ink in my Gladstone bag – I am on holiday while Jane, for once, is doing the work.

But, Jane announces as the train glides past the pretty beaches and sailing boats of Dawlish, I am not on a holiday holiday. I am on a working holiday. While she reviews the Lewinnick Lodge for the paper, I shall be reviewing it for Phileas Dogg. I protest that I am without my fedora with the newshound tag perched in the brim but she is undeterred. I'm a bit BELOW PAR about it as we change trains for Newquay (at Par) but when the cool Cornish air hits my lungs, I perk up. Cornwallshire – my favourite county in the whole kanine kingdom. It would,

263

Attlee's been spotted!

indeed, be criminal if I didn't share it with my readers.

Arriving in Newquay and reaching the Lewinnick is easy – a two-minute walk from the train station to A2B Taxis and then a five-minute, £6 taxi ride. But, when we pull up outside the Lewinnick, it doesn't feel as if we're in Newquay at all – instead, we're on a remote Cornish headland with no houses, just scenery and VIEWS for miles around.

The Lewinnick has been a Newquay favourite for local hounds enjoying post-walk lunches for years but now the owners have opened ten boutique-style bedrooms so holidaying hounds can take advantage of the spot as well. When Jane and I enter our room we gasp, collectively. This room could be just the most basic of kennels and it would still be amazing because of the VIEW.

Four huge windows peer over the cliffs below and then east, along more cliffs, towards Fistral Beach. If I close my eyes and listen to the crashing waves, I'm on a pirate ship in the middle of the ocean.

As it is, the room isn't just the most basic kennel – it's been designed by a top London chap and is tasteful in a subtle way, so as not to detract from the VIEW. There's even a dog bed and some Cornish biscuits for me. But have I mentioned the VIEWS?

For humans, gazing at views is pleasure in itself but we dogs want to get out there – actually into the view. We want to be bang in the middle of it and not just looking at it. So I take the lead and Jane and I are marching out of the hotel's front door and onto the Pentire headland, 100 yards away.

'You can't go wrong,' a local tells us. 'Just keep the sea on your right.'

But, confuse-bonios, the sea is on the left as well – the magnificent, wide Crantock Beach, which we attempt to struggle down the gorse-covered cliff towards. The tide's coming in at quite a clip, though, and Jane becomes nervous so we wander down to The Gannel instead. The Gannel is an estuary and transforms from a sandy beach into a river and then into the sea – all in one day. Even Albark Einstein would struggle with this – in fact, I concentrate so hard trying to work it out that I see spots!

The other amaze-bones walk is along Fistral Beach, left out of the door of the Lewinnick and then down a coastal path for about a quarter of an hour. Fistral Beach has the biggest waves in Europe, some as high as the tallest tree in my local park, which even a squirrel can't reach the top of. I'm generally a brave fellow but we stay at the edge of the beach, by the cliffs, away from the huge waves. Still, I manage to bark at the humans in strange black second skins with white sticks under their arms, called surfers.

That's quite enough barking, Jane reckons so she takes me to Bodhi's Beach Bar, at the cliff side. Once again, I find myself OUTSIDE the view, peering in. But that, Jane says, is what happens when I cause canine chaos INSIDE the view. A lesson learnt, I suppose.

PHILEAS PHACTS: Lewinnick Lodge, Newquay

LEWINNICK LODGE
Pentire Headland, Newquay, Cornwall TR7 1QD:
01637 878117;
www.hospitalitycornwall.com
Price: starting at £130
Charge for dogs: £15 per dog
Extras for dogs: dog beds and treats
Access all areas: not in the restaurant but people can have breakfast in the bar
Number of dogs: no limit as long as dogs are well behaved
Late night pee: the headland – but take a torch to avoid falling over the cliffs!

BODHI'S BEACH BAR
South Fistral Beach, Pentire, Newquay, Cornwall, TR7 1QA:
01637 850793;
www.bodhisfistral.co.uk

Crantock and Fistral beaches are dog-friendly all year round.

ISLES OF SCILLY, BY THE TRAVELLING BEAR

We are at Newquay Airport where I am greeted by a jovial chap who weighs me – a test I obviously pass, unlike Vee's heavy bag, which is gobbled up by a conveyor belt. We walk through machines that beep and then watch a video about flying – isn't that what birds do? – on something called a Skybus. I don't like this, especially when, having walked up the steps to the Skybus as jauntily as possible, putting on a brave face, I'm placed in a crate. Then engines are revving – twenty times as loud as our car – and the ground has disappeared beneath us and we are in the sky. *I repeat – isn't this what birds do?*

I'm a good dog. I don't bark – I grit my teeth and wait for this ordeal to end which, after 30 minutes, it does. Out of the crate, down some steps and I'm back on Terra Firma. I can smell the sea, which is good, and we've arrived on the Isles of Scilly – staying in Tregarthen's Hotel in Hugh Town on St Mary's. The view from our room over the quay is fantastic and the staff are truly dog-friendly, which cheers me greatly. I can relax and enjoy my trip.

Day One: We set off from the hotel after breakfast and stride down to the quay, where Vee buys a ticket from the St Mary's Boatmen Association hut (no charge for me) and we board a boat to Tresco. Across the water we go, taking in the sea smells and waving at other boats along the way.

Tresco is a well-kept island and requires that dogs remain on leads at all times. However, the beaches were mainly deserted, so I played ball and swam as well as sunbathing. I could have stayed at the Ruin Beach Cafe all day – it was so hot – but Vee was determined to see Tresco Abbey gardens. There were all kinds of beautiful sub-tropical plants for her to marvel at and I was chased by a ferocious pheasant – if only I hadn't been on my lead!

Day Two: This time we're off to St Agnes, one of the smallest inhabited islands with a population of around 70. (People – I don't know about dogs!) Landing at Porth Conger, we stride across the island to Troy Town and from there walk along the coastline. St Agnes has a lot to see including the grand lighthouse in the middle, The Punch Bowl and The Nag's Head. Ha – these aren't pubs. They are rocks! There's a beautiful beach too, offering safe, shallow swimming – I jump in. Then we go to The Turks Head, which must be one of the best-situated pubs in the country in terms of VIEWS, for much needed resuscitation.

Day Three: Today my lifejacket is coming with us as Vee's in charge of a fourteen-foot boat. There's a slight steering incident – she stacks the boat in weeds and a rather wild man has to rescue us. (She said I wasn't to mention this but it's too good to miss out.)

Then we're on Samson – a small, deserted island with prehistoric monuments, which we have to ourselves. The Samson Flats give a lovely wide, white sand beach at low tide and I am happy roaring up and down, dipping in the sea and rolling around in the sand while Vee soaks up the sun. Back in the boat, we dot about between Tresco and Bryher, looking for dolphins and enjoying our freedom.

Day Four: We walk right round Bryher and I wave to my cousin Bert in Canada across the ocean! Then I dash into the clear waters at Great Popplestone, before lunch at the swish Hell Bay Hotel, which welcomes dogs.

Day Five: This is my favourite day – on St Martin's, an island of contrasts with wide sweeping bays, cultivated land, wild flowers and soft dunes. We swim and sunbathe at Par Beach and Great Bay and walk along the coast, past Bread, Cheese and Wine Coves.

Day Six: Another highlight of the week – taking a small boat out to the uninhabited islands in search of puffins, gannets, shags, dolphins and seals. We see LOTS! And I bark at seals.

Day Seven: We finish our trip on St Mary's, where The Garrison is teeming with bunnies and a good game of chase ensues.

Deserted sandy beaches and crystal clear waters – it's a dog's life for Bear on the Isles of Scilly

PHILEAS PHACTS: Isles of Scilly

TREGARTHEN'S HOTEL
St Mary's, Isles of Scilly, Cornwall, TR21 0PP: 01720 422540;
www.tregarthens-hotel.co.uk
Price: starting at £95
Charge for dogs: £15 per dog
Extras for dogs: as a lot of people arrive in Scilly by plane, Tregarthen's offers a service whereby beds, toys, bowls and blankets for your dog can be ordered in advance so as not to impact on luggage allowances. (payment is a donation to a local animal charity)
Access all areas: not in the restaurant but breakfast and dinner can be taken in the lounge
Number of dogs: check when booking
Late night pee: the beach

RUIN BEACH CAFE
Old Grimsby, Tresco, Isles of Scilly, Cornwall, TR24 0QG: 01720 424849

THE TURK'S HEAD
St Agnes, Isles of Scilly, Cornwall, TR22 0PL: 01720 422434

HELL BAY HOTEL
Bryher, Isles of Scilly, Cornwall, TR23 0PR: 01720 422947;
www.hellbay.co.uk
Price: £320 and up
Charge for dogs: £12 per dog
Extras for dogs: bowls, blankets and beds
Access all areas: not in the restaurant but welcome in the bar
Number of dogs: three per room
Late night pee: the beach
Owner's dogs: Springer Spaniels Suzy and Jasper

Three beaches on St Mary's have a dog ban during the summer and dogs must be kept on a lead on Tresco.

PLYMOUTH, DEVON

Chips; I see no chips. And I'm far too busy playing bowls on Plymouth Hoe to care even if I do. *Oh bear with me – there is a chip. Best vacuum that up before some other blighter snaffles it.*

I'm rather enjoying my hoe-down on the Hoe. There's green space, a stripey tower, and it's where salty sea dog Sir Francis Drake finished his game of bowls before taking on the Spanish Armada. The numero uno (a nod to Plymouth's Spanish connections there) hotel for dogs in the city is just two minutes from the

Hoe, with built-in chip snaffling time. Dogs are so welcome at The Camelot, in fact, that should our owners wish to leave us for a few hours, the landlady will keep us company, along with her rather large but – and I checked this out with a bark-off – friendly Rottweiler. The Camelot is clean, friendly and serves a decent breakfast – I was allowed in the dining room to claim my rightful share.

Out to explore. First stop – The Barbican, the olde parte of Plymouthe, with cobbled streets and grey stone buildings. It's where people sailed from, in 1620, to start new lives in America, where the President has a Portugese Water Dog called Bo. (A bit different from our Prime Minister who has a rubbish cat called Larry.)

The Barbican boasts a massive metal sculpture of a prawn, which confused me greatly.

I required a sit-down in the Ship Inn overlooking the harbour to contemplate this. And then I required another sit-down, in the dog-friendly Menu Cafe where I was given manifold dog biscuits to contemplate it. But I still couldn't get to grips

Smeaton's Tower on Plymouth Hoe

with the statue of the prawn, so I required yet another sit down at The Queen's Arms. At the end of all this contemplating, I still couldn't work out why anyone would build a statue of a pathetic prawn. A noble hound or even a horse, I'll grant you. But a crustacean?

On to Mutley Plain, which is the opposite of Attlee Handsome, obviously, so I was eager to visit and lord it over poor old Mutley. But Mutley is far from Plain as it has an amazing enterprise on its fair streets – a dog-friendly American-style diner. Never have I set paw in such a place before! Goodbody's, it is called and it

Why not put a prawn on the Barbie?

Jennycliff Cafe, Plymstock, Plymouth, PL9 9SW: 01752 402358
Our Plymouth brethren recommended Jennycliff Cafe as the city's dog-friendliest spot. It's full of Fidos enjoying a fry-up of a weekend and has views of the city to boot. There's no sign of Jenny, though. If I owned this cafe and this cliff, I would be making my presence felt – especially as there are steps down to a sheltered beach with seaweed to snaffle.

Dogs are allowed on Jennycliff beach all year.

is, indeed, a good body.

There are red leather booths set in close proximity to each other meaning the smells from the tables merge together into an amaze-bones aroma which could almost melt a little dog's nose. The fry-ups are huge and the people friendly. So, as anyone who understands basic maths will know, this 'size of portions to friendliness of people' ratio makes the likelihood of scraps for snafflers 99.99 per cent.

Chips – I see a lot of chips!

It's not always sunny in Devon, as Coco discovered on a cold Dartmoor morning.

PHILEAS PHACTS: Plymouth

CAMELOT HOTEL
5 Elliot Street, The Hoe, Plymouth, PL1 2PP:
01752 669667;
www.camelothotelplymouth.com
Price: from £65 although cheaper rates are available for week-long stays
Charge for dogs: no
Extras for dogs: free dog sitting
Access all areas: yes
Number of dogs: three
Late night pee: two minutes' walk to the Hoe
Owner's dogs: Ellie the Rottie

THE SHIP
4 Quay Road, Barbican, Plymouth, PL1 2JZ:
01752 667604;
www.theshipplymouth.co.uk

MENU CAFE
13 The Parade, Barbican, Plymouth, PL1 2JW

THE QUEEN'S ARMS
55 Southside Street, Plymouth, PL1 2LA:
01752 662915

GOODBODY'S 24-HOUR BAR AND CAFE
49 Mutley Plain, Plymouth, PL4 6JQ:
01752 206469;
www.goodbodys.co.uk

HOLSWORTHY, NORTH DEVON

When we arrived at Holemoor Cottage, deep in the north Devon countryside, Jane was stressed. We'd had quite the travel to reach it – bus and train and bus again – and then disaster had struck. Being a Londoner, Jane had imagined the little town of Holsworthy would be brimming with taxis of a Saturday lunchtime to transport us the five miles to the cottage, up on a farm on a hill. But: 'Taxis need to be booked in advance here. This is North Devon,' the lady in the King's Arms told us.

In fact, it took an hour and a half and a free cup of coffee from the manager of Holsworthy Waitrose – who took pity on our hapless situation – before a taxi could be raised. (The driver had given up his day off when faced with Jane's passionate pleas about being stranded.)

So, for the first few hours in the cottage, Jane was tense. She couldn't settle to the idea of being miles from the nearest corner shop or pub. She ate the cream tea Anita, the lovely lady in the farm next door, had left out for us hungrily, as if it might be her last meal on earth. (This despite three Waitrose bags of shopping!) Me – I thought it an adventure on a grand scale. We were stranded on a farm for the whole weekend with countryside as far as my nose could smell!

Then Jane started to relax. There were so many aspects to the farm that she

---

The Bridge Inn is the only pub west of the Tamar in Devon

liked. A Shetland pony (who I did not like). A full size pony. The farm dogs, Billy and Merlin. The big starry sky above us, when dusk fell. At night, Jane enjoyed the sense of being warm and safe in the cottage as a great storm from neighbouring Cornwall battered the top of our hill.

She settled into our seclusion and when Anita kindly offered to drive us somewhere of our choice, Jane said no – she was enjoying pottering about. We walked two miles to the nearest village – Bridgerule – to buy a newspaper in the shop. It had closed half an hour before our arrival, but because Jane was used to North Devon by now, she didn't fret. We went to Bridgerule's pub – the Bridge Inn – where a group of men were discussing the great issues of the day and Jane drank a cup of coffee and shared a packet of crisps with me. Everybody in the pub was friendly and we were invited to the pub quiz, that evening. But Jane politely declined, reckoning that two miles was a long way to walk for the humiliation of coming last.

When the day of our departure dawned and the hour of our pre-booked taxi was upon us, Jane did not want to return to the metropolis of Holsworthy. She wanted to stay stranded on the farm a little longer.

PHILEAS PHACTS: Holsworthy

HOLEMOOR COTTAGE

Holemoor Farm, near Holsworthy, Devon: Book through Toad Hall Cottages on 01548 202020 or 0800 6101122 and at www.toadhallcottages.co.uk 🐾

Sleeps: five
Price: starts at £370 a week
Charge for dogs: £25 per dog per week
Extras for dogs: biscuits and towels
Access all areas: not upstairs
Number of dogs: ask at time of booking
Late night pee: out on to the third of a mile long farm lane (set back from the road). There are also enclosed paddocks where dogs can run off lead
Owner's dogs: Billy and Merlin

Resident Rover: Coco in South Devon

I'm Coco – the 80mph couch potato. It's good to have balance in one's life, so – yes – while I love to run as fast as I can (I might even show off), my all time favourite activity is snoozing in the sunshine. Luckily, I live in South Devon so there's lots of opportunity for that. Here are my top tips for South Devon, as a local lass . . .

First up, the beaches – they're why everyone comes here. My humans like the beach at Beesands because it's easy to park and never crowded. Stroll along the pebbly beach or trot past the houses and up onto the South West Coast Path to nearby Hallsands, which fascinates people as most of the village was washed away in a big storm many years ago.

I'm more interested in what's being washed up on the beach – like bits of tasty old crab. There's a nice dog-friendly cafe in a hut called Britannia@The Beach at Beesands – it does great cakes and ice cream and there's always a bowl of water for us dogs.

If you walk to the other end of Beesands beach and take the coastal path, you'll be heading for Torcross and the beach at Slapton Sands. I particularly like hanging round outside the Torcross Boat House as there are usually yummy bits of fish and chips on the floor. Beware of the pebbles here though – they're even bigger than at Beesands!

Another good walk is at Slapton Ley, which is a big lake close to the beach. It's really tranquil and I paddle in the water – but we're supposed to be kept on leads to stop us chasing the birds. Surely ducks are fair game? BOL!

PHILEAS PHACTS: Coco in South Devon

BRITANNIA @ THE BEACH
Beesands, Kingsbridge,
Devon, TQ7 2EH: 01548 581168;
www.britanniaatthebeach.co.uk

TORCROSS BOAT HOUSE
Slapton Sands, Torcross, near
Kingsbridge, Devon, TQ7 2TQ: 01548
580747; **www.torcrossboathouse.com**

Beesands beach and Slapton Sands are dog-friendly all year round.

Resident Rover: Carrek in North Cornwall

My name is Carrek, which is Cornish for rock, and I'm a Black Labrador. I'm a mover and shaker in the travel industry and I persuaded my bipeds to buy and renovate a cottage to rent to hounds on holiday – and their bipeds too.

The most important thing to make accommodation fit for discerning dogs is location, location, location. No point creating a Ritz for Rovers in the middle of a built-up area with no walks for miles around. Well, here in North Cornwall we're just a few miles from some of the best beaches – and they're dog-friendly all year round too.

Travelling Bear loves a cone of Cornish.

My favourite is Widemouth Bay – 20 minutes away in the car. There's a cafe there named after me – The Black Rock Cafe – so I am always given a right royal welcome. My second favourite beach is Harlyn Bay, which has dramatic cliffs and sweeping sand and, thirdly, I like walking along the harbour at Padstow and on to the green at the top of the cliffs. Afterwards, when the sea's out, I have a romp along the sand.

As for our cottage – well, humans like the little touches when they go on holiday, like a glass of wine on arrival – and us dogs like the little touches too. So I spend my pocket money on things to welcome dogs to Hellangove. There's always a bowl of biscuits – double the amount if two dogs are staying – and a tennis ball on a rope and a card from me, explaining where the best walks are.

I understand, too, that sometimes dogs just want to chill out and find some me-time, away from the bipeds. So my mate Jake – a former resident of Dogs Trust, Ilfracombe – is on hand, if you need a day away from the family, to accompany you on a walk in the Cornish countryside. (His human Lynn goes too – well, you can't have everything.)

PHILEAS PHACTS: Carrek in North Cornwall

HELLANGOVE COTTAGE
Hellangove, South Petherwin,
near Launceston, Cornwall:
01726 850316;
www.hellangoveholidaycottage-cornwall.co.uk
Sleeps: four
Price: starts at £279 a week
Charge for dogs: no
Extras for dogs: biscuits; toys; throws for the sofa; leads and bowls
Access all areas: yes
Number of dogs: ring to discuss if it's more than two
Late night pee: enclosed garden

BLACK ROCK CAFE,
Marine Drive, Widemouth Bay,
Bude, Cornwall EX23 0AG:
01288 361563

The south end of Widemouth Bay and Harlyn Bay are dog-friendly all year round.

Resident Rover: Barnie, the Chocolate Lab

My name's Barnie and I'm an eight-year-old Chocolate Labrador. I've been living on a farm in North Cornwall since I was two. In May 2013 my best friend Benson left me – he was like me but black and seven years older. Two people came to make his pain go away. Without him, I was lonely, even though my owners run a small farm holiday business and lots of other dogs visit. But none of them were

Benson. Some days Mum and Dad called me for walks and I couldn't even be bothered.

Then a lady called Ruth from the Labrador Rescue Trust visited. She drank some tea, looked around – and then drove off. A few days later Dad put me in his truck and we drove to a place where there were lots of dogs in kennels. I was introduced to a one-year-old Golden Labrador called Samson. He was a cheeky young whippersnapper but I put him in his place.

Barnie and Samson enjoy life on the farm

Then Dad put me AND Samson into the truck and brought us both home. I wasn't sure about that but Samson told me that his previous owner was elderly. Even though Samson didn't mean to, he'd forget he was no longer a puppy and knock her over or forget to come back if she let him off the lead. So she decided he needed somewhere with more space, a firmer hand and 'boundaries'. My Dad provides them!

Samson gets us into trouble sometimes – like the day he persuaded me to visit a neighbouring B&B with him. Our dirty paw marks on the carpet meant Mum and Dad were in a little bit of trouble!

Still, I'm much happier now I have a friend who's all mine again and I enjoy introducing Samson to our guests – although Tara, who is a Golden Retriever, was cross when Samson destroyed her 'indestructible' ball. Tara – I've talked to him and he won't destroy your toys if you visit – promise.

PHILEAS PHACTS: Barnie's Farm

HIGHER TREVINNICK FARM,
St Kew, Wadebridge, Cornwall, PL30 3HP: 07866 517645;
www.farmerjames.co.uk
Sleeps: Owl Barn Cottage sleeps four plus cot; Fox Den cottage sleeps five plus cot.
Price: starts at £340 a week
Charge for dogs: no

Extras for dogs: towels; treats; SAUSAGES!
Access all areas: yes
Number of dogs: ask at time of booking
Other pets are welcome as well – once three Hermit crabs checked in!
Late night pee: out on to farmland
Owner's dogs: Barney and Samson

SOUTH WEST ENGLAND DIRECTORY

THE BAKEHOUSE B&B,

1 Acreman Street, Sherborne, Dorset, DT9 3NU:
01935 817969;

www.bakehouse.me.uk

Sherborne is a lovely little town with its impressive abbey, toffee-coloured buildings and thriving independent shops and cafes, but finding a canine canny kip isn't as easy as it could be in a burgh that boasts the wonderfully named Hound Street. Use your loaf, then, and book into The Bakehouse. It's a little shambolic, perhaps, but, if you're willing to put up with a few quirks – on behalf of the 18th Century house itself and the owner Malcolm – then you'll find it friendly and informal.

Price: £40 without breakfast

Charge for dogs: no

Extras for dogs: no

Access all areas: yes

Number of dogs: up to four

Late night pee: grassy area out the back

Owner's dog: Labrador Charlie

BLAGDON MANOR

Ashwater, Devon, EX21 5DF:
01409 211224;

www.blagdon.com

Blagdon has been at the vanguard of the dog-friendly movement over the past decade and, here, dogs really are made as welcome as people. Steve and Liz, dog owners themselves, wanted to create an atmosphere where people could bring their dogs and relax rather than feeling they had to constantly apologise for having their canine companions with them, and they've achieved that – grand-style.

Price: £145 for a double and up

Charge for dogs: £8.50 per dog

Extras for dogs: a bed, bowls, homemade biscuits and personalised Blagdon Manor poo bags!

Access all areas: in all the public lounges and bars but not in the restaurant and conservatory

Number of dogs: three depending on size

Late night pee: 20 acres of grounds

Owner's dog: Chocolate Labradors Cassia and Mace

BLUE BALL INN

Countisbury, Lynmouth, Devon, EX35 6NE:
01598 741263;

www.blueballinn.com 🐾

The Blue Ball is worth chasing – it's a truly dog-friendly digs, with no less than seven circular walks starting from the front door as well as being bang on the South West Coast Path and in the Exmoor National Park. The rooms are comfy in this traditional coaching inn; the portions of pub grub are big; ales are real and staff are friendly – job done.

Price: £78 and up

Charge for dogs: two dogs stay free but the third is £8

Extras for dogs: home-made dog biscuits; hose outside for muddy dogs; blankets on request

Access all areas: everywhere

Number of dogs: three maximum

Late night pee: grass verge at the front of pub

Owner's dogs: Molly, a Rhodesian Ridgeback/Poodle cross, and Poppy, a Labrador Pointer cross

COMBE HOUSE HOTEL AND RESTAURANT

Gittisham, Honiton, Devon, EX14 3AD:
01404 540400;
www.combehousedevon.com

A wonderful Grade I listed Elizabethan manor set in rolling hills, Combe House is a real treat with coal fires and leather sofas to lounge around on in winter and 3,500 acres of grounds to tramp through in summer. Jane and Attlee stayed in the Marker suite, where Alfred Hitchcock once spent a few months while working on a film.

Price: £215 and up

Charge for dogs: £10 per dog

Extras for dogs: a book of walks written by local Dalmatian Toby for canine guests

Access all areas: not in the restaurants but in the bar and lounges

Number of dogs: two per room

Late night pee: all those grounds!

THE COMPASSES INN

Lower Chicksgrove, Tisbury, Salisbury, Wiltshire, SP3 6NR·
01722 714318;
www.thecompassesinn.com

This 14th Century thatched Freehouse is small – just four bedrooms but perfectly formed. Down the bottom of a country lane it can prove rather difficult to locate but is well worth the game of hide and seek. A lot of gun dogs are trained in the surrounding area and the recruits tend to kip at the Compasses, so the staff are very used to catering to the needs of the canine customer.

Price: £85

Charge for dogs: no

Extras for dogs: no

Access all areas: everywhere apart from the beds

Number of dogs: no official limit

Late night pee: fields all around

THE CULBONE

Porlock, Minehead, Somerset, TA24 8JW:
01643 862259;
www.theculbone.com

How could an establishment with the word bone in the title not be dog-friendly? There's a lot going on at this Exmoor restaurant with rooms, including a cookery school. Its food is certainly very fine, and, hurrah for hounds, they're allowed in the restaurant to enjoy it with you.

Price: starts at £65

Charge for dogs: no charge

Extras for dogs: biscuits on arrival

Access all areas: yes

Number of dogs: a whole pack!

Late night pee: car park

Owner's dogs: Pip the West Highland Terrier

DIMORA B&B

Gwel-an-Mor, Mawgan Porth, Cornwall, TR8 4DW:
01637 860511;
www.dimora-bed-breakfast.co.uk

A modern house offers old-fashioned hospitality at the Dimora in the little village of Mawgan Porth. It's a five-minute walk from the beach; the two bedrooms are clean and comfy and the breakfast selection is wide, ranging from locally caught fish to waffles. There's also afternoon tea on arrival.

Price: £75 and up

Charge for dogs: no

Extras for dogs: an outside shower for sandy humans and hounds returning from the beach

Access all areas: no dogs on beds

Number of dogs: maximum two

Late night pee: big, enclosed garden

Owner's dogs: Collie Peppa

THE GNOME RESERVE

West Putford, near Bradworthy, North Devon, EX22 7XE:
01409 241435;

www.gnomereserve.co.uk

One thousand gnomes are at home in three acres of wild garden at Devon's wonderfully eccentric Gnome Reserve and it's free for your dog to visit – he can even wear his very own gnome hat. Just be sure he doesn't lift his leg on one of the little fellow's heads! (Poppy and Holly refused to wear their gnome hats for our photograph!)

HELSBURY PARK

Camelford, Cornwall, PL32 9RH:
01566 781753;

www.helsburypark.co.uk

Helsbury Park's back garden is 100 acres wide – no wonder it has won plaudit after plaudit from pups over the years. Stay for a week and your morning walk through the woods will be different every day. There are four cottages on the site, which also has a swimming pool, sauna and gym.

Sleeps: each cottage sleeps up to six people

Price: starts at £795 for a week

Charge for dogs: £20 per dog per stay

Extras for dogs: treats; poo bags; bowls and blankets; your dog's favourite food ordered in anticipation of arrival – and the services of the local dog whisperer!

Access all areas: downstairs only

Number of dogs: how many have you got?

Late night pee: enclosed gardens

Owner's dogs: Lurcher Solly

THE LOG CABIN

Sheldon, Blackdown Hills, Devon, EX14 4QS
Book through Sykes Cottages on 01244 356666
or at **www.sykescottages.co.uk**

What could be cosier than staying in a log cabin on the edge of a forest, next to a lake? Even though the fairytale connotations of such an idyll might be lost on Fido, there's nothing for him to sniff about at The Log Cabin – and plenty for him to sniff at. Badgers, foxes and deer all share the countryside with you. Sitting on the veranda with a glass of wine in the summer, or sitting round the wood-burning stove in winter, you really will feel you've found your own little piece of Devon Heaven.

Sleeps: four

Price: £232 for a short break and up

Charge for dogs: no

Extras for dogs: no

Access all areas: yes, apart from on furniture

Number of dogs: check at time of booking

Late night pee: step out into the countryside

LONGUEVILLE MANOR

St Saviour, Jersey, JE2 7WF:
01534 725501;
www.longuevillemanor.com
Bear and Vee went upmarket on a recent trip to Jersey – staying at 5-star Longueville Manor, an imposing old stone house standing in 16-acres of ground with an LA style swimming pool and terrace and sumptuous bedrooms and public areas. But, while Longueville is arguably Jersey's poshest pad, the mood is warm and relaxed and the staff are down to earth and helpful.
Price: starts at £175
Charge for dogs: no
Extras for dogs: no
Access all areas: only in the bedrooms and grounds
Number of dogs: depends on size of room
Late night pee: 16-acres of grounds

THE OLD COASTGUARD HOTEL

The Parade, Mousehole, Penzance,
Cornwall, TR19 6PR:
01736 731222;
www.oldcoastguardhotel.co.uk
The Old Coastguard doesn't have televisions in its 14 bedrooms but, with views across to St Michael's Mount and The Lizard, who needs TV? There's an easy grace and charm about the hotel and this extends to the attitude to dogs – they really are welcome.
Price: £120 and up
Charge for dogs: no
Extras for dogs: there's a K9 station providing everything the holidaying hound could require – blankets, bowls and treats etc
Access all areas: everywhere apart from main restaurant
Number of dogs: no limits
Late night pee: coastal path at the foot of the garden

THE OLD CIDER HOUSE

25 Old Castle Street, Nether Stowey,
Somerset, TA5 1LN:
01278 732228;
www.ochc.co.uk
Samuel Taylor Coleridge lived in the village of Nether Stowey for three years – just around the corner from The Old Cider House, in fact – and one of the B&B's two dog-friendly bedrooms is named the Poet's Room in his honour. Every guest who stays in the Poet's Room is invited to take up quill and ink and pen a poem on the wall and Resident Rover Ozy has been the subject of a few of these rhymes. Well he is a dog of letters himself, blogging at www.ozythelabrador.wordpress.com.
Price: £65 and up
Charge for dogs: £3 per dog
Extras for dogs: homemade dog biscuits and tags stating 'I am staying at Old Cider House'
Access all areas: yes
Number of dogs: two
Late night pee: garden
Owner's dogs: Ozy, a Black Labrador (below)

MIDDLEWICK HOLIDAY COTTAGES

Wick Lane, Glastonbury, Somerset, BA6 8JW:
01458 832351;
www.middlewickholidaycottages.co.uk
Pack your cider and your wellies – your dog is off to
Glastonpuppy, camping in a field deep in the Somerset
countryside with a footpath leading up to Glastonbury
Tor. This isn't Glastonbury-style camping though – or, if
it is, it's Glasto in the celebrity field! The site boasts two
luxury e-dens, each with full-size double beds so there's
no waking up on a deflated airbed of a morning.
Sleeps: the e-dens sleep two people in a double bed
Price: starts at £65 per e-den
Charge for dogs: £15 for a weekend and £25 for a week
Extras for dogs: no
Access all areas: everywhere apart from the bed
Number of dogs: two small dogs per e-den
Late night pee: walk up to the Tor on Summer Solstice
Owner's dogs: Maggie and Ellie, mother and daughter
Labradoodles

PENDERRIS B&B

Tintagel Terrace, Port Isaac, Cornwall, PL29 3SE:
01208 880419

Port Isaac is one of Cornwall's prettiest fishing villages
and currently it's enjoying celebrity as the location of
television drama Doc Martin. The eponymous hero of the
series hates hounds but actor Martin Clunes is a real
dog lover and has been known to stop filming to greet
passing pups.
Price: £65 and up
Charge for dogs: Nancy asks dog owners to donate to
an orphanage for disabled children in Nepal in lieu of
a charge
Extras for dogs: towels for muddy paws
Access all areas: yes
Number of dogs: one maximum
Late night pee: the garden

THE PIGS NOSE INN

East Prawle, near Kingsbridge, Devon, TQ7 2BY:
01548 511209
www.pigsnoseinn.co.uk
Your dog's own snout will be twitching at this former
smuggler's inn overlooking the village green in East
Prawle – there's a mutts' menu and, indeed, pigs' noses
to scoff. Look out for regular Rover Roy who props up the
bar with a quarter pint of beer most evenings.

THE SEA TROUT INN

Staverton, Totnes, Devon, TQ9 6PA:
01803 762274;
www.theseatroutinn.co.uk
This has been a pub since the 15th Century so it's fair
to say the Sea Trout has had a while to get it right
– and get it right it has, mixing the old and the new
as effortlessly as it mixes posh with pub grub in the
restaurant. Catch a vintage train to Staverton Station
on the South Devon Railway, a heritage line, and arrive
in style.
Price: start at £85
Charge for dogs: £5 per dog

Extras for dogs: biscuits behind the bar

Access all areas: dogs are allowed in the bar and to breakfast

Number of dogs: two small maximum

Late night pee: the churchyard – torches provided

Owner's dogs: Lily (above), a rescue Dachshund Italian Greyhound cross

STOCKS HOTEL

Dixcart Valley, Sark, GY10 1SD:
01481 832001;
www.stockshotel.com

Until recently, local law on Sark decried that un-spayed female dogs weren't allowed to set paw on the island – only the Seigneur was allowed one. Now all dogs are welcome to enjoy Enid Blyton-esque adventures on the second smallest of the Channel Islands, which, untrammelled by the motor car, has woods and beaches and rural rambles in abundance. Handsome Milo (below) is a regular visitor and the Stocks Hotel offers a classy kip for canines

Price: starts from £170 room

Charge for dogs: £25 per dog

Extras for dogs: blankets, bowls, rugs and bedding

Access all areas: dogs aren't allowed in most of the public areas but are welcome in the (indoors) bar next to the terrace for some poolside posing

Number of dogs: two maximum

Late night pee: step out into woodland and fields

Owner's dogs: Lurcher Bluey

GLEBE HOUSE B&B

Chittoe, Chippenham, Wiltshire, SN15 2EL:
01380 850864;
www.glebehouse-chittoe.co.uk
'We are mother and daughter Silver and Ruby – two
bouncy blondes – and we live in the best B&B in
Wiltshire! We love having doggies to visit but be warned
about our friend Biggles – the grumpy African Grey
parrot!'
Price: rooms start at £80
Charge for dogs: £5 per dog
Extras for dogs: treats for well-behaved dogs on
departure
Access all areas: in the drawing room for breakfasts
Number of dogs: maximum two
Late night pee: Glebe is down a rural track

WATERGATE BAY HOTEL

Cornwall, TR8 4AA: 01637 860543;
www.watergatebay.co.uk
The splendid Watergate Bay is dog-friendly all year
round – no restrictions – so it makes sense that the
super-swish hotel across the road from the beach is
too. It's a study in surfer-chic and a favourite with
metropolitan mutts heading to a hip hang-out for a
weekend break.
Price: £160 and up
Charge for dogs: £15 for the first dog; £5 for each
additional dog
Extras for dogs: water bowls and outside showers
Access all areas: dogs are allowed in one of the dining
areas (Living Space)
Number of dogs: check at time of booking
Late night pee: the beach

WORTHAM MANOR

Lifton, Devon:
Book through Landmark Trust on 01628 825925
or at **www.landmarktrust.org.uk**
The inglenook fireplace at the great hall in Wortham Manor
is big enough for a whole pack of Labradors to settle in
front of – lucky Thorn (below) had it all to himself. The
large medieval manor house, now in the care of Landmark
Trust, is perfect for big parties and
Tudor banquets.
Sleeps: 15
Price: starts at £1205 for a three-
night break.
Charge for dogs: no
Extras for dogs: no
Access all areas: not on furniture
Number of dogs: two
Late night pee: a big garden

Thorn at Wortham Manor

INDEX OF PLACE NAMES

Aberdovey 136–137
Abergavenny 132
Ailsa Craig 42
Aldeburgh 211, 213
Alderley Edge 92
Almscliffe Crag 62
Alnmouth 64–66
Alnwick 84
Alton 170
Altrincham 92, 93
Ambleside 87–90, 96, 107
Amersham 250
Appleby 111
Argyll & Bute 15 -18, 34, 35–38, 44, 46, 48, 49, 51
Arran 40–43
Ashwater 278
Askrigg 58–61
Avoch 20
Bakewell 158–161
Bamburgh 75–77
Barbican Plymouth 269–271
Barnard Castle 72, 74, 83, 84
Barra 31, 34
Bath 152
Beadnell 74–76
Beamish 73, 74
Beesands 274
Bellochantuy 17, 18
Benbecula 31
Bermondsey 221, 222
Bethnal Green 220
Betws-y-Coed 139
Black Isle the 19–23
Black Mountains 145
Blackdown Hills 280
Blackpool 106
Blaenau Ffestiniog 141
Blakeney Point 207
Blockley 154–155
Borders 50
Bowes 52, 53, 71–72
Brackenborough 199
Bradworthy 280
Brancaster 185–189
Brecon Beacons 120–124, 125–126, 131
Brentwood 190–191
Bridgerule 273
Brighton 242–244
Broad Haven –117
Broadstairs 229, 230, 232
Brockenhurst 248
Brodick 40–43
Bryher, Isles of Scilly 267, 268
Buckinghamshire 250

Builth Wells 139
Burnham Market 212
Burnham Overy Staithe 214
Bute Isle of 35-38
Buxton 159, 174
Cadborough Hill 168
Camber Sands 251
Camberwell 217–219
Cambridge 213
Cambridgeshire 210, 213
Camelford 280
Campbeltown 15, 17, 18, 46, 49
Canna Isle of 45
Canterbury 231, 232
Carlisle 107
Carmarthen 127, 144
Carmarthenshire 112–114, 144
Ceredigion 127–130, 139, 144
Chatsworth 159
Chelmsford 212
Chelsea 221
Cheltenham 173
Cheshire 91–94, 101, 106
Chester 106
Chesterfield 174
Chippenham 284
Chipping Campden 146, 151–153
Chirk Bank 162–164
Cirencester 171
Cleddau Estuary 117
Cley-next-the-Sea 212
Clifton 95, 97
Clitheroe 108
Clun 169, 176
Clwyd 138
Coalbrookdale 148–150, 165
Cockle Strand 31
Cold Aston 171
Colintraive 46
Congleton 91-92
Conwy 139
Corbridge 78–79
Cornwall 256–268, 275–284
Cotswolds 146, 151–155, 170, 172, 176
County Durham 52, 53, 71–74, 83, 84
Craig-y-Nos 120–124
Cranborne 262
Crantock 264, 265
Craster 75–77
Crickhowell 125–126
Cromford 158, 160, 161
Cumbria 87–90, 95–98, 102–111
Dedham Vale 203–204
Delamere 94
Denbighshire 164
Derbyshire 156–161, 168, 174, 178, 179
Dereham 210
Derwentwater 89

Devon 269–274, 278, 279, 280, 282, 284
Ditchling 237
Dogmersfield 245
Dorset 252–255, 262, 278
Douglas 105
Dover 228, 232
Dumfries and Galloway 51
Dunwich 205–207
Durdle Door 252–255
Durham 72–74
Easedale Tarn 102
East Dulwich 218–219
East of England 180–215
East Prawle 282
Edinburgh 24-28 45
Edwinstowe 177
Eggleston 73 74 83
Ellesmere 163
Ely 210
Epping Forest 219
Erbistock 138
Essex 190–193, 203–204, 210, 212, 214
Ettrick Bay 36
Farne Islands 75
Fife 50
Finsbury Park 220
Fintry 48
Fishguard 117, 119
Fistral Beach 264, 265
Flatford 203, 204
Folkestone 230
Fort William 49
Fortrose 20, 22, 23, 44
Fowey 259–261
Freshwater West 131, 132
Garndolbenmaen 138
Gigha 17
Glasgow 35
Glastonbury 282
Gloucestershire 146, 151–155 170–173
Godshill 234, 235
Goodwick 117
Goyt Valley 178
Grasmere 88-90, 102-104
Great Cressingham 209, 214
Great Warford 92
Greenwich 218
Guiting Power 170
Gwynedd 136–137, 138, 141, 142, 144
Halesworth 181
Hallin Fell 95
Hampshire 238, 245, 246, 248
Hampstead 218, 219, 223, 246
Hampton Court 224–225
Harlyn Bay 275
Harrietsham 237

INDEX

Harris 32, 33, 34
Harrogate 62–63, 80
Hastings 239–241
Haverfordwest 119, 140, 141
Hawes 59, 61
Hay-on-Wye 138, 142, 143
Heart of England 146–179
Hebden Bridge 83
Herefordshire 171
Herne Hill 218, 219
Hertfordshire 247
Hexham 81, 85
Highgate 219, 220
Highlands, the/Highland 19-23, 44, 48–50
Holkham 187–189
Holsworthy 272–273
Holy Isle 42
Honiton 279
Horncastle 211, 214
Hugh Town, Isles of Scilly 266
Ings 98
Inner Hebrides 45
Inverary 48
Ireby 109
Ironbridge 147–150, 170
Islay 16, 17
Isle of Man 105
Isle of Wight 233–235, 250
Islington 219
Jackfield 149, 170, 177
Jennycliff Beach 270
Jersey 281
Jura 17
Jurassic Coast 252 255
Keighley 85
Kelso 50
Kent 228–232, 236–237, 245, 249
Keswick 87-90, 104, 108
Kilchattan Bay 37
Kilchoan 50
Kildonan 42, 43
Killinghall North Yorkshire 80
Kingston upon Thames 224–225
Kintyre Peninsula 15–18, 49
Kippen 47
Kirkby Lonsdale 111
Knutsford 94
Lake District 87–90, 102–104, 95–97, 98, 102–104
Lamlash 42, 43
Lampeter 139
Lancashire 106, 108, 111
Laugharne 112– 114
Lavenham 214
Leigh-on-Sea 214
Leominster 171
Lerwick 39

Lewis 33
Lifton 284
Lincoln 198–199
Lincolnshire 194–199, 211, 212, 214, 215
Little Bollington 93
Little Haven 117, 119
Liverpool 97-101, 107
Llancayo 141
Llandysul 127, 130
Llangollen Canal 162–164
Llangollen 163–164
Llangwm 117, 119
Loch Fyne 16, 18, 33, 48
Loch Lomond 48, 49
Lochranza 40-41
London 216–223, 246, 247, 249
Long Compton 176
Long Melford 208
Louth 199
Lower Withington 91
Low-Newton-by-the-Sea 64–66
Lowther 95-97
Ludham 201, 202
Ludlow 164–167
Lulworth Cove 252–255
Lymington 238
Lynmouth 278
Macclesfield 93
Maidstone 236
Maldon 210
Malham 83
Mallaig 48
Manchester 108
Margate 228, 230, 232
Martindale 95
Matlock Bath 156 160
Mawgan Porth 256–258, 279
Merseyside 97–101, 107
Midhurst 245
Midlands the 168, 169
Minchinhampton 172
Minehead 279
Molash 231, 232
Monmouthshire 132, 141, 145
Monsal Trail 159
Morfa Nefyn 142
Mousehole 281
Mull of Kintyre 15 – 18, 49
Mull 31
Mumbles 140
Munlochy 20
Mutley Plain Plymouth 270–271
Naburn 81
National Forest the 168
Nether Stowey 281
New Forest 238, 248
Newcastle upon Tyne 81

Newquay 263–265
Newtonmore 44
Norfolk Broads 180, 181, 200–202
Norfolk Broads 180, 200–202
Norfolk 180 185–189, 200–202, 207, 209, 210, 212, 214, 215
North Duffield 85
North East of England 52–85
North Rigton 62–63
North Uist 31, 34
North West of England 87–111
Northumberland 64–66, 74–77, 78–79, 81, 84, 85
Nottinghamshire 177
Oban 31, 34
Oswestry 163–164
Oxenhope 85
Oxford 247
Oxfordshire 247, 248
Oxwich Bay 134–137
Padstow 275
Patterdale 95–97
Peak District 156–161, 178
Peckham Rye 222
Pembrokeshire 115–119, 131, 140–143
Penrith 95, 97, 106
Perthshire 29-30
Pickering 82
Pladda 42
Plymouth 269–271
Pontcysyllte Aqueduct 163
Port Bannatyne 35–38
Port Isaac 282
Porthcawl 144
Porthclais 116
Porthgain 117
Powys 120 124, 125 126, 130, 133, 142
Primrose Hill 221
Raby Village 101
Ramsgate 249
Roadymonoy Cove 260, 261
Reynoldston 135 137
Rhossili Bay 133–137
River Derwent 156, 160
Romsey 248
Rosemarkie 20–23
Ross Back Sands 76–77
Ross-shire 19
Rothesay 35–38
Rowsley 174, 176
Rydal Water 86, 87
Ryde 233
Rye 251
Salisbury 279
Samson, Isles of Scilly 267
Sandown 234, 235
Sark 283

Scalpsie Bay 37
Scilly, Isles of 266–268
Scotland 16-51
Seahouses 74–76
Shalford 251
Shanklin 233, 234, 235
Shap 95
Shell Island 144
Sherborne 278
Sherwood Forest 177
Shetland 39-40
Shincliffe 72–74
Shrewsbury 149, 172
Shropshire 147–150, 162–167, 169,
    170, 172, 176, 177, 179
Skelwith Bridge 96
Skipton 82, 83, 85
Skirrid 145
Skye 31, 33, 34
Slapton Sands 274
Small Hope Beach 234
Snowdonia 136–137, 138, 139
Soho 222, 223
Solva 115–117 119
Somerset 279, 281, 282
South-East 217–252
South Petherwin 276
South Uist 31
South West 252–283
Southend Kintyre Peninsula 17
Southwold 181–184, 185
St Agnes, Isles of Scilly 266–268
St Andrews 50
St Davids 116–119, 142, 143
St Ives 260
St Martin's, Isles of Scilly 267
St Mary's, Isles of Scilly 266–268
Staffordshire 170, 175
Stainburn 63

Stalham 202
Stamford 212, 215
Stirlingshire 45, 47, 48
St-Leonards-on-Sea 240, 241
Stockbridge 26-28
Stratford-upon-Avon 170
Strathcarron 44
Suffolk 181–184, 185, 205–208, 211,
    213, 214
Surrey 224- 225, 251
Sussex 226–227, 237, 239–245, 251
Sutherland 47
Sutton 93
Swansea 140
Swettenham 91–92
Tamworth 175
Tarbert 16, 18, 49, 51
Tarset 85
Taynuilt 44
Teesdale 73, 82, 83
Tenby 117, 118
Tewkesbury 173
Thaxted 192–193
The Gower Peninsula 133–137
Thornham 187, 189
Thornhill 45
Thornhill 51
Thurstaston Beach 110
Ticehurst 226–227
Tintern Abbey 131
Titchwell 185, 186, 189
Torcross 274
Torridon 45
Totnes 282
Tresco, Isles of Scilly 266–268
Trevor 163–164
Ullswater 95
Unst 39, 40
Vatersay 31

Victoria Park 222
Waddington 111
Wadebridge 277
Walberswick 183, 184
Wales 112–145
Walthamstow 220
Warenford 76–77
Wark on Tyne 81
Warwickshire 170, 176
Watergate Bay 257, 258, 284
Weald Country Park 190–191
Wells-next-the-Sea 188, 189
Welwyn Garden City 247
Wemyss Bay 35
West Lulworth 253–255
West Wittering 240
Weybourne 215
Whitby 53–57, 84
Whitesands Bay –118
Whitstable 230, 232, 245
Whittington 164
Whorlton 82
Wickhambreaux 249
Widemouth Bay 275, 276
Wiltshire 279, 284
Winchcombe 154–155
Winchester 246
Windermere 98, 111
Winsor 12
Wirksworth 174, 179
Wirral, the 110
Witney 248
Woodhall Spa 194–197
Wrekin, the 149, 179
Yarmouth 250
York 67–70, 81, 82
Yorkshire Dales 58–61
Yorkshire 53–63, 67–70, 80–85